# Theodore of Mopsuestia
# on the Bible

# Theological Inquiries

*Studies in Contemporary*
*Biblical and Theological Problems*

General Editor
Lawrence Boadt, C. S. P.

PAULIST PRESS

# Theodore of Mopsuestia on the Bible

## A Study of His Old Testament Exegesis

*Dimitri Z. Zaharopoulos*

PAULIST PRESS
New York ● Mahwah, N.J.

Library of Congress Cataloging-in-Publication Data

Zaharopoulos, Dimitri Z., 1924-
  Theodore of Mopsuestia on the Bible : a study of his Old Testament exegesis / by Dimitri Z. Zaharopoulos.
        p.   cm.
    Bibliography: p.
    Includes index.
    ISBN 0-8091-3091-2
    1. Bible.  O.T.--Criticism, interpretation, etc.--History--Early church, ca. 30-600.   2. Theodore, Bishop of Mopsuestia, ca. 350-428 or 9--Contributions in exegesis of Old Testament.   I. Title.
  BS1160.Z34      1989
  221.6′092--dc20                                                                    89-32431
                                                                                          CIP

Published by Paulist Press
997 Macarthur Boulevard
Mahwah, NJ 07430

Printed and bound in the
United States of America

# CONTENTS

To my parents
Zechariah and Maria
in remembrance and gratitude

♦

To my parents
Zechariah and Maria
προσφορά εὔμνῆστος καί εὐγνώμων

# PREFACE

The aim of this work is to present a thorough analysis and evaluation of Theodore's critical methods in Old Testament study on the basis of all the primary sources now available. The methodology which is followed in this study is therefore historical, critical and analytical. Critical examination of the source material involves the analysis of both direct statements and logical implications which are pertinent to the study.

Ancient authors, such as Eusebius, Libanius, Chrysostom, Jerome, Theodoret, Sozomen, Socrates, Malalas, and Leontius of Byzantium, are the main sources for an understanding of the historical, cultural and religious milieu of Antioch where Theodore was born and educated.

Studies concerned with Theodore of Mopsuestia's Old Testament scholarship are scanty. Serious research on the subject began in the latter part of the nineteenth century. This present study is based on the following extant writings of Theodore of Mopsuestia:

*Commentarius in duodecim prophetas minores,* edited by J. P. Migne, *Patrologiae Graecae* (66), 123–632.

*Fragmenta in Vetus Testamentum,* edited by J. P. Migne, *Patrologiae Graecae* (66), 633–714.

*Le commentaire de Théodore de Mopsueste sur les Psaumes* I–LXXX, edited by Robert Devreesse (Studi e Testi, No. 93) Citta del Vaticano: Bibliotheca Apostolica Vaticana, 1939.

*Les fragments grecs du commentaire de Théodore de Mopsueste sur le quatrieme Evangile,* edited by Robert Devreesse as an Appendix to *Essai sur Théodore de*

1

*Mopsueste* (Studi e Testi, No. 141) Citta del Vaticano: Bibliotheca Apostolica Vaticana, 1948.

*Catechetical Commentary on the Nicene Creed,* edited and translated from the Syriac by Alphonse Mingana (Woodbrooke Studies, Vol. V) Cambridge: W. Heffer and Sons, 1932.

*Catechetical Commentary on the Lord's Prayer and on the Sacraments of Baptism and the Eucharist,* edited and translated from the Syriac by Alphonse Mingana (Woodbrooke Studies, Vol. VI) Cambridge: W. Heffer and Sons, 1933.

*Theodori Mopsuesteni in epistolas beati Pauli commentarii.* Vol. I: *Galatians-Colossians.* Vol. II: *Thessalonians-Philemon.* (The Latin version with the Greek fragments) Edited with an Introduction, Notes, and Indices by H. B. Swete, Cambridge: At the University Press, 1880–1882.

Fragments in Greek of Theodore's commentaries on Romans, on I and II Corinthians, and on Hebrews. Edited by Karl Staab in *Pauluskommentare aus der griechischen Kirche. Aus Katenenhandschriften gesamelt und herausgegeben* (Neutestamentliche Abhandlungen, Band XV) Munster: Verlag der Aschendorffschen Verlagsbuchhandlung, 1933, pp. 113–212.

The author's declaration of indebtedness to the publications of previous French scholars is evident throughout the book and it is acknowledged primarily in the footnotes. The writings of Robert Devreesse loom very large. I am particularly thankful to J. M. Vosté, whose translation of the Nestorian Syriac texts has enormously facilitated my job, on account of my ignorance of the Syriac language.

It is a genuine pleasure to express my heartfelt thanks to the Paulist Press and to members of its editorial board for their kindness and patience, as well as their generosity in requesting one of their editors to undertake the preparation and revision of the manuscript, on account of my poor eyesight. For these efforts, a word of gratitude is due to Mrs. Georgia Christo, a former student and now editor of the Paulist Press, who has painstakingly read the entire manuscript and provided editorial guidance. Last but not least, I express my appreciation to my friend and colleague, Professor Demetrios Constantelos, for the stimulus I have received.

*Holy Cross*
*Brookline, 1986*

# INTRODUCTION

In the last few decades the name of Theodore of Mopsuestia has stood in the foreground of patristic studies in the western Christian world. The revival of interest in the work of an ancient heresiarch was stimulated by the discovery in the last forty years of manuscripts and fragments comprising both original writings and Syriac translations of his works.

As a result of these discoveries Theodore's christology has become the focus of contention in the publications that have appeared wherein the views are contentious and dissenting: authors would defend the premise that Theodore's teaching on the nature of Christ's person would pass the test of traditional teaching as it was formulated by the Council of Chalcedon (451), and others would support the opposite view, i.e. Theodore was a Nestorian before Nestorius, or in a more subtle way Theodore in his understanding of the christological problem was guided by a metaphysical moralism which precluded the complete reunion of the superior divine nature with the inferior human one.

Whatever the outcome of this theological debate, our interest in this book lies somewhere else. Its whole range will be concentrating on Theodore's Old Testament scholarship. There is sufficient new material which would support such an undertaking. However, a brief analysis of Theodore's christology has been attempted for the purpose of explaining in a condensed fashion his post-mortem trial and condemnation by the Fifth Ecumenical Council in 553.

Theodore appeared at a time when conventional doctrines and traditional views concerning biblical interpretation were not being challenged by the fathers of the church. Yet, in his theological studies at the school of Antioch, which was simply known to its graduates by the name ἀσκητήριον, i.e. hermitage, Theodore learned a new methodological approach for the study and interpretation of the Bible, the so-called historico-grammatical method. This new hermeneutical procedure cleared away once and for all the relatively old structure of allegory and its fanciful aberrations, as they were practiced by the Alexandrian fathers and still others. This very new method is our own method today. A direct legacy from the Antiochian school, it was revived in the western Christian world in the nineteenth century, and it is applied by all biblical scholars of whatever background and affiliation.

The origin and development of the theological school of Antioch is necessarily treated in this book in a general fashion due to lack of more precise information. Its rival, the school of Alexandria, was more favorably treated by historical circumstances, which means we know a lot more about its beginnings, its curriculum, and its faculty.

At any rate, in the evolution of Christian thought and biblical scholarship the school of Antioch has contributed its considerable share. And Theodore proved to be the foremost expounder of his alma mater. He is still regarded as the number one theoretician of that historic institution who has exemplified in his own writings the basic tenets of his school.

Theodore's age was not conducive to a critical attitude toward the Bible, and yet in his biblical scholarship there is remarkable freedom for research and critical investigation. He seems to have advocated an objective viewpoint which ought to be ultimately based first on historical inquiry, and second on the internal evidence supplied by the text itself. His methodological tools cleared away the structure of biblical misconceptions so far as they then existed. He was particularly critical of the Alexandrian allegorists whom he preferred to name mythologues.

The purpose of this study is to present Theodore's Old Testament scholarship insofar as it has been preserved for us in the primary sources now available and to include every possible evidence and testimony coming from the secondary sources, particularly the Syriac texts which are scattered in different publications. We shall try to present as complete a picture of Theodore's study of the Old Testament as it is possible. We intend to ascertain the method by which he investigated the scriptural texts. For this we have included some attention to traditional Jewish and Christian methods of exegesis for the purpose of contrast. Attention is given to such subjects as canon and text, including the deuterocanonical (the so called apocrypha), as well as his opinion on the Septuagint. An attempt has been made to interpret the Mopsuestian's views on such thorny biblical questions as scriptural inspiration, prophetic call, prophetic inspiration, prophetic ecstasy, and messianic expectation. Theodore's interpretation of the prophetic call and inspiration is highly appreciative of the psychological aspects of the phenomenon of prophecy. In his opinion all the prophets of Israel were ecstatic personalities, and this state of mind resulted from their certainty that they clearly stood in a personal relationship with the eternal God. Prophetic inspiration is not a mechanical communication dictated in Hebrew by the spirit of God but an inner experience known during an ecstatic state when the prophet witnessed unutterable and terrifying experiences.

In conclusion there is clear ground for according Theodore of Mopsuestia a significant place in the history of biblical scholarship. He has anticipated a number of views—however embryonic—which are held by contemporary scholars.

# Chapter One

# EDUCATION AND MINISTRY
# OF THEODORE OF MOPSUESTIA

The life of Theodore is shrouded in obscurity. He was born ca. 350 in Antioch when the Arians were in the ascendency throughout the province of Syria. John Chrysostom informs us that Theodore was a man of noble birth and an heir to large estates.[1] Probably his parents were Christians, and his brother, Polycronius, became bishop of Apamea on the Orontes.[2]

Theodore, with his friend and companion John Chrysostom, and with Maximus, later bishop of Seleucia in Isauria, attended the lectures of the honored sophist Libanius under whose guidance they studied literature and rhetoric.[3] Theodore was also trained in philosophy; in Sozomen's *Church History,* Theodore is described as "a man well versed in the arts and sciences of the rhetors and philosophers."[4] He had developed, from his early youth, eagerness to study the liberal arts and had planned to dedicate himself to the profitable vocation of a lawyer, with the intention of attaining a civic office. His fine intellect had probably caught the attention of his teachers who advised him to carry on his graduate studies in the Forum, after his graduation from the Museum.[5]

No person seems to have exercised more influence over the youthful Theodore than his lifelong friend and colleague John Chrysostom. Theodore left the Museum and, following the example and advice of his former fellow student, John, retired with Maximus to the monastic school of Diodore and Carterius in the vicinity of Antioch.[6] Chrysostom remarks that Theodore's retirement from the noisy life of the Museum and Forum at the age of twenty was sincere and ardent and further suggests that Theodore's intention to practice every form of the ascetic discipline was pure and zealous.[7]

But soon there was to be a change, and Theodore's enthusiasm for the askesis was followed by a sudden reaction. He left the monastic school and order, returned to the Forum, and assumed his juristic studies. When he exchanged his ascetic vow for the Forum, however, Theodore did not fail to justify his decision by citing several examples from the Bible, for he was, according to the remark by the historian Sozomen, "a very learned person."[8] But Chrysostom's eloquence dissuaded him from continuing his studies in the Forum. Chrysostom, bitterly hurt by Theodore's vacillation, sent him a letter[9] in which he tried to persuade Theodore to return to *Asketerion:*

> I shed tears not because you assumed care of your patrimonial affairs, but because you have withdrawn yourself from the list of the brethren and have contemptuously obliterated your covenant with Christ. For this desertion severe punishment awaits you, if you persist in it. . . . A merchant can suffer shipwreck, an athlete can be defeated, a soldier can have recourse to flight; but they can come back again. . . . Of what profit to you the good fortune, power, riches and esteem? All that is but temporary. . . . Now your friends, Valerius, Florentius, Porphyrius and many others, are praying for you. If they do not despair of your salvation, why should you? He who lives for Christ alone enjoys real freedom. . . . Therefore away with despondency and fear, the sharpest weapons of evil. . . . At any rate I will try, with the lifeboat of this letter, to save you from shipwreck. . . . If you have not completely forgotten me, then rejoice me by answering it.[10]

Indeed Theodore listened to the brotherly admonitions of his friend, returned to the monastery and rededicated himself to his obedience with devotion. Thereafter and throughout his lifetime, until the question of Theodore's orthodoxy raised posthumously because a notorious issue for party strife, the record of his dedication and piety is unstained.

When Theodore embarked on the spiritual life, Diodore and Carterius were in charge of the *Asketerion.*[11] And thus Theodore had an excellent opportunity to carry on studies in exegesis and theology under the guidance of the learned Diodore, and in ascetics under Carterius. Diodore is generally considered to have been the founder of the school of Antioch, and his chief claim to fame lay in his meticulous exegetical work and the sound interpretive methods he inculcated.[12] He had pursued his classical studies in Athens, and later studied theology and exegesis in Antioch under the retired bishop of Emesa (Homs), Eusebius.[13] Apparently when Diodore joined the cloister he decided to open a theological school based on a monastic discipline.[14] According to Theodoret of Cyrus, Diodore's friend, Flavian, was most influential in the development of this religious school and made its faculty skilled debaters by providing Diodore and his teaching assistants with biblical manuscripts and doctrinal orientations with which they easily tore apart the nets of the heretics.[15] Diodore was Theodore's teacher, and the brightest period in the history of the school of Antioch opens with Diodore, who taught for a long time at the *Asketerion* before he became bishop of Tarsus in 378.[16] In his writings there are already the basic ideas for his dogmatic system and exegetical methodology, both of which appear later, more fully and more clearly developed, in Theodore's theological scholarship.[17] Unfortunately, information about the statutes of Diodore's school is lacking. Nor do we know much about the character of the instruction and the order of studies. Like the ecclesiastical institutions for the training of the clergy in the eastern church today, the school at Antioch resembled a monastic foundation under the jurisdiction of the bishop of the Syrian capital. The students as well as the ordained teachers lived in the *Asketerion,* and special rules regulated the daily program of this cenobite. This school was not, however, unlike the theological school of Alexandria, a recognized institution with a tradition of brilliant scholars. The students joined the *Asketerion* for ascetic-theological training and promised to remain unmarried. Study hours were long. The principal subject of the curriculum was the

Bible. In addition questions of dogmatics, apologetics, and ethics were studied. Philosophy was taught.[18] Participation in church services was compulsory. The system of interpretation of the Bible, which appealed to the Antiochene teachers, was the historico-grammatical exegesis of the biblical texts, as opposed to the allegorical and mystical theories pursued at Alexandria. Diodore, in contrasting the exegetical methodology of his school with that of the Alexandrians, declared: "We demand them to know that we prefer much more the historical comprehension of the text than the allegorical."[19]

At any rate, during those crucial years for the church at Antioch, the monastic foundation of Diodore and Carterius formed a religious institution of the first magnitude for the needs of the orthodox Christians of Syria, and a center for the cultivation of Christian letters. Here Theodore received his theological education. It was for him a period of growth in biblical and theological learning.

We do not know how long Theodore remained in the school of Diodore. The chronology of his life and its relation to later ecclesiastical happenings poses certain difficulties which cannot finally be solved. Chrysostom's connections with the school of Diodore were broken when he decided to retire to a remote mountain hermitage.[20] Theodore seems, however, to have continued his studies until the elevation of his teacher Diodore to the see of Tarsus in 378. In all probability Theodore remained from 369 to 378 in the *Asketerion* and kept busy expounding the scriptures and refuting heresy.[21]

Theodore had a third period of preparation for his life's work, this time in pastoral work. Theodore had long belonged to the congregation led by Flavian and, after the promotion of his teacher Diodore to the diocese of Tarsus, the future bishop of Mopsuestia attached himself to Flavian of Antioch by whom he was ordained presbyter.[22] Theodore might have been thirty-three years old when he was ordained a priest. As a presbyter he proved to his superior his eagerness to defend the cause of orthodoxy in word and writing. As a preacher he seems to have attained some distinction, especially in his contributions to the dogmatic disputes of that time in which he played an important role, as the testimonies of his contemporaries and the extant fragments of his works prove sufficiently.[23] He fervently opposed the errors of the Arians, Eunomians, Apollinarists, Origenists, and Persian magic, and he mediated in the Antiochian schism, which threw the church into confusion for a whole century.

Through his effectiveness as teacher and presbyter at the principal church in Antioch, and his productive literary work, Theodore's fame and authority grew from year to year. In 392 he was promoted, after the death of Bishop Olympios, to the see of Mopsuestia in Cilicia. As bishop he continued to work for the good of his diocese.[24] Several of his literary works are doubtless living commentaries on and reflections of those pastoral labors. The famous letter of Ibas testifies that Theodore, during his episcopate, eliminated from his ecclesiastical jurisdiction all sorts of errors and deviations from that which he rejected as right and true.[25] He was considered by many as "a herald of truth" and "a doctor of the entire church."[26]

In the year 394 Theodore accompanied Flavian to a synod at Constantinople which was to decide the question concerning the see of Bostra in the patriarchate of Antioch. On this occasion the clergy and the people of the capital were both astonished by the wisdom and eloquence of the Syrian bishop. The fame of Theodore had spread in the city, and Emperor Theodosius I invited him to preach in the imperial court. The sermon made a deep impression, and Theodosius declared that he had never met with such a teacher.[27] Another glimpse of Theodore's episcopal activities is supplied in a letter addressed to him from Pontus by his exiled friend John Chrysostom, the archbishop of Constantinople (404-407). Chrysostom had probably sought Theodore's aid through the latter's uncle, Paeanius, who held a public office in Constantinople.[28] Theodore energetically interceded with the rival parties on behalf of his old friend with a view to reconciling their differences. Evidently Theodore's mediation was strong and appealing for Chrysostom wrote:

> I can never forget thy love, so genuine and warm, so sincere and guileless, a love maintained from early years, and manifested even now. . . . I am not unaware of all

that you have endeavored to say and do on my behalf
my most honorable and God-loving lord. . . . Exiled, as
I am, I reap no ordinary comfort from having in Cilicia
such a treasure, such a mine of wealth, as the love of
your vigilant and brave heart.[29]

A more solemn declaration could not have been made by a
more impartial and unbiased judge, and so damaging was it felt
to be to the motives and machinations of Theodore's avowed
enemies that at the Second Council of Constantinople in 553,
efforts were vainly made to reject the authenticity of this letter.[30]

True to the traditions of the Antiochian church, Theodore
was in friendly communication with the fathers of the church.
Ibas of Edessa, in appraising the work of Theodore, noted: "Even
distant churches received instruction from him."[31] His most
famous pupils were John, bishop of Antioch; Theodoret, the celebrated bishop of Cyrus; Ibas of Edessa; and Nestorius, the archbishop of Constantinople and heresiarch. Toward the end of the
year 428, after receiving Nestorius, who was on his way to claim
the throne of the New Rome, Theodore died in peace and communion with the church, at the end of a ministry of forty-five
years.

Such are the data that history has left us about the life of a
highly gifted man whose intellectuality became proverbial among
both panegyrists and his enemies. It is a misfortune that his personal letters, long known to the Nestorian authors of Syria as *The
Book of Pearls* and doubtless a treasure for the history of his life,
have been lost.

Theodore of Mopsuestia lived and died in the fellowship of
faith, and several famous churchmen showed him great respect
while he was living. No reprimand was heard.[32] His orthodoxy
was not really questioned until three years after his death at the
Council of Ephesus (431) by a certain Charisius who introduced
a deformed creed linked with the name of Theodore. The creed
was condemned by the council, but its authorship did not come
up for discussion.[33] The denunciation of Theodore's orthodoxy
began only with the rise of the Nestorian heresy. Even then the
charges against Theodore's heterodoxy emerged slowly. It was

Rabboula, bishop of Edessa, who started the attacks against the Mopsuestian by charging that in his writings Theodore denied that Mary was *Theotokos*.[34] The Syriac bishop of Edessa, in his fervent animosity against the Mopsuestian, went so far as to order all existing manuscripts of Theodore's writings confiscated and burned.[35] Another person who detested both Nestorianism and Theodore was Acacius, bishop of Melitene in Armenia Secunda. In a letter to Sahak, Catholicos of Armenia, he advised the Armenian Christians to avoid those who are "imbued with the teaching of Theodore of Mopsuestia and the evil poison of Nestorius."[36]

The controversy over the heterodoxy of Theodore gained momentum and seriousness when Cyril of Alexandria, the man who masterminded the deliberations of the Council of Ephesus and exposed Nestorianism, joined the critics of Theodore. Cyril, who had once spoken favorably of Theodore's polemical and exegetical work, now, under the influence of Rabboula, Acacius, and certain Palestinian monks, decided to take a definite stand in opposition. Actually Cyril's opinion about Theodore's christological teaching was hardly any different from that expressed by Rabboula and Acacius. His remark in a letter to Acacius is typical:

> Pretending to detest the teachings of Nestorius, they applaud them in another way by admiring the teachings of Theodore, although these are tainted with an equal, or rather much more grievous impiety. For Theodore was not the disciple of Nestorius, but rather the other way around, and both speak as from one mouth, emitting one and the same poison of heterodoxy from their hearts.[37]

While Theodore was vigorously attacked by the followers of the Cyrillian party, he was wholeheartedly supported by the fathers of the Oriental dioceses. Cyril's judgment on Theodore was not shared by the followers of the school of Antioch. The fight was carried on by Theodore's students: by Ibas of Edessa, who succeeded Rabboula to the episcopacy in 435; by John of

Antioch, who valiantly fought against those who wanted to defame the character of his teacher; and by Theodoret, the most illustrious student of the Mopsuestian who undertook, with his sharp pen, to defend the memory of "the doctor of the universal church."[38] But the fervor of the campaign for the posthumous condemnation of Theodore subsided temporarily through the intervention of Emperor Theodosius II who, at the recommendation of Proclus of Constantinople, issued an edict to John of Antioch and his council of bishops urging them to unity, and urging that all should make it a rule never to assail the memory of persons who had died in the communion of the church.[39]

The issue of Theodore's orthodoxy did not come up for discussion in the Fourth Ecumenical Council of Chalcedon in 451. However, the fathers of this council had an excellent opportunity to hear an echo of Theodore's full name when, attentively, they listened to the letter of Ibas which was read in the assembly.[40] It is a serious question why the fathers of Chalcedon did not attempt to settle the controversy over Theodore's orthodoxy when the name of the late bishop of Mopsuestia was formally introduced into the proceedings of the council by the letter of Ibas. It may be that the council had no time to discuss the subject of Theodore's orthodoxy because it had to deal with more urgent problems. We know, of course, that the fathers of Chalcedon did discuss the fate of such personalities as Dioscorus, Eutyches, Theodoret, Ibas, Domnus, Flavian and others.[41] Some contemporary writers interpret the silence of Chalcedon, regarding Theodore, as a conciliar approbation of his orthodox contribution to the development of the christological dogma.[42] However, it is difficult to view the *Definition of Chalcedon* as a justification of Theodore's view on the incarnation. The claim that the council had many other more immediate and urgent issues to deal with, and preferred to abstain from attempting to solve disputes which were not within its agenda, hardly seems acceptable.[43]

There are clear reasons which would better explain why Theodore was not considered at Chalcedon. First of all, the Mopsuestian, in spite of the charges of Cyril against his christology, does not seem at that time to have been declared by the church a formal heretic. Second, Proclus of Constantinople, Cyril of

Alexandria, John of Antioch, and Emperor Theodosius II had all agreed, only a few years before, never to assail the memory of a person who had died in peace with the church. Third, after the downfall and exile of Dioscorus, the council resumed its deliberations, but in those later sessions the ultra-Cyrillian party was left without a spokesman who would raise the issue.

However, the overriding question is not why Theodore was not discussed in the council, but whether the synod of Chalcedon defined a profession of faith in essentials similar to that of Theodore. The conciliar definition affirms that Christ is one person in two natures which are united unconfusedly, unchangeably, indivisibly, inseparably, in one *Prosopon* and *Hypostasis;* the Virgin Mary is the *Theotokos.*[44]

The Chalcedonian definition represents a moderate statement of faith, worded carefully in order to keep the balance between opposing standpoints in regard to the problem of the union of the divine and the human natures in Christ. The formula of the statement rests upon a theological eclecticism which meets the essential christological viewpoints of the two rival schools of Alexandria and Antioch. As Kelly rightly has remarked: "In its final shape the Definition is a mosaic of excerpts from Cyril's two Letters, Leo's *Tome,* the Union Symbol (of Antioch) and Flavian's profession of faith at the Standing Synod of the patriarchate at Constantinople."[45] The emphasis of the conciliar definition is grounded in the absolute belief that while Jesus Christ is consubstantial with the Father, according to the Godhead, and consubstantial with us, according to manhood, he nevertheless remains one person and one *hypostasis* in two natures. The two natures, the divine and the human, co-exist without division in the oneness of the personality of the Godman. The person of Christ is identical with that of the incarnated external Logos. Because he who was born of the Father before the ages was also born of the Virgin Mary according to the flesh, Mary must be recognized as *Theotokos.*[46]

With these preliminaries, we can turn to a brief consideration of Theodore's doctrine of the incarnation and compare his christology with the conclusions of Chalcedon. The problem of the union of the divine and human natures in Christ engaged

Theodore's continual attention because Arianism and Apollinarianism were in full sway at the close of the fourth century; and
the Mopsuestian, inspired by the example of his teacher, Diodore
of Tarsus, strove mightily to stem the tide of heresy. His major
works on the subject are lost, and an objective appraisal of his
christology is a difficult undertaking. For his views we must
depend on the so-called "hostile florilegia,"[47] which have been
compiled by pamphleteers of the sixth century for securing Theodore's condemnation by the Fifth General Council, and on the
newly-discovered texts of Theodore's works.

The most distinctive aspect of Theodore's christology is its
dualism: Christ is both perfect God and perfect man. A typical
Theodorean sentence runs: "Let us apply our minds to the distinction of natures; He Who assumed is God and only-begotten
Son, but the form of a slave, He Who was assumed, is man."[48]
At a time when proper attention was not always paid to the
humanity of Christ, and there was a strong tendency to reduce
Christ's manhood to a vanishing point, the christology of Theodore emphatically stressed that the incarnated divine Logos
assumed a complete human nature, composed of a body and an
immortal soul. Theodore's christological dualism, favored by all
the Antiochene thinkers, is mainly the product of his opposition
to the teaching of Arians and Apollinarians, who questioned, in
their respective christologies, the reality of Christ's divine nature
and human soul.[49] Gospel revelation, Theodore argued, draws a
sharp line of demarcation between the characteristic attributes of
the two natures, divine and human, in the one Christ.[50] In the
public ministry of the historical Jesus, Theodore pleaded, the
mutual properties of the two natures remained distinguishable.
In harmony with this, he insisted that Christ exists in the duality
of his natures, and thus he was led to distinguish between the Son
of God and the son of David.[51] Alongside the divine nature there
must be a complete and autonomous human nature, which
undergoes real physical growth as well as growth in the discern-
ment of good and evil.[52] Of the complete manhood of Christ
Theodore had no doubt, and that is why he spoke at length about
the weaknesses and defects of the Lord's physical nature.[53] Theodore was no less explicit regarding the existence in Christ of a

perfect divine nature. The distinction between the "assumer" Logos and the "assumed" man is commonplace in Theodore's dogmatic writings and occurs numerous times. The result of this sharp distinction between the divine and the human in the historical Jesus was that it enabled Theodore to assert consistently the independence of the two natures without confusion and without division in the person of Christ.[54] The duality in the God-man, the reality of the two natures in Christ, and the explicit acknowledgement of Christ's normal human psychology are the basic and soundest features of Theodore's christological schema and as such are enshrined and recognized in the Chalcedonian *Definition of Faith.*[55] But beyond this point Theodore's teaching on the two natures in Christ is not free from notable defects. It lacks an important theological feature which was strongly emphasized by the Chalcedonian fathers: the God-man who exists in two natures is one person and *one hypostasis.* The one person affected by the union of the two natures is the unique *hypostasis* of the incarnated Logos, who was born of the *Theotokos* and is consubstantial with the Father according to divinity and consubstantial with us according to humanity. The divine Logos is the unique subject of the Incarnate.

On the contrary, Theodore differed in his understanding of the problems of the unity of Christ. There can be no doubt that he taught that the Incarnate is one person, and that the doctrine of two sons, the Son of God and the son of David, had no appeal to him;[56] nevertheless he never admitted that the one person in Christ is none other than the incarnated Logos in whom there are two natures united into a harmonious *hypostasis.* His Christ was not a person metaphysically dependent on the incarnated Logos. Theodore was a moralistic metaphysician, and his theological presuppositions did not allow him to expound the incarnation in terms of metaphysics. God cannot be present in any heterosubstantial place according to essence because this would be a limitation of his infinity.[57]

How, then, does the unity of Christ's two natures project itself in Theodore's doctrinal system? How is the union between the assumed man and the Logos who assumed him to be defined? Theodore dealt with the problem by using biblical language which excluded any metaphysical implication. The idea of "dwelling" *(skenao)* or "indwelling" *(enoikeo)* provided him with the most satisfying interpretation of the incarnation.[58] It is not a dwelling by essence of hypostasis, but by good will *(eudokia)*. The relevant fragment reads:

> And why is it necessary to say any more? The reason for the union according to essence is true only in the case of consubstantials, but in the case of things not consubstantial it is not true, there being no possible reason for confusion. But the manner of union according to good will, while preserving the natures, demonstrates the one person of both inseparably, and also the one will and one energy, together with one authority and rule which is consequent to these.[59]

The quoted passage shows that Theodore was not indifferent to the problem of the unity of Christ's person. But he rather offered a view of unity which in its essentials suggests a biblical explanation and not a theological one.

However, we cannot charge Theodore with obstinacy and deliberate distortion of Christian truth. There is no indication of anything like a formal heresy. There seems to be evidence that Theodore's intention, in thinking out the christological problem, was to conform to the doctrine of the church as he understood it. One cannot read Theodore's extant dogmatic writings without being thoroughly impressed by his honest intention to think with the church.

The Fifth General Council, held one hundred and twenty-five years after Theodore's death, condemned: (1) the writings of Theodore *in toto;* (2) the writings of Theodoret against Cyril of Alexandria and in favor of Nestorius; (3) the letter of Ibas of Edessa to the Persian Maris. The council pronounced a formal anathema on Theodore. The reasons for the condemnation were largely theological and political. The Monophysite quarrel proved highly dangerous to the Byzantine empire since many of its followers in the granary-land of Egypt mixed nationalistic tendencies with their religion and threatened the rule of Constantinople. Emperor Justinian, in his autocratic religious policy, was determined to reconcile the Monophysite church of Egypt with his court. So he insisted on, and obtained, in 553, the condemnation of Theodore, whom the Monophysites regarded as the originator of Nestorianism, their chief antagonist. The practice of the church, up to that year, was to sanctify those who died in peace and communion with it. In anathematizing Theodore, the Church acted against its own tradition and set a precedent which it has never used again.

## NOTES

1. *Ad Theodorum lapsum* II, Migne, PG (47), 309.
2. Theodoret, *Hist. Eccl.,* 5.40, Migne, PG (82), 1277.
3. Socrates, *Hist. Eccl.,* 6.3, Migne, PG (67), 665–668.
4. *Hist. Eccl.* 8.2, Migne, PG (67), 1516.
5. *Ad Theodorum lapsum* II, Migne, PG (47), 314.
6. Socrates, *Hist. Eccl.,* 6.3; Theodoret, *Hist. Eccl.,* 5:27.
7. *Ad Theodorum lapsum* II, Migne (47), 310.
8. *Historia Ecclesiastica,* 8:2.
9. Actually there are two letters which bear the title *Ad Theodorum lapsum* (cf. Migne, PG [47], 277–308, 309–316). The first is rather an essay which never refers to Theodore by name and is addressed to a person who seems to be much older than the one addressed in the second letter. The second document is a strictly personal letter addressed to a "Dear Theodore," and this title is repeated in the same letter five times. The old church tradition with the exception of Leontius of Byzantium (cf. Migne, PG [86], 1364) speaks of one letter (cf. Sozomen, *Hist. Eccl.,* 8.2 Migne PG [67], 1516).
10. *Ibid.,* 309–316. In Migne, PG (66), 96 there is an answer to this letter, but it is generally considered to be apocryphal and to have been occasioned by Chrysostom's closing remark.
11. Socrates, *Hist. Eccl.,* 6.3, Migne (67), 665–668.
12. J. Ph. de Barjeau, *L'école exégétique d'Antioche,* 34f.
13. Jerome, *De vir. illustr.,* cap. 119, Migne PL (23), 709.

14. Louis Pirot, *L'oeuvre exégétique de Théodore de Mopsueste* (Romae: Pontificii Inst. Biblici, 1913), 28.

15. *Hist. Eccl.* 4.22, Migne, PG (82), 1184–1185.

16. We may assume that the church at Antioch had possessed from early times a religious center for the training of the clergy with a primitive system of education. Such schools and scholastic unions existed in Alexandria, Cappodocia, Carthage, Rome, and Edessa (cf. A. Harnack, *History of Dogma,* trans. N. Buchanan [3rd German ed., London: Williams & Norgate, 1895], II, 321–323). But unfortunately the old church historians say nothing about this school or center at Antioch.

17. Diodore was a voluminous writer, and of his works only scanty fragments exist; he wrote commentaries on several books of the Old Testament (cf. Migne, PG [33], 1545–1628). For a recent bibliography and listing of sources see Johannes Quasten, *Patrology* (Westminster, Md.: The Newman Press, 1960), III, 397–403.

18. Theodoret characterizes the *Asketeria* in and about Antioch as "seminars of philosophy" and the religious education which the trainees received as "sacred philosophy" (cf. *Histor. Religiosa,* Migne, PG [82], 1325, 1340, 1348, 1364).

19. J. Ph. de Barjeau, *L'école exégétique d'Antioche,* 35, n. 3.

20. Palladius, *Dialogue,* Migne, PG (47), 18.

21. H.B. Swete (ed.), *Theodori episcopi Mopsuestini in epistolas beati Pauli commentarii* (Cambridge: At the University Press, 1880), I, lix, n. 3.

22. Our information comes from a letter of John of Antioch (429-441) which is cited by Facundus: "iste ille [Theodori] est Flaviani magni Antiochiensium sanctae Dei ecclesiae pontificis amantissimus discipulus" (*cf. Pro defensione trium capitulorum,* 2.2 Migne, PL [67], 563).

23. *Ibid.,* 722–723.

24. Mopsuestia was a town in the Roman empire built upon the Pyramus, between Tarsus and Issus; the name of this town is explained by Strabo as the dwelling place of Mopsus, the legendary king of the Argives (cf. Strabo, *Geographica,* 14.5).

25. Mansi, *Coll. Conc.,* VII, 247.

26. Theodoret, *Hist. Eccl.,* 5.40.

27. Mansi, III, 857; Facundus, *Pro defensione trium capitulorum,* 2.2, Migne, PL (67), 563: "ile imperator fuit in ecclesia eius doctrinae auditor magnus nec arbitratus est alterum se talem comperisse doctorem superadmiratus quidem eius doctrinam."

28. Chrysostom, *Epist.* 204, Migne, PG (52), 724-725.

29. *Epist.* 112, Migne, PG (52), 668-669.

30. Mansi, *op. cit.,* IX, 272-273: "Praesumerunt vero Theodori defensores etiam Joanis sanctae memoriae episcopi . . . litteras proferre quasi ad Theodorum factas, laudes ejusdem Theodori continentes. Quod vero falsa ista sunt, testimonium praebent qui ecclesiasticas historias studiose scripferunt, aperte narrantes quod ad Theodorum Mopsuestenum, cum a solitaria vite excidisset scripta est epistola ab joanne multorum versum et utilissima . . ."

31. Robert Devreesse, *Essai sur Théodore de Mopsueste* (Citta del vaticano: Bibliotheca Apost. Vaticana, 1948), 51.

32. Theodore is reported, in a letter written by John of Antioch and quoted by Facundus, as having created a scandal among his congregation by some expression he used in a sermon. The reaction of the congregation against that expression was so strong that Theodore later retracted it (*cf. Pro defensione trium capitulorum,* 10.2, Migne, PL [67], 771). Actually we do not know what this expression was which disturbed the congregation. It has been suggested by some modern scholars that Theodore refused to Mary the title of *Theotokos.* For a refutation of this charge, see Francis A. Sullivan, *The Christology of Theodore of Mopsuestia* (Romae: Apud Aedes Univ. Gregorianae, 1956), 4.

33. Cyril Alexandr., *Epist.* 72 *Ad Proclum,* Migne, PG (77), 345 A.

34. Rabboula, in a letter to Cyril of Alexandria, which is preserved in the Acts of the Fifth Council, stated: "Iste primus exposuit non esse Dei genetricem secundum veritatem sanctam Mariam, tanquam Deo Verbo non recipiente eam quae secundum nos est genituram" (Mansi, IX, 247-248).

35. This information comes from a famous document which is known as *The Letter of Ibas of Edessa* (Mansi, VII, 241-249), which was addressed to Maris of Persia about whom we know practically nothing. Ibas at that time was the head of the Syriac-

speaking school of Edessa and later succeeded Rabboula in the diocese from 435 to 457. He was associated with the school at Antioch and translated several works of Theodore into Syriac. In the christological controversies Ibas followed a mediating position between Nestorianism and Alexandrian theology, and championed the cause of Theodore against his enemies. On account of his views and the unfavorable language he used about Cyril in his famous letter, describing the latter's behavior at the Council of Ephesus, Ibas was deposed in the Latrocinium synod in Ephesus in 449. The Council of Chalcedon in 451 reinstated him after he anathematized Nestorius. However, Ibas' letter was condemned a century later by the Fifth Council in 553 in the so-called Three Chapters controversy.

36. F.S. Sullivan, *The Christology of Theodore of Mopsuestia,* 6.

37. *Epist.* 69, *Ad Acacium,* Migne, PG (77), 340 AB.

38. *Hist. Eccl.,* 5.40, Migne, PG (82), 1277.

39. *Synodicon adversus tragoediam Irenaei,* Migne, PG (84), 849-850; Mansi, V, 1009.

40. The tragic vicissitudes of Theodore's orthodoxy with a careful and detailed analysis of the events which contributed to his final condemnation in 553, have been studied by R. Devreesse *(Essai sur Théodore de Mopsueste,* 124–242).

41. Cf. B.J. Kidd, *A History of the Church* (Oxford: At the Clarendon Press, 1922), III, 317–330.

42. Some scholars have recently come up with the conclusion that the Council of Chalcedon with its definition of faith represents a vindication of Theodore's theological reputation. R. Devreesse states: "Le concile de Chalcedoine rehabilitatit Theodoret; il ecoutait, sans manifester le moindre signe de desapprobation, la lecture de la letter d'Ibas contenant l'eloge de Theodore de Mopsueste et rappelait Ibas a son siege d'Edesse, il semblait ignorer qu'il y eut une attaque de Cyrille d'Alexandrie contre Diodore et Theodore; d'un mot, Theodore sortait indemne de la seconde manoeuvre entreprise contre lui" *(Essai sur Théodore de Mopsueste,* 168). Kevin McNamara, on the other hand, claims that the whole standpoint of Chalcedon on Theodore is "significant, as indicating its awareness of his positive contribution to

the development of the doctrine enshrined in its canon" and "as a witness to the Council's conviction of Theodore's good faith in all that he had written" ("Theodore of Mopsuestia and the Nestorian Heresy," *The Irish Theological Quarterly,* XIX (1952), 255.

43. F.A. Sullivan, *op. cit.,* 9–11.

44. The Chalcedonian definition of faith was expressed in the following terms: "In agreement, therefore, with the holy fathers, we unanimously teach that we should confess that our Lord Jesus Christ is one and the same Son, the same perfect in Godhead and the same perfect in manhood, truly God and truly man, the same of rational soul and the body, consubstantial with the Father in Godhead, and the same consubstantial with us in manhood, like us in all things except sin; begotten from the Father before the ages as regards his Godhead, and in the last days, the same, because of us and because of our salvation begotten from the Virgin Mary, the Theotokos, as regards his manhood; one and the same Christ, Son, Lord, only-begotten, made known in two natures without confusion, without change, without division, without separation, the differences of the natures being by no means removed because of the union, but the property of each nature being preserved and coalescing in one *prosopon* and one *hypostasis*—not parted or divided into two *prosopa,* but one and the same Son, only-begotten, divine Word, the Lord Jesus Christ. . . ." See this text in J.N.D. Kelly, *Early Christian Doctrines* (New York: Harper & Brothers, 1958), 339–340.

45. *Ibid.,* 340–341.

46. The term *Theotokos* was widely used by the Alexandrine theologians; it followed as a postulate from the assertion of the *communicatio idiomatum,* and expressed the idea that since Christ's body to which the Logos was personally united was born of the Virgin, He was born after the flesh. The term underlies Cyril's christological teaching and served as the *casus belli* of the controversy between him and Nestorius. Cyril, in receiving the Union Symbol of Antioch in which the Antiochenes recognized the orthodoxy of the term *Theotokos* (cf. T.H. Bindley, The *Oecumenical Documents of the Faith* [3rd ed., London: Methuen, 1950], 274), in his answer to John of Antioch said: "For it is your

absolute duty clearly to understand that well-nigh the whole of our contest for the faith has been waged round our affirmation that the holy Virgin is *Theotokos*" (*ibid.,* 275). Nestorius' preference was for *Christotokos* because of his concern to safeguard the full manhood of Christ and secure the distinction of the two natures in him; but Nestorius was prepared to allow the user of the term *theotokos* under the following conditions: "If any simple soul among you or anywhere else finds pleasure in the term, I have no objection to it. Only do not let him make the Virgin a goddess" (Fr. Loofs, *Nestoriana: Die fragmente des Nestorius* [Halle: Max Niemeyer, 1905], 272).

47. The "hostile florilegia" are to be found in Migne, PG (66), 970–1016; Mansi, *op. cit.,* IX, 203–229.

48. *Commentary on the Nicene Creed* (Cambridge: W. Heffer and Sons, 1932), 89. It is typical of Theodore that he should describe the divinity of Christ as *Verbum assumens* (the Logos who assumed) and Christ's humanity as *homo assumptus* (the man who was assumed).

49. R.A. Norris, Jr., *Manhood and Christ. A Study in the Christology of Theodore of Mopsuestia* (Oxford: At the Clarendon Press, 1963), 202.

50. *Fragmenta dogmatica,* Migne, PG (66), 1004 C.

51. *Ibid.,* 997 C, 1004 D.

52. *Ibid.,* 977 D, 980 A.

53. *Commentary on the Nicene Creed,* 55, 69.

54. *Fragmenta dogmatica,* Migne, PG (66), 1013 A.

55. For the text of the Chalcedonian *Definition of Faith* see J.N.D. Kelly, *op. cit.,* 339–340.

56. *Commentary on the Nicene Creed,* 90.

57. For a discussion of Theodore's moralistic metaphysics, see John S. Romanides, "Highlights in the Debate over Theodore's Christology and Some Suggestions for a Fresh Approach," *Greek Orthodox Theological Review,* V, (Winter 1959–1960), 164ff.

58. *Fragmenta dogmatica,* Migne, PG (66), 972–973.

59. *Ibid.,* 1013.

# Chapter Two

# THEODORE'S LITERARY ACTIVITY
# AND THE PRESENT STATE
# OF HIS WORKS

Theodore's contribution to the patristic literature was substantial. His literary activity began at an early age, possibly while he was still a student under Diodore and Carterius, and continued till at least the end of the second decade of the fifth century.[1] During these years Theodore's pen was unusually productive and his creativity became proverbial among both his friends and his adversaries. John of Antioch, in his attempt to defend the memory of his deceased teacher, mentioned that Theodore "has written immeasurable books against heresies."[2] To this testimony Cyril of Alexandria, Theodore's later adversary, paid this tribute:

> The great Theodore has written perhaps twenty ample books against the Arian and Eunomian heresies, and besides these he has interpreted the gospel and apostolic writings.[3]

Leontius of Byzantium, in his polemic against a deceased Theodore, made the sarcastic remark that he was treating scriptures with insult when he was no more than eighteen years old.[4]

It was as an interpreter of the Bible that Theodore stood supreme among the scholars of his day. In later times, when he was condemned as a heretic, Theodore was known by those who still venerated him as the Mephasqana (interpreter) par excellence.[5] He wrote commentaries on nearly all the books of the

Bible, and these are remarkable for their objective investigations into questions of date and authorship, structure and unity, historical background, canonicity, and inspiration. He composed in addition a large number of dogmatic and apologetic works which prove his keen interest in most of the religious issues of his day and attest that he was engaged in a theological dialogue throughout his lifetime.

Few of what must have been the numerous writings of Theodore have come down to us. This is due primarily to the fact that he was associated with Nestorianism by succeeding generations, and this circumstance led to deliberate attempts to destroy his writings as dangerous to true faith. As noted above, Rabboula of Edessa was the first to anathematize Theodore and to order all existing copies of his works confiscated and burned.[6] Prohibited though they were, parts of Theodore's works were quoted verbatim, even though anonymously, in biblical commentaries.[7] Some of Theodore's writings were translated into Syriac and Latin.

The best sources for the titles of Theodore's writings are two parallel catalogues which have been preserved in Syriac documents from the thirteenth and fourteenth centuries. One of these catalogues comes from the Nestorian metropolitan Ebedjesus, the last important theological writer of the Syriac-speaking church, who died at the beginning of the fourteenth century.[8] The second catalogue of Theodore's works is provided in the so-called *Chronicle of Seert,* which is a Nestorian document from the first half of the thirteenth century and was discovered in Kurdistan and edited in French by Addai Scher in 1909.[9]

Although these two Syriac catalogues were written many centuries after Theodore's death, their historical data may be considered reliable. This is shown by the agreement which exists between the two catalogues on numerous items, although, as indicated by several differences, they were independently compiled.[10] Furthermore, the Christians of eastern Syria made themselves the heirs of Antiochian biblical scholarship, and the writings of the Mephasqana were so much esteemed that after the Council of Ephesus in 431 several of Theodore's compositions were translated into Syriac by the teachers at the school of

Edessa, thus becoming the literary heritage of the Nestorian church of Syria and Persia.[11]

Both catalogues are divided into two parts; in each the first deals with the exegetical commentaries, and the second with dogmatic treatises plus liturgical, didactic, and canon law subjects. According to Ebedjesus, Theodore's commentaries consisted of forty-one volumes and exceeded in size one hundred and fifty times the books of the major and minor prophets combined.[12]

*On the Book of Genesis.* In his catalogue Ebedjesus noted that Theodore the interpreter "published a commentary on the book of Genesis in three volumes which he elaborated with preeminent method and explanation."[13] The Chronicle of Seert tells us that "Aliph requested him to write a commentary on the Pentateuch, something which he did in three volumes."[14]

Photius, patriarch of Constantinople (c. 819–895), seems to have been acquainted only with the first volume of this commentary on the Pentateuch, of which he gives us the following biased opinion:

> Read the work of Theodore of Antioch entitled History of Creation, the first book of which contains seven volumes. The style is neither brilliant nor very clear. Theodore, in this book, avoids the use of allegory as much as possible, being only concerned with the discovery of the historical sense of the book. He frequently writes tautologically, and produces a graceless and unpleasant impression. . . .[15]

This commentary has been lost and only a few fragments have come down to us.[16] Additional parts or fragments of this commentary have been recovered from various Byzantine *catenae* published by Karo and Lietzmann.[17] Different citations from this commentary have been preserved by John Philopon.[18] Some other fragments of the same work have been discovered from the manuscript M or Coislin 113 (Coislinianus) of the National Library of Paris, and have been published by R. Devreesse.[19] And a few fragments have been preserved in a Syriac manuscript which was edited by Sachau.[20] Thus we are now in possession of

Theodore's commentary on Genesis 1–3, covering the act of the creation, the organization of creatures, the invisible powers, day and night and the first day, plants and animals, the creation of man as the image of God, the sabbath rest, paradise and the tree of knowledge, the creation of Eve, the fall and the expulsion.

The determination of the date of this book is extremely difficult. The catalogues make no allusion to historical persons, and the fragments do not provide bases for any such judgment. However, Swete surmises that the commentary could have been written by 405.[21]

*On Exodus.* Did Theodore write a commentary on the Pentateuch? Though Ebedjesus does not mention the other books of the torah, the *Chronicle of Seert* specifies that Alipha requested Theodore to write on the Pentateuch, and he did it in three volumes. Meanwhile the *catenae* have preserved three excerpts which explain Exodus 25:8–20 (the ark of the covenant and the mercy-seat), Exodus 25:23–29 (the table of the showbread), and Exodus 25:30–38 (the seventh-branch menorah).[22] The catenists have also preserved a few lines from Theodore's commentary on Joshua 7:45, and on Judges 13:25 and 16:17.[23] The existence, therefore, of about half a dozen fragments indicates that the commentary on Genesis was not the only one. Leontius of Byzantium affirms that Theodore wrote commentaries on the whole Bible.[24]

*On the Book of Psalms.* Ebedjesus in his catalogue stated, "He expounded (the book of) David in five volumes for Cedron who was his brother."[25] And the *Chronicle of Seert* adds: "and Cedron requested him to write one more commentary on David, something which he did in three volumes."[26] But the most pertinent witness to this commentary comes from Theodore himself. In a book that bears the title *On Allegory and History* our author apologizes to Cedron that his commentary on the Psalms was written in haste because of lack of time, and that was why he neglected to write it more diligently.[27]

Further, Theodore in his surviving commentary on the twelve minor prophets does not fail to refer his readers frequently to his interpretation of the Psalms. These references indicate that Theodore wrote his commentary on the twelve after he had finished his commentary on the Psalms.[28] The treatise on the

Psalms was Theodore's first exegetical commentary, and he probably composed it when he was associated with Diodore in the school of Antioch.[29]

This commentary has been lost, and only recently has Robert Devreesse succeeded in recovering the greater part of the text from a host of manuscripts. The text is in great part in the original Greek, and partly in Latin translation.[30] Thanks to this discovery we are no longer limited to the fragments printed in Migne (PG 66, 648–696), of which about one-half must be rejected as spurious.[31]

The history of the recovery of this work is interesting and may be briefly told. As far back as the end of the nineteenth century (1896), Giovanni Cardinal Mercati announced that a manuscript belonging to the Ambrosian Library at Milan, the Code 301 inf., which was formerly published by G. I. Ascoli (1878–1889),[32] contained a Latin translation of a Greek commentary on the book of Psalms, of which the original was an exegetical treatise by Theodore of Mopsuestia.[33] But this commentary on the Psalms published by Ascoli was not complete, and Mercati supplemented it from another manscript (the F. IV. 1, facs. 5–6.) of the University Library of Turin, which actually was related to the first because both were produced in the eighth century at the celebrated library of the Abbey of Bobbio.[34]

This discovery by Mercati was followed in 1902 by an announcement at the Academy of Berlin: Hans Lietzmann declared that in the National Library of Paris he had found a Greek manuscript (Coislin or Coislinianus 12) which contained comments on Psalms 32–72; he concluded that the work was the lost commentary on the book of Psalms by Theodore of Mopsuestia.[35] After this announcement in the Academy, Lietzmann published in paraphrase the comments on the individual Psalm 46 (H47).

Monsignor Robert Devreesse, guided in his research by Mercati and aided by Lietzmann's pioneering work, was able to edit with great skill and learning almost half of Theodore's renowned commentary on the Psalms.[36] Devreesse was directed to the Theodorean authorship of the recovered commentary partly by the nature of its content, and partly by the character of the Septuagint text and its marginal notes, which bear the name of Theodore. The Greek portions of the commentary derive mainly from the Paris MSS *catena,* Coislin 12. The rest of the original comments are extricated from a host of *catenae* manuscripts, the most important of which are the MS Paris gr. 139, and the MSS Vat. gr. 1682 and 1683. From biblical manuscripts Devreesse succeeded in recovering and reconstructing both the scriptural text and the comments, almost complete, on Psalms 32–80.[37]

Moreover, a large portion of the commentary on Psalms has been recovered from a Latin translation in the Ambrosian manuscript C. 301 inf., and from the code of the University of Turin F. IV. 1, fasc. 5–6. These Latin manuscripts enabled Devreesse to restore in its entirety that portion of Theodore's commentary that covers Psalms 1:1–16:11, and large portions for Psalms 16:12–40:13.

*On the Twelve Prophets.* His commentary on the minor prophets is the only one of Theodore's many exegetical compositions surviving in its original text, perhaps because it offers almost nothing of christological import.[38] Its text has come down to us in a manuscript of the tenth century preserved in the Vatican Library and registered as Vat. gr. 2204. It was published first by the paleographer Angelo Cardinal Mai in 1825, and in 1854 Jacques Migne reprinted Cardinal Mai's publication in his Patrologia Graeca (Vol. 66, 123–632).

*On 1 and 2 Samuel.* Both of these Syriac catalogues state that Theodore wrote a commentary on the books of Samuel at the request of a friend. Ebedjesus states, "He commented on Samuel in one volume for Ma[ma]ri[a]nus,"[39] and the chronicle adds, "Babai requested him to write a commentary on Samuel."[40] Such is the witness of the Syriac sources, and not one single fragment has come down to us from this writing.

*On the Book of Job.* The Acts of the fifth general council in 553 have preserved five extracts from Theodore's commentary on Job which are reprinted in Migne.[41] Ebedjesus states that Theodore dedicated this commentary to Cyril of Alexandria. In addition to this information, a Nestorian author of the ninth century, Isho'dad of Merv, supplies us with valuable information concerning Theodore's views on the person of Job and the date and authorship of that book.[42]

*On the Book of Ecclesiastes.* The Syriac sources inform us that Theodore wrote a commentary on Ecclesiastes, and this information is confirmed by a passage cited in the Acts of the Fifth Council in which Theodore is charged of having taught that Solomon did not write the books of Proverbs and Ecclesiastes with the prophetic charisma, but through his wisdom and experience.[43] Also a Syriac translation of Theodore's commentary on Ecclesiastes was discovered before the First World War in the *qubbet el-hazne* (treasure dome) of the grand mosque of the Ommayyads at Damascus, Syria. It was seen by E. von Soden, who accompanied Kaiser Wilhelm II during his good-will tour to the near east.[44] But this manuscript has remained unavailable to modern scholarship.

*On the Song of Songs.* The Syriac catalogues do not mention this book among Theodore's writings. However, the Acts of the Fifth Council have preserved in a Latin translation a few passages from one of Theodore's letters which indicate that he dealt with the Song of Songs at the request of a friend, who is not mentioned in the passages.[45] Further, Leontius of Byzantium noted:

> In his [Theodore's] impudent and immoderate reckless-
> ness, having understood the Song of Songs according to
> his prostituted language and judgment, he cut it off from
> the Holy Books.[46]

If Theodore excluded the Song from his Old Testament canon, then the fragments may be excerpts from a letter which was written and addressed to an unknown friend who had asked Theodore for certain explanations concerning the book. This is exactly what the first fragment suggests.[47] But the three remaining fragments give the impression that they belonged to a commentary which was comparatively short. It actually consisted of a succinct exposition of the meaning of the Song of Songs in the form of an historical paraphrase. Theodore, in these fragments, considers the book a nuptial poem written by Solomon concerning his marriage to an Egyptian princess, and refuses to grant it a deeper meaning. The book is simply an epithalamium or love poetry and any allegorical or mystical interpretation must be given up.[48]

*On the Major Prophets.* We have lost Theodore's commentaries on the major prophets. Ebedjesus noted: "He expounded and elucidated Isaiah, Ezekiel, Jeremiah, and Daniel; each one in one volume. And with this he finished his labors on the Old Testament."[49] The *Chronicle of Seert* remarks, "He commented on Jeremiah, Ezekiel, and Daniel."[50]

From Theodore's commentaries on the major prophets not even a single fragment survives. After a fresh examination of the sources, Vosté reached the conclusion that Theodore did not comment on the major prophets. Vosté's conclusion is based on the following arguments:

> If Theodore had expounded the four major prophets [including Daniel], he would have referred his readers to these commentaries in his later writings as it was his practice to do. Besides, none of the ancient sources, such as the Greek *catenae,* the Acts of the Fifth Council, and the church historians, gives us a slight vestige which would indicate that Theodore had expounded the major prophets. One might object that this negative process of reasoning is ultimately based on arguments *a silentio;* it is true, yet these arguments *a silentio* have the value of probability or moral certainty in our daily life as well as in history.[51]

These are hardly grounds for stating so categorically a conclusion, as Vosté does on this issue, at least insofar as Theodore's commentary on the book of Isaiah is concerned. A sixth century author, Facundus of Hermianae, seems to confirm that Theodore had written a commentary "in expositione quoque Hesaiae prophetae libro quarto sic ait."[52]

The year 383 marks a turning point in Theodore's literary career. His entrance into the priesthood forced him to interrupt, at least temporarily, his exegetical commentaries on the Old Tes-

tament, and he turned his attention to the christological controversies of his time. This concern led him necessarily to study the
New Testament. He now dedicated himself to a polemic against
heresies by writing theological books and New Testament
commentaries.[53]

According to Ebedjesus, Theodore expounded Matthew in
one volume for Julius; Luke and John in two volumes for Eusebius.[54] His commentaries on the synoptic gospels have been lost;
only a few fragments exist, some of which are printed in Migne's
*Patrologia Graeca,* and the rest are scattered in different catenae.[55] The situation, however, is entirely different with Theodore's *Commentary on the Gospel of John;* it has reached us in a
complete Syriac version, which was discovered in 1868 by G. E.
Khayyat in the Chaldaean monastery of St. George near Telkef
in the vicinity of Mosul.[56] This commentary in its Syriac version
was edited by Chabot in 1897,[57] and in 1940 it was translated into
Latin by Vosté.[58] Later on, Monsignor Devreesse discovered
from several *catenae* more than a hundred pages of Theodore's
original commentary on the gospel of John.[59]

With regard to Pauline literature, Theodore gave Paul
impressive recognition in his scriptural work by commenting on
all of his epistles. Before Theodore, that had been done only by
Origen and Chrysostom. A considerable number of Theodore's
writings on Paul have come down to us. His commentaries on
the minor epistles, i.e. from Galatians to Philemon, have been
preserved in a Latin version of the fifth century. This version was
long attributed to Ambrose, the sanctity of whose name helped
to preserve it from being disregarded. The discovery of their
Theodorean authorship was made by Jacobi of Halle who proved
that the entire work is a translation of a Greek commentary, of
which the original was written by Theodore of Mopsuestia.[60] The
work was edited and published in two volumes by Swete together
with several Greek fragments found in the Paris manuscript
Coislin 204.[61] Finally, Staab compiled and edited from various
manuscripts an important series of Greek fragments from Theodore's lost commentaries on Paul's major epistles, i.e. Romans,
1 and 2 Corinthians, and including the epistle to the Hebrews,[62]
which Theodore considered to be a Pauline writing.[63]

The historians of dogma and liturgics cannot pass by Theodore unheedingly. The Mopsuestian is reported to have written a considerable amount of books and essays on various theological, liturgical, apologetic, polemic, and catechetical subjects, but only a few fragments are preserved in hostile sources. Ebedjesus gives us the following information in regard to the titles of Theodore's literary activities:

> There still is his book on the Sacraments and another on Faith;[64] he wrote one volume on the Priesthood and a book on the Holy Spirit[65] in two volumes; one volume on the Incarnation,[66] and two volumes against Eunomius[67] and two volumes against those who affirm that sin is innate in the human nature;[68] he wrote two books against *Magic* and one book on *Monasticism;* he also composed one treatise on the *Obscure Diction* (of the Scripture) and one on the *Perfection of Works;* he also wrote volumes against the *Allegorists;*[69] one defending *Basil,* and another on the *Assemente and Assumpto;*[70] also the book of *Pearls* in which his letters were collected;[71] finally a sermon on *Legislatio,* by which he terminated his writings.[72]

## NOTES

1. J.M. Vosté, "La chronologie de l' activité de Théodore de Mopsueste," *Revue Biblique,* XXXIV (1925), 78–79; H.B. Swete (ed.) *Theodori Mopsuestini in epistolas Pauli commentarii,* I, lx.

2. Facundus, *Pro defensione trium capitulorum,* Migne, PL (67), 562.

3. This tribute, which begins "Theodore the great . . . ," has been preserved by the courageous North African bishop Facundus who had visited Constantinople in 546 during the ecclesiastical turmoils which were stirred by Theodore Askidas, Theodora, and the Emperor. He departed from there in 548 with the intention to complete his work on the defense of the Three Chapters in his own diocese (*ibid.* p. 589).

4. *Contra Nestor. et Eutych.,* Migne, PG (86), 1364.

5. Joseph S. Assemani, *Bibliotheca Orientalis* (Romae, 1726), lll, cap. CIX, 30: "Theodore the interpreter had written forty one volumes."

6. Mansi, VII, 241–249. In his narrative which bears the title, *Cause de la fondation des écoles,* the Nestorian Barhadbeshaba Arbaya states: "Rabboulas had burned all the writings of Theodore in Edessa, and nothing had escaped the fire except . . . those which had not been yet translated into Syriac." *Patrologia Orientalis,* IV, 381.

7. M.V. Anastos, "The Immutability of Christ and Justinian's Condemnation of Theodore of Mopsuestia," *Dumbarton Oaks Papers,* No. Six (1951), 133–134.

8. *Bibliotheca Orientalis,* III, 30–35.

9. *Patrologia Orientalis,* V, 289–290.

10. J.M. Vosté makes the following remark in regard to the reliability of these two Syriac sources: "In the enumeration and in the titles of these two writings there are striking resemblances. These two documents, the one independent from the other, have a real historical value," *Revue Biblique,* XXXIV (1925) 61. H. Kihn is of the same opinion as far as the authenticity of Ebedjesus' catalogue is concerned, because the *Chronicle of Seert* had not yet been discovered (see *Theodor von Mopsuestia and Junilius als Exegeten,* p. 53).

11. *Bibliotheca Orientalis,* III, 85.

12. *Ibid.,* III, 30.

13. *Ibid.*

14. *Patrologia Orientalis,* V, 289.

15. Migne, PG (103), 72. While he blames Theodore for his obscure language, Photius does not yet fail to join, unwittingly of course, the multitude of modern times scholars in praising him for his attachment to the historical sense of the biblical text.

16. Migne, PG (66), 635–645.

17. Georgius Karo and Iohannes Leitzmann, *Catenarum graecorum catalogus,* Heft I, 21ff.

18. *De opificio mundi,* ed. Gaulterus Reichardt (Lipsiae, 1897), 1, 8ff.

19. "Anciens commentateurs grecs de l'Octateuque, "*Revue Biblique,* XIV, (1936), 364–384.

20.  Ed. Sachau (ed.), *Theodori Mopsuestini fragmenta syriaca* (Leipzig: Sumptibus Guilelmi Engelman, 1868), 1–21.

21.  *Theodori episcopi Mopsuestini in epistolas Pauli,* I, lx.

22.  Louis Pirot notes that the famous paleographer Angelo Mai has discovered in the Vatican and other European libraries several fragments of Theodore's writings on Leviticus and Numbers (cf. *L'oeuvre exégétique de Théodore de Mopsueste,* 77).

23.  For the text of these fragments see R. Devreesse's *Essai sur Théodore de Mopsueste,* 25–37.

24.  Migne, PG (86), 1221. H. Kihn maintains that he has no doubt that Theodore had also commented upon Joshua and Judges because according to the historical testimonies he had highly praised the books of history. The fact that these commentaries are not mentioned in the Syriac catalogues does not warrant the conclusion that Theodore had not written them. See *Theodore von Mopsuestia als Exeget,* 57.

25.  *Bibliotheca Orientalis,* III, 30.

26.  *Patrologia Orientalis,* V, 289.

27.  Facundus of Hermiane, *Pro defensione trium capitulorum,* in Migne, PL (67), 602.

28.  Twenty references to his commentary on the psalms were cited by Theodore in his commentary on the twelve minor prophets. See Migne, PG (66), 124 A, 176 C, 225 C, 397 A, 560 A, etc.

29.  Leontius of Byzantium, *Contra Nestor. et Eutych.,* Migne, PG (86), 1364; L. Pirot, *L'oeuvre exégétique,* 72.

30.  *Le commentaire de Théodore de Mopsueste sur les Psaumes I–LXXX, Studi e Testi,* 93 (Citta del Vaticano: Bibliotheca Apostolica Vaticana, 1939), pp. xxxi and 572.

31.  *Ibid.,* xi; see also R. Devreesse, *Essai sur Théodore,* 29.

32.  *Il codice irlandese dell' Ambrosiana edito e illustrato,* Vol. I (Roma-Firenze: Ermano Loescher, 1878–1879).

33.  *D'un palimsesto Ambrosiano contente i Salmi esapli e di un' antica versione latina del commentario perduto di Teodoro di Mopsuestia al Salterio* (Atti. R. Accad., XXXI, 1896), 655–676. This publication was followed by Mercati's Unpublished Fragments in the Ancient Latin Version of the Commentary on

Psalms by Theodore of Mopsuestia (Rome: 1903), Studi e Testi II.

34. Bobbio is a small town in northern Italy famous for an abbey which was a center of learning in the medieval ages; it had a rich collection of ancient manuscripts, most of which have been transferred to the Vatican Library, the Ambrosiana Library, and the University Library of Turin.

35. *Der Psalmencommentar Theodor's von Mopsuestia, Sitzungsberichte der Wissenshafter zu Berlin* (April 1902), XVII, 334–346.

36. Devreesse acknowledges his indebtedness to the publications of Mercati with the following remarks: "The reconstruction of this work owes its point of departure to a remarkable discovery by his eminence Cardinal Mercati. My singular debt goes beyond that: from the day I had undertaken to restore this commentary by Theodore, the cardinal had surrendered to my hands an important dossier which for a long time was open and growing rich constantly. He ought to be thanked from the bottom of my heart" (*Le Commentaire,* VI–VII). His courtesy to H. Lietzmann is shown by the citation: "A manuscript existed, which indeed preserved the Greek text and which was recovered by the translation of Facundus: Coislin 12, which H. Lietzmann had had the inspiration to point out the interest" (*Essai sur Théodore,* 29).

37. Devreesse's restored commentary has been reviewed favorably by H. Lietzmann in *Literaturzeitung Worchenschrift für Kritik der Internationalen Wissenschaft,* 61 (1940), 841–843; by A. Vaccari, *Biblica,* XXII, (1941), 209–210. See also E. Amann, "Un nouvel ouvrage de Theodore de Mopsueste," *Revue des Sciences Religieuses,* XX (1940), 492–499.

38. The Syriac sources refer to this commentary. Ebedjesus states, "He commented upon the twelve in two volumes for Mar Touris (*Bibliotheca Orientalis,* III, 31); and the *Chronicle of Seert* notes, ". . . after he expounded the twelve on the request of Mar Touba" (*Patrologia Orientalis,* V, 289).

39. *Bibl. Orientalis,* III, 31.

40. *Patr. Orientalis,* V, 289.

41. Mansi, IX, 224–227; Migne, PG (66), 697–698.

42. See *Revue Biblique,* XXXVIII (1929), 390–393.

43. Mansi, IX, 223.

44. *Sitzungberichte der Akademie der Wissenschaften zu Berlin,* XX (1903), 825–830.

45. Mansi, *op. cit.,* IX, 225–227.

46. Migne, PG (86), 1365 D.

47. Mansi, *op. cit.,* IX, 225.

48. H. Kihn, *Theodor von Mopsuestia und Junilius Africanus als Exegeten,* 59.

49. *Bibliotheca Orientalis,* III, 32.

50. *Patrologia Orientalis,* V, 290.

51. J.M. Vosté, "La chronology de l'activité litteraire de Théodore," *Revue Biblique,* XXXIV, No. 1 (Janvier 1925), 69–70.

52. *Pro defensione,* 11.7, Migne, PL (67), 819; R. Devreesse, *Essai sur Théodore,* 35–36.

53. It has been claimed by Vosté that Theodore's ordination divided his interpretive work into two periods: the first period extending to 383 is devoted to the Old Testament, the second starting at 400 is dedicated almost exclusively to the New Testament. However, he assigns the commentaries on Job and Ecclesiastes to this second period (cf. *Revue Biblique,* XXXIV [1925], 78).

54. *Bibliotheca Orientalis,* III, 32; *The Chronicle of Seert* notes: "He explained the gospels of Matthew, Mark, Luke and John" (*Patrologia Orientalis,* V, 290).

55. Migne, PG (66), 705–728; R. Devreesse, *Essai sur Théodore,* 36–38.

56. J.M. Vosté, "Le commentaire de Théodore de Mopsueste sur s. Jean, d'apres la version Syriaque," *Revue Biblique,* XXXII, No. 4 (Octobre 1923), 522–551.

57. J.B. Chabot, *Commentarius Theodori Mopsuestini in Evangelium Iohannis* (Parisiis: Ernestum Leroux, bibliopolam, 1897).

58. *Theodori Mopsuestini commentariis in Evangelium Iohannis apostoli,* Corpus Scriptorum Christianorum Orientalium, scriptores Syri (Louvain: E Typographeo Reipublicae, 1940), series quarta, tom. iii.

59. *Essai sur Théodore,* 287–419.

60. J.L. Jacobi, "Ueber zwei neu entdekte exegetische Werke des kirchlichen Alterthums," *Deutsche Zeitschrift fur christliche Wissenschaft und christliche Leben,* August 5–12 (1854), cited by H.B. Swete whose work is mentioned in the next footnote. F.J.A. Hort was led to the same conclusion independently in an article which appeared in *Journal of Classical and Sacred Philology,* IV (1859), 302–308.

61. H.B. Swete (ed.), *Theodori episcopi Mopsuestini in epistolas beati Pauli commentarii,* The Latin Version with the Greek Fragments (Cambridge: At the University Press, 1880–1882), I and II.

62. Karl Staab, *Pauluskommentare aus der griechischen Kirche, Aus Katenenhandschriften gesamelt und herausgegeben* (Munster: 1933).

63. Ebedjesus gives the following information about Theodore's writings on Paul: "Also he explained the epistle to the Romans for Eusebius. And he expounded and elucidated the two epistles to the Corinthians in two volumes at the request of Theodore. Eustathius asked him to write on the following epistles: Galatians, Ephesians, Philippians, and Colossians. The two epistles to the Thessalonians had been commented upon at the request of James. He expounded the two epistles to Timothy at the request of Peter. At the request of Cyrinus he explained both the epistle to Titus and that of Philemon; he likewise elucidated the epistle to the Hebrews for the same Cyrinus. Theodore finished his commentaries on all the epistles in five volumes" (Assemani, *Bibliotheca Orientalis,* III, 32–33). The chronicle gives almost identical information (see *Patrologia Orientalis,* 289–290).

64. Previously we had known both books from isolated fragments; now the full text of both writings have been discovered in a complete Syriac translation which was rendered into English by Alphonse Mingana in the series of Woodbrooke Studies, Volume V: *Commentary of Theodore of Mopsuestia on the Nicene Creed* (Cambridge, 1932); Volume VI: *Commentary of Theodore of Mopsuestia on the Lord's Prayer and on the Sacraments of Baptism and Eucharist* (Cambridge, 1933). Raymond Tonneau has published a French translation of the same writings with a pho-

totypic reproduction of Mingana's MS Syriac 561, *Les homelies catechetiques de Théodore de Mopsueste,* Studi e Testi 145 (Vatican, 1949). The *Chronicle of Seert* reports: "he even left us an exposition of the creed of the 318 fathers and of the eucharist," *Patrol. Orient.,* V, 290.

65. The essay in question has reached us in a Syriac version which bears the title: *A Controversy with the Macedonians.* This Syriac manuscript belongs to the British Museum (Code 6714). Its text was edited by F. Nau in the series of *Patrol. Orientalis,* IX, 637–667. The Nestorian Berhabdeshaba Arbaya in his chronicle states: "In the episcopal see of Anazarbos in Cilicia Theodore defended the divinity of the Holy Spirit against the Pneumatomachi" (*Patrol. Orient.* IX, 507–508).

66. The chronicle mentions: "Theodore wrote a treatise on the humanity of our Lord." And Gennadius of Marseille states: "Theodore a presbyter of the Antiochian church, a man careful in knowledge and skillful in utterance, wrote against the Apollinarians . . . about the Lord's incarnation in fifteen books . . . in which with the purest reason and scriptural testimonies he proved the Lord Jesus to be indeed a complete deity, and just so true a complete human" (*De viris illustribus,* Migne, PL [58] 1067–1068). Addai Scher in 1909 identified Theodore's work on the incarnation in a Syriac version, but this manuscript perished during the First World War, *Revue Biblique,* XXXVIII, (1929), 383.

67. Photius makes the following statement: "I read the twentyfive books of Theodore against Eunomius; his style is somewhat obscure, but the work is full of ideas and sound reasoning" (Migne, PG 103, 52).

68. Marius Mercator, a Latin writer of the fifth century, accused Theodore, on account of this writing, of being the "father of Pelagianism"; for a detailed exposition of the truth see R. Devreesse, *Essai sur Théodore,* 161–168, 98–103; also *Patrologia Orientalis,* IX, 505.

69. The *Chronicle of Seert* adds: "He wrote one volume against those who cannot see, in reading the books of the scripture, but the parabolical aspect." This book would have been a valuable source to the study of Theodore's exegetical methodol-

ogy if it had been preserved. The only fragment which is preserved by Facundus reads: "In libro de allegoria et historia, que contra Origenem scripts" (cf. Migne, PL [67], 602 B).

70. The surviving fragments are printed in Migne, PG (66), 994–1002.

71. *Chronicle of Seert:* "He composed a book in which he refuted every single innovator; he filled it with excellent things and named it 'The Book of Pearls' because it looked like precious pearls placed in good order"—*Patrologia Orientalis,* V, 290.

72. Assemani, *Bibliotheca Orientalis,* III, 35.

# Chapter Three

# THEODORE'S VIEW OF THE OLD
# TESTAMENT CANON AND TEXT

The early Christian church, which sprang from Palestinian Judaism, received its first scriptures from the Jewish synagogue. However, since many Gentile converts to Christianity could not read Hebrew, the Greek Bible of the Alexandrian Jews (called the Septuagint) was widely employed in the church. Because of the antagonism between the synagogue and the church, the Jews abandoned the use of the Septuagint and strongly supported the new versions of Aquila, Theodotion and Symmachus.

It is important to notice here that the new Greek versions of the Old Testament made by Hellenistic authors included only the twenty-four books of the standard Hebrew scriptures, and disregarded the apocrypha because the Palestinian rabbis never considered them canonical.[1] Jewish rejection of the apocryphal books was unheeded by the church, which continued to reckon all books in the Alexandrian Bible as sacred scripture. It was only at a later date (ca. 180) that the church generally became conscious of its divergence here from Judaism. The issue had not been settled for the Greek-speaking church by conciliar decision, because it had not been included in the schema of an ecumenical council. It appears that the subject was informally introduced in the deliberations of the Trullan Council in 692; but that council failed to define the exact bounds of the Greek Old Testament and did not list the separate book.[2]

The case among eastern Christian scholars, however, was quite different. Their position concerning the books of the Old Testament shows that instead of following the indifferent tradition of the church, they preferred to follow solely the books acknowledged as canonical by the Jews themselves. They were probably informed by their Hebrew teachers or from polemics with Jews. It appears strange that the first list of canonical books given by a Christian writer, that of Melito, omits not only the apocrypha but also the book of Esther. Melito of Sardis (d. ca. 180), in response to a request from a certain Onesimus, gives the following information:

> Having therefore gone up to the East and come to the place where these books were proclaimed and done, and having exactly learnt which are the books of the Old Testament, I send you the list as given below. . . .[3]

Then follows his list which does not include Esther or the apocrypha. The second list comes from Origen who also states: "But be it known that there are twenty-two books according to the Hebrew tradition."[4] Athanasius, in his 39th Festal Epistle, draws up a canon in which he recognizes only the Jewish canonical list, except that he rejects Esther and retains Baruch, the epistle of Jeremiah and all of Daniel.[5] Gregory of Nazianzus supports the Palestinian canon and rejects the book of Esther.[6] John Chrysostom, in his treatises and sermons, often quoted the Old Testament, but the books which are never represented among his nearly seven thousand Old Testament citations are: Judith, 1 Esdras, Ezra, 1 and 2 Maccabees, and Ruth. The following are seldom quoted by him: Judges, 1 and 2 Chronicles, Tobit and Esther. He also reckons the Song of Songs as being of doubtful canonicity. In full agreement with the Antiochene tradition he considers Ben Sirach's Ecclesiasticus authentic and canonical.[7]

Theodore's canon of the Old Testament has not been preserved for us either in the original writings or in the Latin and Syriac translations which survive. Therefore, in order to form an opinion about Theodore's view of the Old Testament canon, we must examine the information which has come down to us from different ancient sources.[8]

According to Leontius of Byzantium, Theodore had suppressed two thousand verses from the book of Job. And yet this book in the Massoretic original has altogether 1070 verses, while in Origen's time the book of Job in the current LXX text was shorter than the Hebrew by some four hundred lines. And Origen supplied the missing lines from Theodotion's translation. Leontius' assertion is rather a gross exaggeration inspired by his ill will toward Theodore.[9]

The Acts of the Fifth General Council accuse Theodore of denying divine inspiration to the book of Job, for he supported the view that the book was the product of human wisdom. Job was an historical person who lived all his life outside of Israel, for he was an Edomite, and as such he was diligently versed in the pagan myths and fictions, and for this reason he has named his third daughter Amalthaea's horn. The story of Job goes back to antiquity, but an author introduced the story of the just in Israel. The intervention of Elihu at the very end was unnecessary, for he has uttered arrogant words against Job. The book as it stands today is not history but an invention and the product of the author's imagination.[10]

But the record vis-à-vis the authorship of the book of Job is straightened out by the ninth century author Isho'dad of Merv who has explicitly stated Theodore's teaching. The name of Job was famous among all the Semitic people; his virtues as well as his ordeals were transmitted by word of mouth from generation to generation and in all the languages of the ancient near east. An anonymous Israelite author utilized the orally circulating story as a framework, and following the sample of the dramatists he composed an exquisite book. The date of its composition is post-exilic. Although the identity of the Israelite author is unknown to us, he was a well educated person because he knew the science of the Greeks. And in order to make the story of Job more attractive he had borrowed the literary idiom of the non-Israelite poets. Isho'dad's quotation is as follows: "On the evidence of many, among whom I include John Chrysostom, it was the divine Moses who wrote the book of Job during the forty years that the Israelites spent in the desert.[11] But the opinion of the blessed interpreter (i.e. Theodore) was different. The name of the blessed Job, said he, was famous among all the people, and his virtuous acts as well as his ordeals were related orally among all the people and all the nations from century to century and in all the languages.[12] Now, after the return of the Israelites from Babylon, a learned Hebrew who was especially well versed in the science of the Greeks committed in writing the history of the just, and in order to make it larger he mingled the story with exquisite utterances borrowed from the poets, because he composed his book with the purpose of making it more pleasant to the readers."[13]

In addition Isho'dad provides Theodore's understanding of the mythological animal Behemoth: "Behemoth is a matchless dragon. However, the interpreter calls it a dragon of pure fiction created by the author according to his own thoroughly poetic manner; it is thus that he has composed also many speeches in the name of Job and his friends, and in the name of God, which neither agree with nor correspond to reality.[14]

The foregoing information suggests that Theodore has significant place in the history of biblical studies, and it matters little if his attempts to investigate the book of Job critically for the purpose of determining the date and the origin of its component parts have been considered neither traditional nor pious. For the first time in the history of the church a book of the Bible was expounded from the perspective of a critical method by a scholar. Theodore based his study upon the investigation of the internal evidence furnished by the book itself and reached conclusions some of which are still noteworthy and advocated by modern scholars; he did not deny the historical existence of Job, whom he regarded as a *homo barbarus et Edomitanus genere*[15] (a barbarian man and of Edomite genre). Job's undeserved sufferings had become a folklore among the people of the ancient near east, and his story in its oral version goes back to an unknown antiquity. The dialogues are not historical but the product of a poetic imagination and were written down in the beginning of the post-exilic era. Nothing is known of the poet-author. The speeches of Elihu are not an interpolation, but they were introduced by the very same poet-author at a later time.[16]

Theodore has proved himself to be a pioneer in the field of Old Testament studies because he advocated an objective and historical investigation of the Bible; it was inevitable that some of his teachings and conclusions should have been interpreted by his conservative enemies as an attack on the biblical books. But contrary to the prevailing opinion there are grounds for believing that Theodore did not omit the book of Job from his Old Testament canon. And this is confirmed by the second canon of the Nestorian Council of Iso'iahb (A.D. 585) which, in defending the writings and the doctrine of our author against those who charged him with heresy, makes the following point in regard to his commentary on the book of Job:

> They are slandering the Interpreter on account of the commentary he wrote on the book of the blessed Job [written] in the spiritual sense, [saying] this commentary is written with adulteration and with ostentation by one of those sophists which have no concern for the truth, but they force and amplify history with inventions that are created by fictions ... for, with the exception of a small part, [the commentary] is full with sayings which are manifestly blasphemous and deceitful.[17]

Further, in his commentary on the book of Psalms Theodore quotes the book of Job three times.[18] Devreesse has also discovered among the *catenae* on the book of Job a fragment of Theodore's commentary on Zechariah in which the Mopsuestian elucidates a point by referring his readers to the book of Job.[19]

Similarly impressive is Theodore's view concerning the superscriptions to the individual psalms in the psalter. Leontius reports that Theodore

> rejected all the titles of the most sacred psalms, hymns, and odes; and following usage of the Jews he referred all the psalms to Zerubbabel and Hezekiah. He applied to the Lord only three psalms.[20]

Isho'dad of Merv has stated the matter accurately when he says:

> We must know that all the psalms were written originally without superscriptions. The titles were added

later according to the personal view of some people but they do not correspond to the content of the psalms.[21]

Theodore's commentary on the book of Psalms and particularly his commentary on the fiftieth psalm (H 51) is instructive; in connection with his treatment of the psalm superscriptions, we get some sense of Theodore's critical thought:

> If the superscription happens to be different from the text let no one be astonished; because we have not been uncritical of the superscriptions, we have talked only about those which we accepted after we found them to be true. Whatever was necessary to be said in regard to this subject we have stated it in the Introduction before we started the literal exegesis.[22]

From this observation we can glimpse Theodore's critical insight in treating problems of biblical introduction. Theodore rejected the titles of the psalms as no part of the inspired text and as historically worthless.[23] He based his objective research on the internal evidence furnished by the text and came to the conclusion that an exegete should not be guided by the authority of the titles since they had been added to the original composition at a later time. Robert H. Pfeiffer, calling attention to this point, makes the following statement:

> Theodore of Mopsuestia, a theologian belonging to the school of Antioch, not only perceived that the titles and superscriptions of the Psalms were added to the original compositions, but also that a number of Psalms (seventeen, in his opinion) were Maccabean in date.[24]

Theodore's opinion about the Song of Songs, judging from the Acts of the Fifth Council, was radical.[25] Despite the teachings of the rabbis and the earlier fathers, who were so strongly convinced of the allegorical meaning of the Song of Songs, Theodore rejected its spiritual meaning and preferred to expound it historico-grammatically. He viewed it as a secular poem of love which was written on the occasion of Solomon's marriage to Pharaoh's daughter.[26] He could not interpret the book in terms of an allegory of the love of Christ for his church. Isho'dad of Merv in the following passage has preserved for us Theodore's interpretation of the Song, when he says:

> The blessed Interpreter and all those who followed in his steps understood the Song of Songs as [referring] to the Pharaoh's daughter. Solomon, indeed, in his wisdom had become the son-in-law of all the adjacent kings—not because of voluptuousness, but chiefly with the intent to secure the peace for himself and his people, then in order to find the opportunity to build the Lord's temple and the royal palace—he took Pharaoh's daughter as his wife. But since she was dark, as all the Egyptian and Ethiopian women are, and because the Hebrews and their beautiful wives, and the other princesses as well, ridiculed her on account of her unseemliness, her small height, and her dark complexion, to avoid any irritation on her part, and no hostility resulted between him and the Pharaoh, Solomon exclusively built for her a house of valuable stones [and decorated it] with gold and silver; and during the meals he chanted it (i.e., the Canticle) in her presence in order to honor her; and he made known with it that she was dark yet beautiful and loved by him.[27]

This is another trait which assures us that Theodore was not only the most original and radical biblical scholar in the Patristic age, but also in some respects, a forerunner of the modern biblical scholarship. It is this spirit of free inquiry demonstrated by the Mephasqana in his study of the individual books of the Old Testament that made Pfeiffer remark:

> Although declared heretical by the Church when proposed by Theodore of Mopsuestia (d. ca. 428) and St. Castellio (d. 1563), the literal interpretation of the Can-

ticles has finally prevailed, but in two radically different forms, dramatic and lyrical.[28]

The typical Christian interpretation, paralleling Jewish tradition, explained the Song of Songs as an allegorical representation of the love of Christ for his church or else as an allegory of the mystical union of a believing soul with God or Christ. If the Song of Songs symbolizes God's love for Israel, it must also symbolize Christ's love for his church. The historico-literal interpretation of the Song of Songs has never been popular in the Greek and Roman churches.

The heterodox exegesis of the Mopsuestian, who refused to see an allegory in the Song and maintained that it celebrated Solomon's marriage with the Egyptian princess, was condemned by the Second Council of Constantinople. But the conciliar fragment in its present Latin version does not inform us that our author rejected the Song of Songs from his canon. It was only his avowed adversary Leontius who made that claim.[29] And in modern times, the charge that Theodore rejected the Song of Songs has been revived by H. Kihn and L. Pirot on the evidence afforded by Junilius Africanus' Instructions of Guidance of the Divine Law (or *Instituta regularia divinae legis*).[30] They both claim that Junilius' curious views on some canonical books in the Bible reflect Theodore's teachings about the Old Testament canon; the Song of Songs, and the Chronicles and Ezra, which according to Leontius were also rejected by Theodore, are excluded by Junilius from the books of "primary importance" *(primae auctoritatis)* and they are listed among the so-called books of "secondary importance" *(mediae auctoritatis)*.[31] The *Instituta,* the Catholic authors assert, had been prepared and put together by Paul the Persian, who had studied at the Nestorian school of Nisibis, where the east Syrian church possessed at a very early date nearly all of Theodore's writings in a Syriac translation, because the Nestorian church accepted him as the master of Nestorius. At Nisibis his authority on biblical subjects was so great that no Nestorian teacher could contradict Theodore's views on the Bible. Louis Pirot has concluded that one must take account of the permanent influence which Theodore exercised on the school at Nisibis in explaining the fact that Paul the Persian placed all the books rejected by Theodore under the so-called category of "secondary importance" books of the *Instituta.*[32]

Since there was no clearly fixed canon in Antioch, it was perfectly logical for a keen expounder of the Bible to have his own views on certain Old Testament books. While Theodore regarded the Old Testament as the word of God, he nevertheless recognized the human element in it, and at the same time he was emphasizing that in the Old Testament could be found books of pure human origin based on wisdom and experience. This distinction between books of revelation and books of human wisdom is attested by an extract which has been preserved in the Acts of the Fifth Ecumenical Synod.[33] Judging the whole issue of the Canticle's origin in the light of the conciliar fragment (cited in note 33) we may conclude that Theodore considered all the books which tradition has ascribed to Solomon, including the Canticle, as products of Solomon's wisdom. It was Theodore's common practice in dealing with problems of introduction to discuss carefully and with boldness the personality of the biblical writers and their idiosyncracies of thought and language. It is through a recognition of this approach that one should try to explain the reason why Theodore debated the origin of the Song of Songs and considered the literary genre to which it belonged in his short commentary on this book.[34] However, he had little use for the book just because he could not discover any deeper meaning which would be useful for the instruction and edification of the Christian soul.[35]

As for Leontius' further charge that Theodore excluded the Chronicles from his Bible, we observe that the Mopsuestian, in his short essay *Synopsis of Christian Doctrine,* which has been discovered in Syriac translation, quotes 1 Chronicles 5:2 as scripture, and the whole passage where the quotation is referred to reads as follows:

> The Lord appeared from the tribe of Judah in order that the prediction of the prophets might be fulfilled. Jacob said in his prophecy, 'the sceptre shall not depart from Judah, nor a prophet from between his feet, until the

Christ to whom government belongs comes, and Him shall nations expect' (Gen. 49:10). Another book says: 'The King Messiah will come out of Judah' (1 Chron. 5:2).[36]

The citation is in agreement with the Peshitta of Chronicles and not with the Septuagint version which was Theodore's Old Testament; from this variant we may infer that the Syrian translator allowed himself a certain amount of freedom in his translation. But still the claim can be made that the whole passage is characterized by the same biblical erudition that stamped Theodore's interpretive work. Furthermore, in commenting on Psalm 29 (H 30), Theodore explicitly stated: "As it is written in the Chronicles, and Hezekiah bowed himself down, out of the exaltation of his own heart."[37] Finally Theodoret of Cyrrhus in his commentary on the Chronicles not only makes no complaint against his teacher but it seems to us he echoes his master's voice when he says:

The writing is post-exilic. . . . He who writes history never says what will happen in the future, but he narrates facts of the past as well as of contemporary times. It is only appropriate for the prophets to predict the future.[38]

So far as the books of Ezra are concerned it is difficult to see grounds for Theodore's rejection of them.[39] It is true that the Peshitta, as it existed in the third century, lacked Chronicles, Ezra, Nehemiah, and Esther, as well as the Apocalypse; these books, however, were soon added.[40] Our study leads to the conclusion that it was only the legendary work ascribed to Ezra by the pseudepigraphic II (IV) Esdras that preoccupied the thoughts of certain Christian scholars in the patristic age, and not the canonical books of Ezra and Nehemiah.[41] None of the Latin and Greek fathers expounded the books of Ezra.

Finally, it is generally assumed that Theodore omitted the book of Esther from his Old Testament canon.[42] However, this claim seems to be unwarranted because of the fact that Theodore's enemies in their manifold charges against him nowhere imply that the bishop of Mopsuestia refused to accept Esther as a canonical writing.[43]

In conclusion, because of a rigid conception of canonicity Theodore was rather inclined to accept only those books which were recognized by the Jews. His numerous commentaries on Old Testament books suggest that Theodore accepted the limits of the Palestinian Jewish canon. He nevertheless allowed himself a fair amount of freedom to discuss problems of biblical introduction with intellectual sincerity. He endeavored to study problems of authorship of the biblical books and to call attention to the actual motives and thoughts of the men who wrote them. A spirit of free inquiry in matters of biblical scholarship was the basic characteristic of Theodore's biblical methodology. The results of this method were highly productive; in many respects Theodore anticipated many of the basic tenets of modern higher criticism.

In his historico-critical approach, Theodore rejected the titles of the Psalms as not being part of the original text and as having little historical value. He treated the Psalms historically and referred a number of them to the Maccabean period. He viewed the book of Job as the work of a sage disclosing a surprising knowledge of pagan wisdom, and regarded the Elihu speeches in Job as a later addition by the same author. The books of Proverbs and Ecclesiastes were, in Theodore's judgment, the products of Solomon's wisdom and experience. As suggested, Theodore gave careful attention to the origin and literary genre of the Song of Songs.

Undoubtedly there were some grounds for the view among his contemporaries that Theodore was radical concerning the Old Testament canon; however, his over-zealous adversaries often exaggerated this radicalism in order to secure Theodore's posthumous condemnation. Such labels as impious, blasphemous, and heretical were frequently used by Leontius and others in their writings against Theodore.

Theodore's position concerning the Old Testament apocrypha is clear although he has not left us an explicit list of inspired

THEODORE'S VIEW OF THE OLD TESTAMENT    55

Old Testament writings.[44] Neither Theodore's friends nor his numerous adversaries tell us whether he rejected or retained the apocrypha. Nevertheless, Theodore's extant writings provide considerable evidence for determining his position in regard to the apocrypha. In the first place, Theodore in his extant writings does not appear ever to have cited the apocrypha by name.[45] Secondly, for the purpose of illustrating his viewpoints Theodore often introduces into his commentaries and theological writings numerous Old Testament citations, but among these there is no direct or implicit quotation from the apocrypha. Finally, in his commentary on the Psalms Theodore refers a number of individual psalms to Maccabean times and prefaces each with a prologue purporting to illustrate the religious conditions of the Jews under the Seleucids as they are reported in 1 and 2 Maccabees, which he cites as "Maccabean history."[46] In his rapid review of the Maccabean period, Theodore carefully selected historical material mentioned in the apocryphal books of Maccabees, but the manner in which he handles such material gives the impression that he felt he was using extra-biblical sources. For example, he introduces the Maccabean books to his readers in the same manner in which he introduces Josephus' *Antiquities*, and he places both on the same level.[47] The apocrypha obviously did not belong to Theodore's canon.

Rightly, then, it may be said that Theodore, owing to a rigid conception of canonicity, was the only one among the early Christian commentators who restricted his Old Testament to the limits of the Bible of Palestinian Judaism, not only in theory but also in practice. The attitude of the fathers about the Old Testament apocrypha was not consistent; the same fathers, who held that canonicity and inspiration were confined to the Palestinian canon, in practice highly esteemed and quoted as scripture all the books of the Septuagint version. Even Jerome, in his later works, quotes as having scriptural authority books which he had termed apocryphal.[48]

We have already noticed that Theodore wrote commentaries on the four gospels, Acts, and what he regarded as the fourteen epistles of Paul. Extant fragments from Theodore's lost commentary on the epistle to the Hebrews show that he accepted it as a Pauline writing. But nothing is directly known of his judgment on the New Testament Apocalypse or the seven Catholic epistles.

John of Maiouma, in the beginning of the sixth century, stated in very obscure language that Theodore rejected "the epistles which are in the Acts of the Apostles and the gospel of John."[49] Less obscure, however, is the language of Leontius: "Because Theodore suppressed the book of Job by two thousand verses I should think that he renounced the epistle of James and the test of the Catholic epistles."[50]

The ambiguous statement by Leontius seems to imply that Theodore rejected the canonicity of the following New Testament writings: the epistle of James, the first and second epistles of Peter, the first, second and third epistles of John, and the epistle of Jude. But it is well known that the Antiochenes excluded from their New Testament canon only the Apocalypse, the second epistle of Peter, the second and third epistles of John, and the epistle of Jude.[51] The books which are not represented in Chrysostom's eleven thousand quotations from the New Testament are the ones just mentioned. Theodoret of Cyrrhus used the same canon as Chrysostom and has nowhere quoted the four Catholic epistles or the Apocalypse which were always disputed at Antioch.[52]

The evidence supplied to us by the writings of Chrysostom and Theodoret gives us the right to claim that Theodore's New Testament canon agreed with the canon of the rest of the Antiochenes, probably because they all followed the common opinion held in the school to which they belonged. In other words, Theodore retained the epistle of James, 1 Peter, and 1 John, but he never quoted from them.[53] However, he ignored the book of Revelation, 2 Peter, and 2 and 3 John because they were also ignored or rejected by the church of Antioch in the fourth century.[54]

Some scholars have expressed the opinion that Theodore was showing Jewish tendencies in his Old Testament studies because he explained the Jewish scriptures through the original Hebrew text and not from the Greek Bible of the Christian church.[55] Other contemporary writers are of the opinion that Theodore knew some Hebrew but was not as proficient as Jerome.[56] Our contention on this very subject is that Theodore knew no Hebrew, because he spent no time in learning this language. Occasionally Theodore drew attention to variant readings, but he never attempted to explain them in the light of any personal knowledge of the Hebrew language. On the contrary, he makes it clear that all his information concerning textual variations rests on the authority of sources to which he alludes with the formulas "they say," "it is said," "they speak," but he never names those to whom he refers. For example, in discussing the meaning of the prophet Jonah's name, Theodore quite bluntly noted: "Here again they say that the name Jonah in the Syriac means dove; these Syrians are marvelous legend tellers."[57] It is remarkable that Theodore makes no attempt to give his own translation of the name Jonah. That Theodore's acquaintance with Hebrew was only by report of associates seems to be indicated further by his translation of Malachi as an angel "because in the Hebrew language the angel is named Malachias,"[58] and, again, by his treatment of Zephaniah 1:5. In this passage Theodore is totally unaware that the same Hebrew consonants with a slightly different vocalization could mean either *Malkam* or *Melchom*. But Theodore insisted on the evidence of the Septuagint text that Melchom means an idol.[59]

But if Theodore did not know Hebrew, one is tempted to ask what Theodore meant by such terms as "Hebraic voice" and "Hebrew idiom" which are found so often in his extant writings. Does he designate a definite Hebrew source when he uses these terms? Unfortunately, his use of these terms in the text is not accompanied by references to any recognizable sources or persons. Nor do the contexts in which the terms are used offer any suggestion that he is referring to the original Hebrew text. Therefore, we can by no means be certain what these terms signify. Further, Theodore's bent for *textual* criticism is evident almost solely in his commentary on the book of Psalms, and his remarks afford evidence of his awareness that the original Hebrew text should be the basis for a faithful interpretation of scripture.[60]

It would appear that Theodore had little knowledge of Hebrew beyond the few scraps of information he was able to gather from intermediary sources.[61] The fact that many fathers reveal some Hebraic information in their writings in no way implies that they knew Hebrew. Verbal tradition played a significant role in these cases. Origen's Hexapla allowed for widespread though superficial knowledge of the variants as between the Jewish and Christian Old Testament. With the clear exception of Origen and Jerome, and perhaps of Lucian, none of the fathers appears to have possessed any considerable knowledge of Hebrew. The learning of Hebrew was not encouraged in fourth century Antioch, where anti-semitism against the "wretched, good-for-nothing Jews" had reached a climax.[62] Unhappily, several writings directed against the Jews originated in the school of Antioch. Theodore's master, Diodore of Tarsus, wrote a treatise which bore the title "Against the Jews,"[63] and Chrysostom composed a series of homilies under the same title.[64] Chrysostom, the most anti-semitic of all the Christian writers in the patristic age, made the following charge against the Jews and their synagogues:

> The Jews collect the choruses of voluptuaries, the rabble of dissolute women, and draw the whole theater with all its actors into the synagogue. For there is no difference between the synagogue and the theater. The synagogue is not merely a theater, it is a whorehouse, a robbers' cave and a place of refuge for unclean animals, a dwelling place of the devil. And it is not merely the synagogues that are the dwelling places of robbers, swindlers, and devils, but also the souls of the Jews themselves. . . .[65]

On the other hand many rabbis strongly objected to the idea of Gentiles studying the torah and expressed their objection in terms which make it clear that they deplored heathen slanderers and enemies of the Jews who were studying the torah merely in order to misinterpret its teachings and use this in their theological battle against the Jews. Rabbi Johanan, who taught in Sepphoris and Tiberias, and who was a contemporary of Origen, displayed his enmity toward the Christians who were eager to study Hebrew: "A heathen who studies the torah is deserving of death."[66] Similarly, Rabbi Ami, a contemporary of Diocletian, warned: "You must not impart the law to a heathen."[67]

As they lacked the aid of Hebrew textbooks on grammar and lexicons, it was practically impossible for the fathers to master Hebrew without oral instruction. In Theodore's day a rabbi in Antioch would hardly be willing to teach a Greek Christian Hebrew so that the latter could carry on a theological skirmish against the Jews with an intimate knowledge of Hebrew as one of his most effective weapons. In any case the disposition as well as the motivation for a Christian to learn Hebrew in Theodore's time and long after his time were completely non-existent.[68]

Certainly, if Theodore had known Hebrew he would not have claimed that the name of Job's third daughter "Keren-happuk" (horn of antimony) was a pagan name and not Jewish. In effect, he bases his argument upon the Septuagint version which renders the two Hebrew words as "Amalthea's horn," i.e. the she-goat which, according to Greek mythology, was the nurse of Zeus when he was a baby and fed him with her horn.[69]

So far as the Syriac is concerned, Theodore, dealing with problems of textual criticism, introduces now and then variant readings borrowed from the Peshitta, but the way he presents them leaves no doubt that he largely ignored the Syriac and relied on oral information. In commenting on Habakkuk 2:11b he made the following characteristic remark:

> Some have said that the Syrian version reads "peg"; but it would be nonsense to disregard the voice of the Hebrew [language]—in which the prophets spoke and which the Seventy [Septuagint] with their own translation have made clear to us, for they were notables and perfectly knew that language—and pay attention to the Syrian who has altered the voice of the Hebrews into that of the Syrians. Besides he [the Syrian] often wants to raise his own mistakes to a linguistic law, without knowing what he is talking about.[70]

In elucidating Zephaniah 1:5, Theodore again rejected the variant reading found in Peshitta, which reading he happens to know through hearsay evidence, and then went on to say:

I happen to know several mythological stories concerning those who rely with pride on the Syriac [Peshitta], but I have passed them by because I did not want it to look as if I were going to fill my commentary on the sacred Scripture with silly stories. The Syrians say that *Melhom* signifies the king, because according to the language of the Syrians and Hebrews the king is named *Melhom:* so those who translated *Melhom* idol were led astray. The Syrians should be very conscious of the fact that the contents of the sacred Scripture were written in the Hebrew language; and they [the contents] have been translated into Syriac by someone whose identity even today remains unknown.[71]

From the two passages quoted above it becomes evident that Theodore had no formal education in Syriac. His knowledge about the Syrian Bible was based on oral information. It seems that he gathered his information from Greek-speaking Syrian clergymen.[72] The Nestorian authors, in all their laudatory comments about this great interpreter, never suggest that Theodore was versed in Syriac or Hebrew.

H.B. Swete has suggested that Theodore possessed some acquaintance with Latin.[73] His suggestion is based on evidence from Theodore's commentary on 2 Timothy 4:13. Swete's suggestion seems to us to be plausible because Theodore attended the school of Libanius where both Latin and Roman law were taught as a part of the curriculum. There was not, however, an established chair for Semitic languages in the university system of Antioch.[74]

The earliest and most important translation of the Old Testament into Greek ("The Interpretation of the Seventy-Two Elders" or "The Septuagint") was considered by the Christians of the patristic age as an authoritative transcript of divine revelation, and as such it still continues to enjoy the same status not only in the Greek church, but also in several churches whose versions of the Old Testament were made directly from the Septuagint.[75]

Theodore, following the tradition as well as the practice of his church, accepted the Septuagint as the authoritative version of the Old Testament. He treated the Septuagint with high respect and made it no secret that of all the Greek versions of the Old Testament, the Septuagint was most faithful to the original text. This does not, of course, mean that he followed the Septuagint uncritically, because he very often introduced, especially in his commentary on the Psalms, variant readings borrowed from Symmachus,[76] Aquila,[77] Theodotion,[78] and occasionally from the Syriac.[79] Theodore also realized the authority of the original Hebrew text which he accepted as the most important source, and on which, he held, an exegete should base his writings.[80] He never appears to have spoken against the Hebrew language; on the contrary, he accepted it as a well-formed vehicle of speech through which the utterances of revelation were spoken. And yet, because of his ignorance of Hebrew, Theodore was forced to rely on translations, and particularly on the Septuagint, which he too believed was introduced to the church by the apostles.

Strictly speaking, the Septuagint according to Theodore is not an unknown entity but the official undertaking of the seventy elders who had been commissioned by the high priest with the approbation of the people of Israel.[81] Theodore's information concerning the origin of the Septuagint rests on the legendary explanation given in the pseudepigraphic letter of Aristeas. And while he never mentions the letter, he seems to accept its content, but with an unusual sobriety. It is true that he failed, as did all of the fathers with the exception of Jerome, to discern that the letter of Aristeas referred only to the Greek Pentateuch, and he connected not only the Pentateuch, but the translation of the entire Old Testament, with the work of the seventy. But nowhere does Theodore appear to have accepted the other legendary details with which the story of the translation was embellished by pseudo-Aristeas, Philo and some of the fathers.[82]

The most important thing to be stressed in regard to Theodore's use of the Septuagint version is the fact that he considered it to be an undertaking of purely human origin. The authority of the Septuagint as the authentic translation of the Old Testament used exclusively by the apostles, and by his church as well, did not lead him to declare it a miraculously inspired translation, having equal authority with the original.[83] In sharp contrast to the prevailing belief that the Septuagint was a divinely inspired transcript of revelation, Theodore in his use of the translation demonstrates a surprisingly modern spirit by accepting it as a scholarly achievement of some men who were eminently qualified for the undertaking because of their brilliant achievement both in Hebrew and in Old Testament scholarship.

Theodore's view of the Septuagint is reflected in his contrasting of the version of Symmachus with that of the seventy concerning a particular variant reading:

> Therefore, the seventy translators earnestly labored to preserve the emphasis of the Hebraic text without a difference, while Symmachus demonstrated a greater care in the clarity of the text, and in his own undertaking he did not succeed completely.[84]

It is evident that the notion of a miraculously produced translation is strange to Theodore. He relied on the Septuagint not because he accepted it to be an inspired version, but because he thought it preserved the literal meaning and force of the original Hebrew better than the other Greek versions. If Theodore had believed that he was dealing with a miraculously produced text he would have stated so when he compared the Septuagint version with that of Symmachus. Further, the fact that he did not hesitate to consult other Greek versions indicates that in the eyes of Theodore the Septuagint never appeared as an infallible text.

The view that Theodore considered the Septuagint as the only faultless and infallible translation was held for the first time by H. Kihn.[85] In point of fact the German scholar claims that the Mopsuestian regarded the translation of the seventy as an infallible text produced miraculously, and a text which coincided word-for-word with the original Hebrew, making the latter dispensable and comparison of it with the other three Greek versions superfluous.[86]

The textual discrepancy between the Septuagint and Peshitta over the name Milcom in Zephaniah 1:5 afforded Theodore the opportunity to make the following remarks concerning the origin of the Septuagint:

> The sacred scripture has been translated into the Greek language by seventy elderly men of the people, who had a scholastic training in their own native language and who were also scholastically versed in the contents of the sacred scriptures; they had also been approved and approbated by the priest and the whole people of Israel as the most worthy of all for the task of the interpretation. That the blessed apostles accepted their interpretation and edition is very obvious; the sacred scripture which was translated into the Greek language by the seventy was handed over by them [the apostles] to the Gentile congregations which before this paid no attention at all to the contents of the Old Testament. All the Gentile believers in Lord Christ, having received it [the scripture] from them [the apostles], possess it now, and we read it in the churches and keep it at home. Would it not be nonsense to hold that the seventy, who were many and had been approved as fitted for the task, could have been mistaken in regard to a word? They certainly knew the text of the sacred scripture and they could tell whether it meant "king" or "idol" before they resumed the translation.[87]

It is on the evidence of this rather lengthy passage that Kihn has reached the conclusion that Theodore considered the Septuagint faultless, infallible, superhuman, and divine. But the passage speaks for itself. In point of fact, Theodore seems to treat all the legends connected with the origin of the Septuagint with a measure of sobriety and moderation. He does not even mention the letter of Aristeas. He nowhere appears to claim that the Septuagint as a whole is a faultless version but only a scholarly translation produced by competent scholars. As far as the term "infallible" is concerned it should be noted that the Greek fathers were not accustomed to using it. As for the terms "superhuman" and "divine," it may be noted that Theodore often used the word "sacred" in order to distinguish the original scripture from the version of the Septuagint which he always calls "The Seventy" or "The Interpretation of the Seventy" or "The Edition of the Seventy."[88]

On the contrary, we think that Theodore's use of the Septuagint is to a certain extent modern. He emphatically stresses that it was achieved by men of academic scholarship without the intervention of any divine agency. The Septuagint for years declared the ideals of the Old Testament to the world but the Gentiles persisted in their idolatry.[89] It was through the teaching of the apostles that the Septuagint was introduced to the Christian church.

During recent decades, Septuagint studies have been deeply influenced by the theories of Paul de Lagarde.[90] In turn his theories have been based on a statement that Jerome made in his *praefatio* to Chronicles. In referring to the diversity of the editions of the Greek Old Testament, Jerome declares:

> Alexandria and Egypt in their Septuagint praise Hesychius as its author; Constantinople as far as Antioch approved the copies of Lucian the martyr; the provinces between these read Palestinian codices which, edited by Origen, were popularized by Eusebius and Pamphilus; and the whole world is in a state of mutual strife about this threefold variety.[91]

According to the explanation of Lagarde, this passage from Jerome indicates that Hesychius, Lucian, and Origen had produced three independent recensions of the existing Septuagint text, transforming it by additions, omissions or stylistic changes according to the respective sources on which they based the revision of the old Septuagint text. The church fathers in Egypt quoted the Septuagint in the Hesychius recension; those in Antioch and Constantinople in Lucian's.[92] That the Antiochene fathers based their biblical studies on Lucian's recension is a fact supported by all textual critics.[93] The principal witnesses for the reconstruction of the Lucian text are the biblical quotations of the Antiochene fathers of the fourth and fifth centuries, who almost certainly used the Antiochian Bible. Chrysostom and Theodoret are our primary witnesses to Lucian's recension through their extensive biblical quotations. Theodore's original biblical writings that have been preserved are so sparse that he could not possibly be included with the other two.[94]

So far as Theodore's form of the LXX text is concerned, this has been demonstrated by Emil Gross-Brauckmann in a study of Theodoret's psalter text which appeared in the Communications of the Septuagint Undertakings.[95] According to the German scholar the Mopsuestian had based his commentary on the psalter on the very same LXX text which his colleagues Theodoret and Chrysostom had used for their own commentaries on the Psalms. Lucian's recension came to be recognized as the accepted text *(textus receptus)* throughout Asia Minor and Constantinople. It would be logical to conclude that Theodore belonging to this very same milieu would have remained faithful to the same Lucian LXX. He, too, was monolingual and very much isolated after his elevation to the diocese in Cilicia. For there is no evidence in his remaining writings that he ever consulted Origen's hexaplaric text. On the contrary, his disciple Theodoret does not hesitate to emend the text he was commenting upon with the help of Origen's Hexapla.[96] The versions of Symmachus and Aquila were nothing but a kind of encyclopedia supplying Theodore with help in elucidating obscure verses. He very seldom used textual sources to improve his own text because he was convinced that the Hebrew text was the only authentic source on which the exegetes should base their commentaries.[97]

Significantly, in his commentary on the twelve prophets, Theodore showed little interest in textual criticism. He first quoted the prophetic verses (naturally in Greek) and then commented upon them. Consequently in this particular commentary the entire book of the minor prophets has been preserved. Louis Pirot claims that his review of the text of Amos and Malachi used by Theodore proves that Theodore is one of the important witnesses of the Lucianic text. Pirot collated the texts used by Theodore and Theodoret and noticed that the latter diverges widely from the text of the former. In Amos, Pirot discovered that out of the 134 passages he collated, Theodoret introduces 36 variant readings, which are to be found in Codex Vaticanus.[98] In the text of Malachi, Theodoret, while he follows to a very large extent that of Theodore, nevertheless indicates a remarkable influence of the codices Vaticanus and Marchalianus. But in 42 passages Theodoret's renderings cannot be found in Theodore's text.[99] The differences between the texts of these two eminent Antiochene exegetes can be explained by the fact that Theodoret's text, while it was originally a Lucianic text, underwent a revision according to the textual tradition of the western sources.[100] This does not mean necessarily that Theodore's type of text is purely Lucianic; there seems, however, to be substantial evidence to prove that Theodore preserved a fairly pure form of Lucianic readings. Thus, our principal witness for the reconstruction of the Lucianic text of the twelve minor prophets, in addition to ancient manuscripts, is Theodore of Mopsuestia.[101]

## NOTES

1. Although at this time and later several rabbinical scholars debated the authority of certain canonical books, such discussions are thought to have been largely academic, and few Jews, after A.D. 100, argued about the exact bounds of the Hebrew scriptures. The sole exception was Ben Sirach's Ecclesiasticus which was still read and copied in some Jewish circles as late as the twelfth century. Of course the Jewish sectarians had their own secret books, the authority of which was axiomatic among members.

2. The Trullan Council tried to work out a compromise between antagonistic traditions in regard to the exact bounds of the Greek Old Testament by referring to older authorities, such as Athanasius, the Roman African Council of Carthage in 397, and the famous 60th Canon of the provincial Council of Laodi-

cea in Asia Minor (365), which omits the apocrypha (see Mansi, *op. cit.*, II, 603–604). Unlike the Roman and Protestant churches the question remains unsettled in the Greek church; the subject has already been placed among the problems which will be discussed in the Pan-Orthodox Council which is to be convened by the patriarchate of Constantinople in the near future.

3. Melito's epistle to Onesimus has been preserved by Eusebius in *Church History* 4.26, Migne, PG (20), 395–398.

4. *Ibid.*, 6.25, Migne, PG (20), 579–582.

5. Migne, PG (26), 1176.

6. *Carmina* I, 1, 12, Migne, PG (33), 472–474.

7. Chrysostomus Baur, *John Chrysostom and His Time,* trans. Sr. M. Gonzaga (Westminster, Md.: The Newman Press, 1959), I, 316–317.

8. The sources of information are: (1) Leontius of Byzantium, *Against Nestorians and Eutychians,* Migne, PG (86), 1365–1368; (2) The Acts of the Fifth Council, Mansi, IX, 224–27; (3) Junilius Africanus, *Instituta regularia divinae legis,* lib. I, cap. iii–vii; (4) the exegetical commentaries of Isho'dad of Merv, a Nestorian bishop of the ninth century who echoes the views of Theodore in his brief commentaries. The passages related to the subject under discussion have been translated from the original Syriac into French by J.M. Vosté in his article, "L'oeuvre exégétique de Théodore de Mopsueste...," *Revue Biblique,* XXXVIII, (1929), 382–395, 542–554.

9. Leontius' view is expressed as follows: "From the book of Job, God's great servant, and the vivid example of courage, and for centuries the inscribed monument he (i.e. Theodore) washed off and crossed out about 2,000 verses" (Migne, PG [86], 1365).

10. The Acts of the Fifth Council has preserved in a Latin translation five excerpts taken supposedly from Theodore's commentary, which was dedicated by its author to nobody else but Cyril of Alexandria. The very first one reads: "What a petty shame has Theodore stated! This is what he has said: Job has named his third daughter Amalthaea's horn, and this is nothing else but to show that Job approved of the pagan fables and he was diligent with the fictions of idolatry; in fact Theodore con-

firmed with certainty that Job was in a position to know about
Jupiter and Saturn, and Juno, for Job was a barbarian and of
Edomite descent. Job decided to name his daughter after the
pagan myths of idolatry in order to make her sound beautiful"
(Mansi, IX, 224). Is this a direct quotation? I doubt it. In the
LXX version of Job, there is a brief apocryphal addition at the
very end providing the following biographical information: "The
town of Uz is located on the borders of Edom and Arabia. . . .
Job was a king of Edom, his wife was Arabic, his three friends
were monarchs."

11. Even the Babylonian Talmud written at a later time supported the Mosaic authorship of the book of Job: "Moses wrote
his own book, and the passage about Balaam, and Job; Joshua
wrote his book, and eight verses in the Torah," *Baba Bathra*, 14b.

12. A comparison of Theodore's view with that of R.H. Pfeiffer is instructive: "The original Edomitic tale of the innocent suf-
ferer is an example of ancient Oriental folklore. The theme of a
man suffering undeserved indignities or torments, whether
through human (as in the story of Ahikar) or through divine
agencies (as in the Indian story of King Harrischandra and in the
Babylonian poem 'I will praise the Lord of wisdom'), is common
in Oriental folklore, which to some extent is international"
(Introduction, 670).

13. Our English text is based on J.M. Vosté's French translation of the original Syriac. Both can be found in *Revue Biblique*,
XXXVIII (1929), 391f.

14. *Revue Biblique*, XXXVIII (1929), 392.

15. This expression must be taken in the sense that Job was
neither a Hebrew nor a Gentile who shared with Theodore the
way of life of the western world, but that he was an Asiatic.

16. "To be sure he (the author) introduced Elihu at a later
time, and he spoke against the just (i.e. Job) by causing so much
injury, and in that person (Elihu) the greatness of the divine
nature was restricted by those utterances, and furthermore he
added the image of a sea-monster" (Mansi, IX, 225).

17. *Synodicum orientale*, 137–138, 399. J.M. Vosté has pro-
posed a textual emendation to this translation which instead of
"in the spiritual sense" should read "with an intelligence illumi-

nated by the Spirit"; while M. Draguet has corrected the last sentence of the canon as follows: "for he admitted that only a small part was not full of erroneous sayings possessing blasphemy and deceit" (cf. R. Devreesse, *Essai sur Théodore*, p. 34, n. 4).

18. *Le commentaire*, 75, 1.2: 147, 1.17; 152, 11.2–23.

19. *Essai sur Théodore*, 302–303 n. 1.

20. Migne, PG (86), 1365 D.

21. *Revue Biblique*, XXXVIII, No. 4 (Octobre 1929), 542.

22. *Le commentaire*, 334, 11.27–30.

23. George F. Moore, "The Theological School at Nisibis," *Studies in the History of Religions*, edited by D.G. Lyon and G.F. Moore, and presented to Crawford H. Toy (New York: Macmillan, 1912), 261.

24. *Introduction*, 43.

25. Mansi, *op. cit.*, IX, 225–227.

26. 1 Kgs 3:1.

27. The present translation is based not upon the original Syriac text, but on the French translation which has been produced by J.M. Vosté, "L'oeuvre exégétique de Théodore," *Revue Biblique*, XXXVIII, No. 3 (Juillet 1919), 395.

28. *Introduction*, 715.

29. *Contra Nestorianos*, Lib. III, Migne, PG (86), 1365: "Theodore, in his impudent and immoderate recklessness, having understood it according to his prostituted language and judgment, cut it off from the holy books."

30. *Instituta regularia divinae legis*, Lib. I, cap. 3–5; edited by H. Kihn as an appendix in his book *Theodor von Mopsuestia and Junilius Africanus als Exegenten*, 472–476.

31. The *Instituta* is an early example in Latin of a "school book" composed in the form of a dialogue between teacher and student. The manner of its transmission is interesting. Probably between the years 541–542 Junilius, a native of Africa who held the office of quaestor in the imperial city of Constantinople, met with a certain Paul the Persian who had studied at Nisibis and who belonged to the Nestorian sect. At the request of Primasius, the bishop of Hadrumentum, who came to the city to defend the interests of his jurisdiction, Junilius compiled his Instituta as they were prepared for him by Paul. The book purports to be a

short introduction to the study of the Bible and theology. All the books of the Bible are divided into four categories of literature: historical, prophetic, wisdom and didactic. And from the canonicity point of view the books are classified in three groups: "primary importance, secondary importance, and of null importance." But under the third division no biblical document is listed. All the books, however, which Leontius testifies that were rejected by Theodore are placed by Paul under the category of "secondary or medium importance." The opinion originally put forward by H. Kihn that the Instituta is nothing else but a compendium of Theodore's theological system has gained a good deal of currency among modern authors. It has been challenged though by Robert Devreesse, who, after a detailed study, reached the conclusion: "It would be wiser to conclude, if one wants to conclude, that the Instituta represents very simply a part or an average teaching of the head teachers at Nisibis" (*Essai sur Théodore,* p. 272).

32. *L'oeuvre exégétique,* pp. 146, 148.

33. "In favor of the human doctrine are written and he (i.e. Theodore) attributed to Solomon's books, that is, Proverbs and Ecclesiastes which were written by him for the benefit of others, which he (Theodore) did not accept, indeed, to have been written by the prophetic grace, but truly by the influence of sagacity which appears plainly between the two, in accordance with the voice of the blessed Paul" (1 Cor 12:8). See Mansi, IX 223; Migne, PG (66), 697.

34. "With me I feel reluctant to read aloud the Song of Songs, because neither according to the prophetic notion could be defined, nor according to the traditions of the historical books, for instance, the writing of the kingdoms (Israel, Judah) and not even it demonstrates the study of admonition" (exhortation); see Mansi, IX, 223.

35. "At this point it seems essential to cite Devreesse's conclusion on the subject: 'Theodore measured the degree of inspiration of Ecclesiastes. Did he go yet much more daringly with the Canticle of Canticles? Was it not, in his eyes, but a song of love which had no place in the canon?' The accusation is supported by a doubtful caution and by one passage coming from Isho'dad

of Merv which allows us to understand that Theodore did not perhaps exclude the Song as much radically as one is led to believe" (*Essai*, 35).

36. Alponse Mingana, "Synopsis of Christian doctrine in the Fourth Century," The Bulletin of the John Ryland Library, V, No. 3 and 4 (April–November 1919), 304.

37. *Le commentaire sur les Psaumes*, 135.

38. Migne, PG (80), 805.

39. The charge that Theodore rejected the books of Ezra from his canon comes from Leontius (cf. Migne, PG [86], 1368).

40. R.H. Pfeiffer, *Introduction*, 69, 120f.

41. The story from 4 Esdras that the entire Old Testament had been lost when Nebuchadnezzar destroyed Jerusalem and had been rewritten seventy years later by Ezra during forty days made an impression on several church fathers, among them Tertullian, Irenaeus, Clement of Alexandria, and Theodoret. Even Jerome accepted it without question (cf. R.H. Pfeiffer, *Introduction*, 42).

42. Ernest C. Colwell, *The Study of the Bible* (Chicago: University of Chicago Press, 1946), 35; R.H. Pfeiffer, *Introduction*, 69. This charge was originally advanced by H. Kihn (*op. cit.*, 47) and L. Pirot (*op. cit.*, 148) on the evidence affirmed by Junilius Africanus' *Instituta regularia divinae legis*. Junilius listed the book of Esther under the group of mediae auctoritatis of the Instituta (pp. 272–280).

43. Leontius of Byzantium, *Adversus incorrupticolis et nestorianos*, 3.17, Migne, PG (86), 1368 A.

44. According to the Greek Orthodox Church the books which Protestants call apocrypha are named *anaginoskomena* (readable, in private or public) or deuterocanonical; for the Greek church the term apocrypha designates the books which Protestants call pseudepigrapha.

45. One brief reference to the history of Susanna has been found; in that reference the text seems to be quoted with great liberty (*Le commentaire sur les Psaumes*, 392). On the other hand Daniel, in both the Septuagint and Theodotion's version, includes the apocryphal additions lacking in the Massoretic text, and the entire book of Daniel was considered canonical by all the

fathers. The canonicity of Susanna's history was questioned by Junilius Africanus in 240 in a letter addressed to Origen from Palestine (Migne, PG [11], 44); Jerome also expressed some misgivings in his preface to Daniel (R.H. Pfeiffer, *History of the New Testament Times* [New York: Harper Brothers, 1949], 442).

46. *Le commentaire sur les Psaumes,* 306. Theodore believed David to be the author of all the psalms in the Hebrew psalter.

47. *Ibid.,* 184, 422, 542.

48. For a helpful discussion of Jerome's inconsistent views of the apocrypha, see R.J. Foster, "The Formation and History of the Canon," *A Catholic Commentary on Holy Scripture* (New York: Thomas Nelson and Sons, 1953), 17.

49. *Patrologia Orientalis,* VIII, 1, p. 97.

50. Migne, PG (86), 1365 C.

51. B.F. Westcott, *A General Survey of the History of the Canon of the New Testament* (London: Macmillan & Co., 1870), 409–411; Cosmas Indicopleustes, an Alexandrian of the sixth century who was first a merchant and then became a monk, states in his *Topographia* that only three Catholic epistles were received by the Syrians, i.e. the epistle of James, 1 Peter, and 1 John (Migne, PG [138], 372D–373B).

52. B.F. Westcott, *op. cit.,* 411; C. Baur, *John Chrysostom and His Time,* I, 317.

53. Our opinion is supported by Isho'dad of Merv, who in his commentary on the epistle of James noted: "Also Theodore does not mention any part (of James, 1 Peter and 1 John), and he cites them not in any of his writings" (J.M. Vosté, "L'oeuvre exégétique de Théodore de Mopsueste," *Revue Biblique,* XXXVIII, [October 1929], 390).

54. B.F. Westcott, *op. cit.,* 410–411.

55. H. Kihn, *Theodor von Mopsuestia,* 87f. Leontius of Byzantium charged Theodore with Judaic tendencies (Migne, PG [86], 1365).

56. Rowan A. Greer, *Theodore of Mopsuestia: Exegete and Theologian* (Westminster, 1961), 100; Mingana, *Synopsis of Christian Doctrine,* 2.

57. Migne, PG (66), 465 D–468 A; 280 B.

58. *Ibid.,* 597 B.

59. *Ibid.*, 452 D.

60. *Le Commentaire sur les Psaumes,* 127, 133, 195, 249.

61. Dudley Tyng, "Theodore of Mopsuestia as an Interpreter of the Old Testament," *Journal of Biblical Literature,* I (1931), 298–299.

62. John Chrysostom, *Against the Jews,* orat. 1, Migne, PG (48), 844–845.

63. Migne, PG (33), 1587–1588; J. Quastin, *Patrology,* III, 399.

64. *Against the Jews,* I–VIII, Migne, PG (48) 814–942.

65. Migne, PG (48) 848. The Greek text has been translated into English by S.M. Gonzaga in Chrysostom Baur's *J. Chrysostom and His Time,* I, 332.

66. Harry Orlinsky, "The Colummar Order of the Hexapla," *The Jewish Quarterly Review,* XXVII, No. 2 (October 1936), 145, n. 23.

67. *Ibid.*

68. One might raise the example of Jerome as a refutation of our argument. While Jerome spent considerable time in Antioch (374–376), he did not learn Hebrew there but only Greek, by attending the lectures of Apollinaris of Laodicea. He did not start learning Syriac until he settled for more than four years as a hermit at Chalkis in the Syrian desert. At Chalkis he was obliged to learn the local language in order to facilitate his communication with the natives; and this language helped him later in his study of Hebrew (Epist. XVII, 2) which he began with the aid of a baptized Jew in Chalkis (Epist. CXXV, 12). However, it was in Bethlehem where he finally settled as the head of a monastery where he devoted himself seriously to the study of Hebrew.

69. Theodore's comment upon Job 42:14 has been preserved by the Acts of the Fifth Council (Mansi, *op. cit.,* IX, 224: "In fact Theodore said that Job's third daughter was called Amalthea's horn, and this was not strange, but it manifested that he (Job) agreed with pagan fables and esteemed highly the images of idolatry.") It has been suggested that Theodore in his usage of the expressions "Hebrew voice" and "Hebraic idiom" was referring to Aquila's version which provided the reader with a slavish word-for-word translation of the original Hebrew (see J. Philip

de Barjeau, *L'école exégétique d'Antioche,* 57). But whenever Theodore quoted Aquila's translation he mentioned his name.

70. Migne, PG (66), 437 C. The passage (Hab 2:11b) in Hebrew reads: "and the beam from the wood will answer." The Septuagint renders the beam "beetle," and the Peshitta reads "peg." Theodore rejects the evidence offered by the Peshitta.

71. *Commentarius in Sophoniae* 1:6, Migne, PG (66), 452 D.

72. R.H. Pfeiffer holds that the origins of the Peshitta were as obscure to Theodore as they are to us *(Introduction,* 120).

73. *Commentarii in epistolas b. Pauli,* I, lxxvi; II, 228–229.

74. J.M. Walden, *The Universities of Ancient Greece* (New York: Charles Scribner's Sons, 1912), 275ff.

75. With the exception of the Peshitta, Jerome's Vulgate, and Saadia Gaon's Arabic version, all other Christian Old Testament versions were made either directly or indirectly from the Septuagint. The Greek church with the Coptic, Armenian, Georgian, and the Slavic Orthodox churches still are using the respective versions which were produced from the LXX, although in their present Bible some books have been revised with the benefit of the Vulgate, the Syriac or the Hebrew (H.B. Swete, *An Introduction to the Old Testament in Greek* [Cambridge: Cambridge University Press, 1900], 117ff; R.H. Pfeiffer, *Introduction,* 114–119).

76. *Le commentaire sur les Psaumes,* 52, 1.1; 55, 1.5; 58, 11.32–33; 69, 11.29–30; 92, 11.21–22; 127, 1.11; 139, 11.3–4; 140, 1.28, 144, 1.1; 253, 1.8 etc.

77. *Ibid.,* 53, 1.17; 54, 1.1; 108, 1.8; 140, 11.26–27; 150, 11.1–2; 207, 1.25; 214, 11.19–20; 245, 11.22–23; 321, 11.1–2 etc.

78. *Ibid.,* 140, 1.8; 214, 11.20–21; 225, 1.17; 363, 1.2.

79. *Ibid.,* 91, 1.9; 92, 11.7–8; 93, 11.16–17; 134, 11.9–10; 134, 1.18; 395, 11.16–25; 419, 1.15.

80. *Ibid.,* 195, 11.23–25.

81. *Commentarius in Sophoniae,* 1:6, Migne (66), 453 A.

82. Philo circulated the story that the Seventy were segregated in different cells on the island of Pharos in Alexandria, and that at the end of seventy-two days, in which each one completed his own translation, the seventy-two separate versions were found to be marvelously in full agreement with each other. Philo also informs us that every year the Jews commemorated this

miraculous event with great festivities on the island (Philo, *Life of Moses*, 2:5f). The stories of Philo have been accepted by such fathers as Pseudo-Justin (*Exhortation to the Greeks*, Migne, PG [6], 268); Irenaeus (*Adversus Haereses* 3, 21); Tertullian (*Apologia* 18); Clement of Alexandria (*Stromateis* A, 22, 148); Eusebius (*Hist. Eccl.*, 7, 32); Cyril of Jerusalem (*Catechesis*, 4, 34); Epiphanius (*De mensuris*, 3, 6), etc.

83. Philo considered the seventy-two translators to have been divinely inspired and gifted with the spirit of prophecy (*Life of Moses*, 2:7). Even this Philonic hyperbole left upon the fathers a tremendous impression.

84. *Le commentaire sur les Psaumes*, 364. A contemporary scholar, J.W. Wevers, states the following in regard to Symmachus' translation: "His work can easily be recognized by its elegant and bombastic style. Its periphrastic character renders it somewhat less useful . . ." in *Interpreter's Dictionary*, IV, 275.

85. Louis Pirot has supported the very same view in his monograph, *L'oeuvre exégétique de Théodore de Mopsueste*, p. 101.

86. Henrich Kihn has stated Theodore's view on the origin of the Septuagint as follows: "He extols the Septuagint as the only accurate and infallible version, which agrees perfectly with the original Hebrew text. It makes the original (Hebrew) text unnecessary and its comparison with the Syriac translation superfluous. Its accuracy and superhuman authority is guaranteed by its amazing origin. The authority of its translators is guaranteed by the esteem with which the apostles held it" (*Theodor von Mopsuestia*, p. 88).

87. *Commentarius in Sophoniae*, ch. 1:5, Migne, PG (66), 452 D–453 A. At another instance in his commentary on Zephaniah, Theodore makes the following point over a variant reading between the Septuagint and the Peshitta: "About the Seventy that they could not be misled we have enough spoken formerly; it would be more justifiable to hold that it could have happened to the one who has translated it into Syriac" (*ibid.*, 468 A). Theodore refers his readers to the above quoted passage.

88. R. Devreesse in his essay on Theodore does not even discuss the subject as an issue because he thinks that the Septuagint

was for Theodore just a Greek Vulgate (*Essai sur Théodore,* 55).
R.A. Greer supports the view that Theodore's authorized text
was the Septuagint but that he never accepted it as divinely
inspired translation (*Theodore of Mopsuestia: Exegete and Theologian,* 99).

89. R.H. Pfeiffer, *History of New Testament Times,* 189.

90. Paul Anton de Lagarde, *Ankundigung einer neuen Ausgabe der griechischen Uebersetzung des A. T.* (Gottingen: Ahoyer
W.F. Kaestner, 1882); *idem, Septuaginta Studien,* Erster Theil
(Gottingen: Dietrische Verlags-Buchhandlung, 1891).

91. *Preface to Chronicles,* Migne, PL (28), 1392 A. The Latin
text has been translated by R.H. Pfeiffer, *Introduction,* 111.

92. The pioneering work in the field of Septuagint textual
studies, initiated by the polymathic Paul de Lagarde, has been
adopted and continued by his able disciple Alfred Rahlfs and his
collaborators, and as a result of it we have now the famous *Gottinger Septuaginta-Unternehmens* (see P.L. Hedley, "The Gottingen Investigation and Edition of the Septuagint," *The Harvard
Theological Review,* XXVI, No. 1 [January 1933], 55ff). In contrast with the majority of critics, Paul Kahle and his student
Alexander Sperber regard the Hesychius and Lucian texts, not as
recensions of the Septuagint, but as two independent translations
produced from Hebrew with the help of other Greek versions (see
Alexander Sperber, "The Problems of the Septuagint Recensions," *Journal of Biblical Literature,* LIV, Part II [June 1935],
73–92).

93. Frederick G. Kenyon, *Recent Developments in Textual
Criticism of the Greek Bible* (London: Published for the British
Academy by the Oxford University Press, 1933), 65–66, 110.

94. From the great uncial MSS only Codex Venetus and various ancient Old Latin sub-versions are based on a text similar
to that of Lucian. Certain cursive MSS can be classified as
Lucianic; they are: 19, 82, 93, 104, 144, 147, 233, 246, 308. See
Bruce M. Metzger, "Lucian and the Lucianic Recension of the
Greek Bible," *New Testament Studies,* VIII (1962), 189–203.

95. "Der Psaltertext bei Theodoret," *Mitteilungen des Septuaginta-Unternehmens,* by the Göttingen Gesellschaft, Heft 3
(1911), p. 85.

96. Theodoret, *Expositio in psalmos,* Migne, PG (80), 864, 913, 1029.

97. *Le commentaire sur les Psaumes,* 195, 1.23.

98. *L'oeuvre exégétique de Théodore,* 110–111.

99. *Ibid.,* 111.

100. Alexander Sperber, "The Problems of the Septuagint Recensions," *Journal of Biblical Literature,* LIV, Part II (June 1935), 81.

101. L. Pirot, *L'oeuvre exégétique de Théodore de Mopsueste,* 111–112.

# Chapter Four

# THEODORE'S DOCTRINE OF REVELATION AND INSPIRATION

The notion of inspired scripture is a contribution of Judaism, and it grew out of the Old Testament concept of prophecy. The conception of inspired scripture was gradually extended from the time of the exile to include every word of the Old Testament.[1] In the Old Testament itself there is no clear theory about the manner of inspiration. According to the rabbis, however, the individual books of the Bible attained final form through three stages: first, the divine revelation; second, the inspired utterance of a prophet; third, the exact transcript through a scribe.[2] Thus the ultimate author of each sacred book was God who, through his spirit, first spoke his revelations, then dictated them in propositional form.

This old belief in the verbal inspiration of the scriptures had been inherited from Judaism by the apostolic church along with the scriptures themselves. The New Testament writers shared the common Jewish view of the nature of the inspiration of the scriptures, and they quoted the Greek Bible or Septuagint as inspired scripture. For the New Testament authors the inspiration of the Old Testament was beyond question, and they referred to it as the direct utterance of God.[3] In the New Testament the term "inspired scripture" ($\theta\epsilon\acute{o}\pi\nu\epsilon\upsilon\sigma\tau\sigma$) occurs only once (2 Tim 3:16) and does not suggest any particular theory of the operation of the Spirit of God upon the minds and souls of the writers of the scriptural books. No quality is more characteristic of the New Testament writers than their belief in the supernatural. They all live in the same supernatural atmosphere and refer to the mystical operations of the indwelling spirit which infused them with the light of the knowledge of the glory of God.[4]

Not only with the New Testament writers, but in the patristic age too, the idea of inspiration carries the same signification. All of the fathers lived in the same supernatural atmosphere and related scriptural inspiration to the operations of the Holy Spirit from outside the human realm. The biblical authors, according to the fathers, had been possessed by the force and energy of the Holy Spirit, and the Spirit in them was its own authority. And while the church in its early creeds and councils was more concerned with the equal status of the Old Testament and New Testament, and with the divine authorship of both, than with theories of inspiration as such, the church fathers intensified their inquiry into the nature of inspiration and formulated theories which attempted to explain the mystery of revelation. No distinction was drawn between the giving of the revelation and the writing of it; biblical authors had no personal share in the writing of the Bible. Inspiration was identified with infallibility, and the written record with revelation. In the Bible there is nothing without purpose, not a syllable, not an iota, not the smallest dash.[5] The ancient ecclesiastical writers insisted so strongly on the divine action in the composition of the individual books of the Bible that they regarded the human authors as passive instruments receiving the dictation of the Spirit. Thus, Justin Martyr regarded the prophets as the lyre upon which the Holy Spirit plays such music as he will,[6] and Athenagoras in discussing the doctrine of inspiration made this statement:

> The words of the prophets guarantee our reasoning . . . for they, while the reasoning power within them was at a stand, under the motion of the divine Spirit, spoke forth what was being wrought in them, the Spirit working with them, as it were a piper who breathed into his pipe.[7]

The immediate consequence of this view is that both Testaments form but one single saving book, given by one God by means of the Holy Spirit and which, in spite of the diversity of ages and generations, extends from the creation of the world unto us.[8] Because of the common origin of both Testaments, it was held, the teaching of the law and the prophets is in perfect agreement with that of the apostles. Clement of Alexandria describes this perfect agreement of the Old and New Testament in terms of a comparison borrowed from music: the two Testaments constitute an ecclesiastical symphony of two choirs.[9] Following this metaphor, which certainly is not lacking in charm, Origen declares:

> The whole of scripture is but one single instrument of God, perfect and harmonious, which renders one consonance that is formed of different saving sounds.[10]

In point of fact the fathers stressed the harmony of both Testaments to the extent of claiming that they are identical. The Old Testament as a whole has to be considered as "a book of the generation of Jesus Christ, the son of David, the son of Abraham." The Old Testament represented the period of promises and expectation, the time of covenants and prophecies; it was not only the prophets who prophesied—events also were prophecies. The whole biblical history was prophetical or "typical," a "sign" pointing toward approaching consummation "in Vetere Testamento Novum latet et in Novo Vetus Pate."[11] Cyril of Alexandria, on the other hand, in order to show that the two Testaments are intimately connected, wrote:

> The New Testament is sister to and closely related to the Mosaic oracles; indeed it is composed of the selfsame elements. We can show that the life in Christ is not remote from conduct in accordance with the law, provided that the ancient ordinances are given a spiritual interpretation.[12]

On another occasion the same father confesses that he feels

> . . . inclined to crown Isaiah not only with the grace of
> prophecy but also with the prerogatives of the apostles.
> He is at once a prophet and an apostle; and his pro-
> phetic writings share the luster of the evangelical
> kerygma.[13]

This interpretation of the Old and New Testaments rests, according to the patristic viewpoint, on the notion that the message of both is divine; it comes from God; it is the word of God in book form. It was the people of the covenant to whom the word of God has been entrusted under the old dispensation; and it was the church of the Word Incarnate that received the fullness of God's message to men. But the Old Testament retained its authority in the new covenant because the two together formed a single and final record of God's revelation of himself. Jesus, the Christ, belongs to both. He is the fulfiller of the old and the inaugurator of the new dispensation. This divine truth was contained in the scriptures of the Old and New Testament. The Bible is thus the only source-book for our knowledge of revealed truth. In it, the Holy Spirit speaks to us and indeed in the same way through all the holy books. The true author of the Bible was the Holy Spirit. The Bible was dictated by the Spirit of God. Revelation is a body of propositional truths contained in an inspired record which was supernaturally written through the plenary and verbal inspiration of the Holy Spirit. The use of the metaphor of the human writer as the pen in the hand of the Holy Spirit becomes frequent in the patristic literature, and it comes to be regarded as of little importance whether or not the scriptural author understood the words which he recorded.[14]

The fathers as a whole insisted so much on the divine action in the composition of our Bible that they came to view inspiration as being a mechanical dictation of truths into the scripture. According to this view of "plenary and verbal inspiration" the biblical writers were divinely secured against any and all mistakes by virtue of absolute supervision by the Holy Spirit which was using them as passive instruments and not as intelligent and active collaborators. Whatever the Bible contains must be true because it was dictated by the Spirit. Divine inspiration of the Bible was generally held by the fathers to require belief in the truth of all its assertions on matters not only of religious doctrine and ethics, but also of cosmology, astronomy, history, and biology.

The foregoing account of the nature of inspiration presents in a very broad outline the patristic standpoint on the subject as it is represented in the theologies and the exegetical systems of individual fathers. It was never precisely formulated, in part because it was not seriously challenged by any school of religious thought, except by Marcion and the Manichees. This view became the generally accepted position of Christian theology in the patristic age.[15]

In consequence, one is not surprised to learn that Theodore subscribed to tenets and views to which his predecessors and contemporaries had committed themselves. Together with the entire church of his day, Theodore was firmly convinced that the Bible was divinely inspired and that the two Testaments were given by one God in spite of the diversity of ages and generations.[16] Inspiration was attributed by Theodore to God or to the Holy Spirit, and for him scripture was, so to speak, supernaturally written.[17] But at several important points Theodore states a notion of inspiration which is more flexible than that of his predecessors. This flexibility on the part of Theodore, which to a certain extent can be explained as a modification of his original conception of inspiration, can only be discovered in his later writings; in all of his earlier works he adheres to the doctrine of plenary and verbal inspiration.

From this assertion we must turn to a discussion of Theodore's notion of plenary inspiration as it is stated in his earlier writings; after that we shall be able to consider how he formulated a more comprehensive and exact conception of scripture and revelation.

Theodore's commentary on the book of Psalms is one of the earliest works which the future bishop of Mopsuestia wrote after he graduated from the theological school of Antioch.[18] Since questions about the authorship and date of each book of the Bible were of fundamental importance and were carefully studied by Theodore, he assumed with a juvenile certainty that David was the author of the entire book of Psalms.[19] In his commentary Theodore adopted a very curious method of interpretation. He held that the book of Psalms was written by David and that each psalm is a literary unit through which David speaks, sometimes personally, and sometimes in the name of other notables in Israel's history. According to Theodore, David, the author of the psalter, was not only a warrior who later became king of Israel, but also a saint, a righteous being, a prophet; as a prophet he was deeply concerned with the destiny and religion of his people.[20] In his daily life the king-prophet was constantly praying and asking God about the future of Israel, and God answered David's prayers by revealing to him through an illumination of his mind the future of the Israelite kingdom.[21] Thus the psalter, instead of being a collection of religious lyrics or a codification of Israel's psalmody for cultic and devotional purposes, was regarded as a collection of oracles.[22] This does not necessarily mean that Theodore regarded each psalm as a prophetic utterance:

> The purpose of all the psalms of the blessed David is to become a source of profit for the people, and they were not written by the same single fashion; there are certain in which David sets forth doctrinal sayings, there are others in which he sings hymns of praise to the Lord of creation. There still are others in which he suggests, as a subject of discussion, circumstances relating to the future and by prophesying them he indicates the benefit which will come from them. . . . There are other psalms by which David tries to instruct his readers through his personal experiences; he teaches them how they are supposed to behave and what is proper for them to recite whenever they find themselves in sin and calamities. There also are exhortatory psalms which are not based upon a concrete "argument"; in these he tells his readers from what they should be abstaining or he advised what is befitting to practice.[23]

From the foregoing it is clear that Theodore was the first Christian commentator who recognized that the Hebrew psalter comprises psalms of different types, and who tried to classify them according to their spirit and content.[24] David's mission as prophet, according to Theodore, was both to predict the future and to teach his contemporaries and future generations. In point of fact, Theodore regarded the prophets as the greatest and truest teachers of Israel.[25] He regarded David as being first in the line of the great prophets and as marking a new era in the history of Israel's religion.[26] David is the herald and teacher of a pure religion, and through his autobiographical and doctrinal psalms he preaches *paedeia*. The book of Psalms in its scope and perspective, according to Theodore, is thoroughly Israelitic. David's inspiration, however, reached its highest degree when he started revealing the future history and destiny of Israel. It was in the prophetic psalms that God revealed to David the fullness of Israel's consummation in history.[27] In Theodore's opinion, revelation enabled David to transcend history and predict the various phases of *Heilsgeschichte* with a telescopic view extending above time and space. Divine inspiration elevated David's soul and spirit to a supernatural sphere, and from there he was able to anticipate the development of future events which were to take place in succeeding centuries. The range of this telescopic vista extends from the era of Solomon to the Maccabean insurrection. There is no messianic expectation involved in this contemplation of time and history.[28] The prophetic psalms are thoroughly theocentric and not christocentric. David predicts and writes through the grace of God's Spirit.[29] To the illuminated intellect of David the Spirit of God unfolds the history of the political forces of the world which will try to shape the course of events in the center of monotheism where the supreme God of history has his temple.[30] By virtue of this spiritual illumination David visualizes the Assyrian monarchs, the Chaldaean conquerors, and the Seleucid invaders marching through the land of Israel given to him by God with the promise that David's throne would endure forever. David did not foretell all the events of Hebrew history but only a certain number of them which, however, had great significance in the development of Israel's historical drama. He particularly dealt with the Syro-Ephraimitic war and Sennacherib's invasion of Judah during the reign of Hezekiah,[31] with the captivity and return from Babylon,[32] and finally with the Seleucids and Maccabeans.[33]

In foretelling the various vicissitudes of his nation through his prophetic oracles, David spoke on behalf of the nation of Israel or in the name of various Old Testament personalities who were involved in the different crises of his nation and showed them the example that should be followed in each decisive turning point of Israel's destiny. Thus David, in the opinion of Theodore, lived by anticipation the most important circumstances of the history of his people and he wrote down, for the benefit of his nation, all the oracles that God had spoken to him because he was conscious of being led by the Spirit to a knowledge of future situations in Israel's life and history. He regarded all knowledge of the future as emanating from God. This principle was applied not only to the psalmic oracles of David but also to the oracles of the Old Testament prophets.[34] Theodore regarded the prophets as obedient servants of the Spirit; they had been called to the ministry of the word to restate and re-emphasize what David had long before prophesied.

This knowledge of future events was conveyed, according to Theodore's understanding, through the channel of revelation. Revelation is an illumination of mind imparting inspiration in propositional form. Theodore makes no distinction between revelation and inspiration. The essence of Theodore's understanding of revelation is based upon a view that all the content of the psalter emanates from a divine initiative which was communicated supernaturally to the human author by the intervention of a divine agent. And thus inspiration becomes a verbal dictation in the mechanical sense. Psalm 45 afforded him an opportunity to elaborate his understanding of this supernatural intervention on the part of the spirit of God. In commenting upon Psalm 45:1, Theodore made the following *scholium:*

But the reed-pen needs ink, and it also needs a scriber both to add the ink and set it in motion in order to model the letters. David views the tongue as a reed-pen;

and the Holy Spirit is called by him a scriber so that the sayings which are shaped by the Spirit be in the spot where the ink stays. Because the Spirit, just like a perfect writer, fills, as if it were ink, the human heart with the perceptions of revelation and from there allows the tongue to speak loud and clear and to formulate the sayings in letters and articulate them distinctly for those who are willing to receive the benefit which stems out of them.[35]

In this passage Theodore considered the notion of inspiration in terms of dictation. The Spirit of God breathed the precise words of God's message into the human organism. Thus the ultimate authority of the psalter was God, who activated the biblical writer and by his pen communicated the perceptions of propositional truth. So the activity of God's Spirit in the heart or in the mind of biblical writers worked either by illumination or by dictation. The recipient was, however, conscious of the divine activity in him and bore witness to it by praying for the instruction and edification of God's people.[36]

Our discussion thus far has proved that Theodore, in his commentary on the book of Psalms was, as a child of his age, an advocate of the plenary view of verbal inspiration which was the viewpoint of the church from the days of the apostolic fathers until the rise of biblical criticism in the nineteenth century.[37] Over against this general affirmation, however, must be placed the statements that Theodore made when dealing with the content and texts of other biblical writings in his later commentaries. There is strong evidence that Theodore attempted to break with the traditional theory of inspiration by modifying it and minimizing the role that God's Spirit played in the composition of the autographs of the Bible.[38]

It must be noted that this plenary notion of inspiration was somewhat modified by Theodore's understanding of prophecy. In his commentary on the twelve minor prophets, Theodore gives such prominence to the human factor that prophecy becomes a collaboration between God's Spirit and man. The state of prophetic inspiration, far from suppressing the mental faculty of the human author (as the Platonic-*mantic* doctrine of the Alexandrians maintained), actually makes it stronger and more receptive to the message of God. The "word of the Lord" is an energy or voice in inward experience.[39] The Spirit of God awakens in the inmost soul of the prophet a disposition of thoughts and images without audible communication.[40] Prophetic experiences are not communications of propositional truths, and the oracles of the prophets are not written by mechanical dictation:

> It is quite clear, and we have said it several times in the past, that the sayings of the prophets have not been compiled in the form of a book following a harmonious pattern, but separately, and the prophecies were spoken by the prophets when they received the revelation.[41]

The most important information concerning Theodore's modification of the idea of plenary inspiration comes from the Acts of the Second Council of Constantinople. According to the conciliar record Theodore taught that all the books of the Old Testament were not equally inspired; he recognized different kinds and degrees of inspiration. For example, the inspiration of Proverbs and Ecclesiastes was different from that of the prophets. The peculiar religious structure of the wisdom books could not be placed on the same level with the prophetic books. Israel's wisdom literature is of human origin, and it could not be compared with the revelation of God's mighty deeds and acts. Sound teaching and advice for getting on in the world were very different from the revelation of God's redemptive dealings with his people. Theodore ascribed Proverbs and Ecclesiastes to Solomon but at the same time claimed that both books were written out of the author's human experience and sagacity: "and he (Theodore) attributed to Solomon books, that is, Proverbs and Ecclesiastes, which were written by him for the benefit of others, which Theodore, indeed, did not accept to have been written by the prophetic grace, but truly by the influence of sagacity which appears plainly between the two, in accordance with the voice of the blessed Paul" (1 Cor 12:8).[42] This interpretation was condemned by the Fifth General Council in 553.

Theodore's numerous commentaries on the historical books of the Bible have been lost and we do not know what his approach was to the subject of inspiration in relation to the composition of the historical books of the Old Testament. Fortunately, his student Theodoret, in a brief commentary on Chronicles, makes an important remark which sounds typically Theodorean:

> He who compiles a history never records matters of posterity, but only facts of the past or present. Only the prophets foretold matters pertaining to the future; this was their characteristic.[43]

In the light of Theodoret's testimony we maintain that Theodore's view concerning the authorship of the historical books of the Old Testament, with the exception of course of the Pentateuch,[44] was that their respective authors were gifted priests who, by utilizing the available source material which was stored in the temple scriptorium, composed the history of the people of Israel from a religious viewpoint.

Theodore explained the authorship of the book of Job in a similar way. In post-exilic times a Jew, well-versed in the letters of the Greeks, took up an Edomitic folklore which was in circulation for generations in the whole near east and committed the history of the just to writing, fashioning it after the models of Greek poetry.[45]

It was especially in his writings dealing with the New Testament that Theodore gave the human factor such prominence that we cannot credit him anymore with a traditional view of inspiration. The autonomy of the authors was explicitly emphasized. Thus in his commentary on the epistle to the Galatians he criticized Paul's style and diction as abrupt and obscure, and blamed Paul for a passionate indignation against his adversaries that had caused the textual abruptness.[46] Also, in his commentary on Philemon, he complained that Paul's textual obscurity arose from his tendency to write too succinctly.[47] And again in commenting upon Matthew 1:1 he says:

> Matthew would not have taught this at the beginning of his gospel had he known that our Lord did not approve of it; indeed he who took so much trouble to write faithfully his gospel according to the orders of Christ would not have dared to put down in writing a statement that was detrimental to Christ.[48]

We also observe how Theodore interprets the origin of the fourth gospel:

> And thus the blessed John settles in Ephesus, visiting the whole Asia Minor and rendering great services to the local congregations through his own preaching. In the meantime takes place the edition of the rest of the evangelists, i.e. the Gospels of Matthew and Mark, and even that of Luke, and which were spread within a short time all over the Christian world and were studied by all the congregations, as it was expected, with great promptness.
>
> But the congregations of Asia Minor, having judged that the blessed John was more trustworthy than the rest to bear witness to the evangelical testimony because he had been with the Lord from the very beginning . . . brought the books to him in order to learn from John what his opinion was in regard to them.
>
> John praised the evangelists for having recorded the truths, but at the same time he found them to be short and to have omitted things pertaining to the most important miracles and doctrines.
>
> Thereupon the brethren begged John entreatingly to choose the things he estimated to be of great value for the interpretation of the doctrine which had been omitted by the rest and commit them to writing immediately. And this is what he did.[49]

These quotations speak for themselves: Theodore clearly shows that the idea of a purely mechanical inspiration through the Spirit of God was no longer dear to him. The authors of the gospels were not merely clerks, nor passive tools of the Spirit. Theodore explicitly states that in writing their accounts the evangelists drew on their own memories, and each one assumed full responsibility for his own work. The human element in the Bible exists because the personalities of its writers are safeguarded. The Bible is not the exclusive work of God's spirit. The divine meets the human element in the midst of man's religious experience. Thus the Bible becomes the realm of the divine–human encounter. Theodore's final word is that we must distinguish between revelation and inspiration. Beyond that the *Mephasqana* did not theorize. He even anticipated the modern concept of progressive revelation, though, of course, the doctrine is not expressed in any nineteenth century evolutionary sense. Theodore asserted explicitly that the two persons of the Trinity, the Son-Logos and the Holy Ghost, did not reveal themselves as independent *prosopa* in any respect whatever to the writers of the Old Testament.[50] He likewise taught that the doctrine of resurrection of the dead was an entirely unknown idea in pre-New Testament times, and it was the conception of sheol—the shadowy realm of the underworld where the departed spirits of the dead remained—that prevailed in the teaching of the old dispensation.[51] Another aspect to be emphasized concerning Theodore's teaching on Old Testament revelation is that the Mopsuestian considered the prophets of Israel to be teachers of monotheism, progressive revealers of God's true character, and preachers of a true and perfect religious knowledge.[52] From a critical point of view, Theodore's standpoint reflects a remarkable faithfulness to the text and teaching of the Old Testament.

In Theodore's theology of the Bible the Old Testament contains the revelation that God is one. The religious teachings of the Old Testament have a great value and significance even apart from Christ.[53] The providential and everlasting God of creation who revealed himself in the Old Testament gave that revelation in such a manner that it would be profitable and meaningful for his people. The Old Testament does not present Christ to us; it rather prepares the way for Christ. It records God's visitation of a particular people. According to Theodore it was only the God-head who revealed himself to those who had received the religious *paideia* before the parousia of the Lord Christ.

Theodore prefaced his biblical commentaries with long prologues in which he treated problems of biblical introduction, but the prologue to his commentary on the minor prophets has not come down to us. His views on the mode of prophetic call and inspiration have been compiled from such information as we have been able to glean from different comments he made in expounding the text of the twelve.

Theodore's view on the prophetic call is a sound interpretation of the phenomenon. He held that prophecy is not an art or an institutionalized profession which can be learned and practiced for the purpose of exploiting religion. It is not a hereditary office which can be inherited from one's father.[54] Prophecy is independent of any particular state of life because it is an action of God without the medium of a sacrament. And he who has been the object of that divine action can only point to a call that originated in the will of God. A prophet cannot appeal to any religious or national institution. It was the irresistible command of the deity which forcibly took Amos from his life as herdsman and pruner of sycamore figs and made him to prophesy the message of God concerning the people. The ministry of the prophets was not open just to any man of good will who wanted to constitute himself a prophet; it came to those who were called through the manifestation of God's grace.[55] The prophets were raised and sent forth by a divine force emanating from the will of God. So the original call was independent of the will of men, and therefore the call to the prophetic ministry came from God alone. This feeling and conviction is confirmed by the content of the prophetic books.

From the moment of their call these men were prophets; this does not mean, however, that they were under the influence of the prophetic charisma at every moment. They experienced this charisma only at certain times—whenever they felt that they were inspired by the living God.[56] The prophets were the confidants and spokesmen of God because they made known the will of God and events of the future. In commenting upon Amos 3:7 Theodore makes the following point:

> Accordingly we prophets do not utter our voice without reason, because we say as much as God has given us to tell. God wants the things which he intends to bring out for your own instruction as well as the events which will take place in the future to be made known to you by us the prophets.[57]

It is interesting to note that Theodore refers to the seers of the Old Testament as the spiritual forerunners of the great eighth century prophets. He even alludes to the fact that the earlier visionaries of Israel did not enjoy a high reputation among the people. They prophesied because of certain gifts of temper and natural disposition. Among such enthusiasts Amos must not be reckoned:

> Amaziah in his impertinent mood said to Amos: "O thou seer, go, flee thou away into the land of Judah. . . ." Amaziah used the term seer sarcastically because the people beforetime called the prophets by that name, for they claimed to see some extraordinary sights through divine energy and revelation. The book of Kings says: "For he that is now called a prophet was beforetime called seer." Amaziah said seer in order to provoke antagonism; he should have said instead: "O thou who are pronouncing and proclaiming by authority."[58]

Theodore held that it was only in Israel that God raised true prophets who spoke inspired words. The will of God for all humanity is historically conveyed through Israel by way of election. Only to one people on earth did God mediate his providential interest for mankind. He called Abraham and instituted circumcision in order to distinguish Abraham's descendants from the rest of the nations; and then God revealed his law unto Moses and provided a country for Israel. All these privileges came from God alone; there was no human merit involved.[59] Yet all these

providential blessings granted to the Israel of old came for the
sake of man because they were subordinate to the ultimate purpose of God in history: the salvation of all men. Universal salvation had been decided by God from the beginning, but it was
carried out by means of election or by setting apart. The Old Testament looks forward; it is oriented toward the future because it
is a history of a redeeming drama which arrives at its terminus
with the advent of the Lord Christ. But universal salvation
through the Lord Christ could not appear as an innovation or
novelty which God had decided as an afterthought. God, in order
to avoid that impression among men, raised the prophets.[60]

God persistently addressed himself to men through the
prophets. David was the first in the line to whom God revealed
the future history of his people. Then came the prophets whose
preaching was purely oral.[61] And after that God from time to time
raised the great writing prophets whose primary mission consisted in retelling and re-emphasizing what David had long
before prophesied. Every prophet was called upon to minister in
a particular historical situation, and their message in its primary
significance had to do with contemporary circumstances and the
immediate future. Prophets applied their messages to a certain
and specific stage of Israel's drama in history; they never left their
own world and their peculiar religious interest. It was only occasionally, Theodore holds, that the prophets referred to distant
future events. This foretelling, however, resulted from a certain
historical context:

> Each of the prophets seems proclaiming oracles the
> issue of which looked to be nigh at hand; they joined
> together some oracles which referred to the future for
> they were led to that from a certain context.[62]

Prophetic inspiration, according to the understanding of
Theodore, means human possession by the Spirit of God.[63] This
possession is explained by the Mopsuestian as a psychological
state which the prophet experiences in a particular confrontation
with the deity, and in objectifying it the charismatic person

speaks in his own human tongue the words of God. It was the energizing power of God's Spirit that inspired the prophets:

> The energy of God is called by the prophet "word of the Lord," because by this energy the prophets received the revelations of the things to come through a spiritual grace. This sacred revelation also is called by the prophet "vision" because through this they were receiving knowledge of obscure things.
>
> Since the prophets were accepting in the depth of their own souls unspoken thoughts and images through a spiritual energy, and they understood the instruction of what they learned as if it were someone speaking to them—during the energy of the divine spirit in their inner soul—for this reason the prophet calls it both "vision" and "word of the Lord."[64]

The passage bears ample witness to the author's conviction that prophetic inspiration is not a communication of truths dictated in conceptual words and forms but a psychological experience, the spirit of God awakening in the inward part of a prophet's being, thoughts and images by a spiritual perception without sensible forms. The God of the prophets is not God *absconditus,* but God *revelatus.* He reveals his will in the soul of the prophets as an inner vision. The inward vision becomes equivalent with the "word of God" because it is articulated as an experience. The "word of God" is not imposed on the human senses as an audible communication. It is not expressed in Hebrew or Aramaic, and yet the prophetic experience is articulated and transmitted in the idiom of human speech. We cannot grasp in what manner the prophets understood their revealed experience or how they could transmit it in the idiom established by the prophetic language. But since the vision was taking place in the inner soul of a personality, the mental faculty of the human organism was there to attend and perceive. Thus human speech became the vehicle of inspiration. The prophets believed in the reality of what they saw and heard. The power of such inspiration lay in the prophets' conviction that God was speaking to them and through them. The decisive characteristic is that the charismatic person must have living intercourse with the Lord. The hearing of the voice of God was the prophet's self-legitimation. And that which had to be reproduced by the human tongue, says Theodore, was not a corporeal voice of God but a psychological experience which created in the mind of the prophets the impression that someone was speaking to them: "If God had spoken to the prophet from above in human voice it could have filled all the inhabited world."[65]

We must turn briefly from this account of Theodore's understanding of prophetic inspiration to his notion of prophetic ecstasy. Theodore does not treat the subject in terms of a nineteenth century evolutionary interpretation. The various physiological, psychological, and possibly pathological states which accompanied or preceded the ecstasy of the prophets are not considered in his extant writings. In point of fact these very states in antiquity were considered important characteristics of the prophetic charisma and, hence, were to be expected in diverse forms even when not reported. On the other hand Theodore's general view on the mode of the prophetic ecstasy, as it was experienced by the classical prophets, is a careful interpretation of the phenomenon.

In commenting upon the word "burden" *(lēmma),* which in the Septuagint is used to render the Hebrew *massā',* Theodore finds the opportunity to discuss the various biblical terms employed by the prophets in describing their experiences. The energies of God's Spirit, asserts Theodore, were manifold; the prophets experienced oracles, visions, burdens, and sights. But the highest type of spiritual experience was obtained in ecstatic states:

> The inborn energies by which the prophets received the revelations from the Spirit were manifold and according to the circumstances. By ecstasy all of the prophets were receiving the knowledge of the most unutterable things; for it permitted them, by keeping their minds out of the earthly conditions, to hold fast and attach themselves to the view which was shown to them. If it is impossible

for us to learn with accuracy the instruction of our teachers without concentrating on their teaching, how could it ever be possible for the prohets to endure such terrifying and unutterable views if their intellects did not go out of the present conditions of life during the time of vision?

The Bible says, the blessed Peter, by falling in ecstasy, saw a great sheet descending from heaven. This was made possible because the grace of the Spirit took his intellect away from the present situation and helped him to view what was to be shown.

The grace of the Spirit by removing their minds to a different state enabled the prophets to view the indicated vision. But whenever the prophets found themselves in this state of mind the Spirit granted them such an instruction that it created the impression that they were hearing someone speaking and teaching them.[66]

In this passage Theodore considers the prophetic ecstasy as a state of tension. He says there are in both the Old Testament and the New Testament phenomena of ecstasy. Such ecstatic experience came especially when the prophet was in isolation and solitude. The Spirit drove the prophets into isolation by suppressing their consciousness. Their senses were overtaken by the force and tension of the theophanies.[67] The ecstatic states were personal and no sort of external influence was required; God placed the prophets in this state of tension. Theodore claims, as many modern critics do, that the ecstatic element could be found even in the noblest of the prophets.[68] It resulted from the certainty of truly having stood in personal relationship with God. The invisible God assured the prophets that they were his messengers. In the high tension of the ecstatic state meaningful pronouncements were forthcoming without the prophets being asked. The experiences were terrifying and unutterable. And yet they presented themselves into a flash of verbal messages transmitting the will and requirements of God. It was not a real corporeal voice in the human idiom but the impression of a voice.

And when the terrifying experience receded into the background the articulated prophetic utterance burst forth.

Finally, we should note that Theodore has been accused of having an anthropomorphic understanding of inspiration.[69] This charge has arisen from Theodore's teaching that the prophets, during the states of inspiration, had the impression that someone was speaking to them. But the prophetic data relevant to inspiration are so complex and many-faceted that a proper definition of the prophetic inspiration is practically impossible. However, we find anthropomorphic expressions and experiences throughout the pages of the prophetic literature. God is represented, in his relation both to Israel and to his prophets, as a living and feeling being, as a person who acts in nature and history and reveals his message "by divers portions and divers manners" to his servants the prophets. No matter how refined it becomes in the prophetic books, anthropomorphism is firmly seated in the prophetic consciousness; it is more psychological than physical in nature. The prophetic consciousness testified to what it saw and heard; the forcefulness of the prophetic consciousness in many cases lies in an inner conviction which resulted from the certainty of having stood in God's council. It was in Yahweh's council that the divine and the human encounter took place. The typical prophetic oracle begins with "The Lord said unto me. . . ." Jeremiah did not consider a man to be a true prophet unless he spoke "from God's mouth" rather than "from his own heart." Above all, prophets heard sounds, voices, words, and commands addressed to them. The hearing of "the word of God" was the secret of the prophets' power and influence. And when the prophets proclaimed the word of God in human idiom they did not feel that the frailty of the human speech betrayed the nature of God's majesty.

Out of the foregoing observations of Theodore's views on scriptural revelation and inspiration, we come to these conclusions. The Mopsuestian started with a high traditional doctrine of inspiration; he stressed the divine origin of inspiration to such an extent that he obliterated the human factor in the writing of revelation. But there is evidence that Theodore later attempted to break from the plenary notion of inspiration by emphasizing the role that human involvement played in the composition of the autographs of the Bible. In his later exegetical writings, Theodore gave such prominence to the human factor that inspiration became a collaboration between God's Spirit and man. This emphasis on the human element was brought about by a better understanding of the historical significance of biblical revelation. Prophetic inspiration, Theodore asserted, is not a communication of truth dictated in conceptual words but a psychological state which the prophet experienced in a confrontation with the deity at a particular time and place in history.[70] In that state of confrontation the divine did not sweep away the human; on the contrary the human element was growing stronger and more receptive because the mighty spirit of God was placing it in an ecstatic tension. In the high tension of the ecstatic state the prophet experienced terrifying and meaningful pronouncements which he articulated and interpreted with the help of human idiom. Theodore assumed, as many modern critics do, that all prophets were ecstatic men.[71]

## NOTES

1. Divine visitations to Old Testament personalities (from Adam to Samuel), who heard with their own ears Yahweh's words spoken in person or by his angel, are enclothed in pious legends and should not preoccupy us here.

2. R.H. Pfeiffer, *Introduction,* 42.

3. Heb 1:1; Eph 4:8; Acts 3:21; 28:25.

4. 2 Cor 4:4–6.

5. John Chrysostom, *In Isaiam,* cap. I, Migne, PG (56), 13–14.

6. *Dialogus cum Tryphone judaeo,* 7, Migne, PG (6), 492 BC.

7. *Legatio pro Christianis,* 9, Migne, PG (6), 905 D–908 A.

8. Clement of Alexandria, *Stromatum,* lib. vii, cap. 17, Migne, PG (9), 552 B, 328 B.

9. *Ibid.,* 309 C.

10. *In evangelium Matthaei,* 2, Migne, PG (13), 832 C.

11. Augustine, *Questionum in heptateuchum* 2, 73, Migne, PL (34), 623.

12. *De adoratione in spiritu et veritate,* Migne, PG (68), 137 A.

13. *In Isaiam,* Migne, PG (70), 13B.

14. Theodore of Mopsuestia used the same metaphor, but only once in his commentary on the book of Psalms (*Psaumes,* 282).

15. This understanding of inspiration developed by the church fathers was shared for many centuries by Orthodox, Catholics, and Protestants alike. It was only in the nineteenth century that the whole question of inspiration and revelation was opened anew by the biblical critics as a result of their literary and historical criticism of the various books of the Bible.

16. *Commentarius in Jonam* (Prologue), Migne (66), 317 C.

17. *Commentarius in Nahum,* Migne (66), 401 B; R. Devreesse, *Le Commentaire,* 282.

18. Facundus, *Pro defensione trium capitulorum,* Migne, PL (67), 602B. Theodore was barely twenty years old when he composed his commentary on the book of Psalms.

19. *Le commentaire sur les Psaumes,* 470.

20. *Ibid.*

21. *Ibid.,* 43: "Sancti spiritus gratia revelante in contemplationem futurorum adductus."

22. We must recognize that in the latter part of the Old Testament David is represented as the organizer and promoter of Israel's psalmody (1 Sam 16:17–23; Ez 3:10; Neh 12:24; 1 Chr 16:7–36; 2 Chr 23:18; 29:25–30; Sir 47:7–9). In the midrashic additions to the "Late Source" of the book of Samuel David lays claim to divine inspiration (2 Sam 23:1–7). In the New Testament Christ is reported to have regarded David as inspired, and in a sense he considered the psalms as oracles (Mt 22:42–45; Mk 12:36; Lk 20:42; 24:44–46). For the apostles the psalms were regarded as prophecies by which they tried to justify their faith in the messiah and to convert the Jews to the new faith (Acts 2:22–36; 4:8–12; 13:33–37).

23. *Le commentaire sur les Psaumes,* 205–206.

24. In the patristic age this approach to the psalter was uncommon; for most of the fathers the psalter was just a book of divine

100 THEODORE OF MOPSUESTIA

promises addressed to the "true Israel," and they found prophetic oracles on almost every page of it. Theodore's opponent, Cyril of Alexandria, claims that David foretold in the psalms everything recorded in the entire New Testament: Christ, his life and doctrine, and the events which led to the spread of the gospel among the Gentiles (Alexander Kerrigan, *St. Cyril of Alexandria Interpreter of the Old Testament* [Roma: Pontificio Instituto Biblico, 1952]; 230–231.

25. *Le commentaire sur les Psaumes,* 517.

26. According to Theodore the prophets of Israel were called by God to ministry in order to restate and emphasize what David had long before prophesied. Theodore stated this view in the beginning of his commentary on the twelve (*In Oseam,* Migne, [66], 124–125; 212 A B; 244 A B).

27. *Le commentaire sur les Psaumes,* 43, 260, 261, 269, 301, 307, 334.

28. In the commentary on the book of Psalms, Theodore discovers only four Davidic psalms (2; 8; 44; 109) prophesying Christ. Since David's prophetic horizon did not extend beyond the Maccabean age the *Mephasqana* adopts a method of interpretation which has little to do with the one which was popularized by the early ecclesiastical writers. His views are much loftier. All four psalms, according to Theodore, refer to the terminal redemptive act of God in human history: the incarnation and the church. We shall reserve a separate chapter in this study in which to discuss Theodore's teaching about Israel's messianic hope.

29. *Le commentaire sur les Psaumes,* 260.

30. *Ibid.,* 260, 301.

31. Psalms referred by Theodore to the Assyrian age are: 13; 14; 15; 28; 29; 31–33; 39–40; 45; 47; 51–53; 74; 75.

32. Psalms of the exile and return, according to Theodore, are: 5; 22; 23; 25; 33; 39; 41; 42; 50; 60; 65–66; 70; 72; 76; 80.

33. Theodore referred the following psalms to Maccabean times: 43; 46; 54–59; 61; 68; 73; 78–79.

34. *In Oseam* (Prologue), Migne (66), 124–125 A.

35. *Le commentaire sur les Psaumes,* 282.

36. *Ibid.,* 470, 477.

37. Dewey M. Beagle, *The Inspiration of Scripture* (Philadelphia: The Westminster Press, 1963), 111ff.

38. Prophetic inspiration as it was understood by Theodore will be discussed in a subsequent division of this chapter.

39. *In Nahum,* 1:1, Migne, PG (66), 404 B.

40. *In Aggaei,* 2:6, Migne, PG (66), 485 A.

41. *In Oseae,* 3:1, Migne, PG (66), 144 C.

42. Mansi, *op. cit.,* IX, 223.

43. Migne, PG (80), 805 A.

44. Theodore believed in the Mosaic authorship of the Pentateuch and maintained that it was an inspired document (cf. R. Devreesse, *Essai sur Théodore,* 20, n. 2).

45. *Revue Biblique,* XXXVIII, No. 3 (Juillet 1929), 391. This information comes from a Nestorian commentator of the ninth century and it has been dealt with above.

46. "His sayings to the adversaries in Galatians are found to be covered with obscurity and the diversion of sense is manifest; at present certainly this, now to be sure that, all are said frequently briefly, none is in place and distracts the sense" (see H.B. Swete [ed.], *Commentarii in epistolas Pauli,* I, 93).

47. *Ibid.,* II, 282: "Certainly it is excessively obscure what is said by reason of brevity in expression; oftentimes the apostle is inclined to some briefness and that explains the obscurity in which his sayings are enveloped."

48. *Commentary on the Nicene Creed,* 82.

49. R. Devreesse, *Essai sur Théodore,* 305–306.

50. *In Aggaei,* 2:1–5, Migne, PG (66), 484 C–485 C; *In Zachariae* 1:8, Migne, PG (66), 501 C–505 A.

51. *Le commentaire sur les Psaumes,* 386–387.

52. *Commentary on the Nicene Creed,* 25–28.

53. *In Jonam* (prologue), Migne, PG (66), 320 B, 328 D.

54. *In Amosi,* 7:14–17, Migne, PG (66), 292 AB.

55. *Ibid.,* 244 A; *In Malachiam* (prologue), Migne, PG (66), 597 B.

56. *In Oseae,* 1:1, Migne, PG (66), 125 D–128 A.

57. Migne, PG (66), 261 C.

58. *In Amosi,* 7:13, Migne, PG (66), 289 D–292 A.

59. *Ibid.,* 241 A.

60. *In Amosi,* 1:1, Migne, PG (66), 241 AB.

61. *In Oseae,* 1:1, Migne, PG (66), 128 B; *In Amosi,* 7:11, Migne, 289 D; *In Malachia,* 4:6, Migne, 652 A.

62. *In Joelis* (prologue), Migne, PG (66), 212 B.

63. *In Zachariae,* 13:7, Migne, PG (66), 585 C.

64. *In Abdiam,* 1:1, Migne, PG (66), 308 CD.

65. *In Zachariaea,* 1:9–10, Migne, PG (66), 509 A.

66. Na 1:1, Migne, PG (66) 401, 404. The word *lēmma* is derived from a root idea *(eilemmai)* which denoted "to receive," "to take." And in the case of prophecy it suggests the receiving of a prophetic oracle.

67. *Ibid.,* 404 B: "Blessed Isaiah says he saw God and the seraphim; he also heard voices coming toward him. For this reason he sometimes says, 'The word of God' which was upon so and so, and by word he means the energy by which he had the impression that he was learning by a voice what was necessary; and other times he says 'vision,' which he saw here and there, meaning by this the revelation, according to which, believing to see something, he was taught the proper."

68. Some modern students of Old Testament prophets who have come to this same conclusion are: Alfred Guillaume, *Prophecy and Divination Among the Hebrews and Other Semites* (London: Hodder and Stoughton, 1938); R.B.Y. Scott, *The Relevance of the Prophets* (New York: Macmillan, 1947); Johannes Lindblom, *Prophecy in Ancient Israel* (Oxford: Basil Blackwell, 1962).

69. H. Kihn, *Theodor von Mopsuestia und Junilius Africanus als Exegeten,* 110f; John S. Romanidis, "Highlights in the Debate over Theodore's Christology," *The Greek Theological Review,* V, No. 2 (Winter 1959–1960), 179f.

70. *In Nahum,* 1:1, Migne, PG (66), 401 C–404 D; see also J.N.D. Kelly, *Early Christian Doctrines* (New York: Harper and Brothers, 1958), 64.

71. William F. Albright uses the term "rhapsodic" in order to describe the nature of this prophetic experience (cf. *From the Stone Age to Christianity* 2nd ed.; Baltimore: The John Hopkins Press, 1957, 309f).

# Chapter Five

# THEODORE OF MOPSUESTIA
# AS A CHRISTIAN EXEGETE

As early as the second century before the Christian era, Jewish religious authorities held that Judaism in every detail had been divinely revealed in the law and the prophets; no word or letter therein was useless or superfluous.[1] The conviction that God had recorded his mind and will in the Pentateuch and in a series of sacred books, and the insistence that Jewish national recovery would not be realized until the people lived in accordance with God's law, made it imperative that the meaning of scripture be taught to every Jew. The need for general education created two institutions, the synagogue and *beth ha-midrash*.[2]

Palestinian teachers intended to show their fellow Jews what the divine revelation recorded in the torah should mean to them, and how they could rightly follow it in their lives. But changing theological needs required some method of bringing the torah up to date. Once the law had been fixed as divinely authorized (ca. 400 B.C.; see Neh 8–10), the simplest way of making it applicable for a later generation with new ideas and different practices was to develop an unwritten law of interpretations. It is from this point of view that interpretation in Judaism is to be understood. Assuming the legitimacy of oral law, the Jewish religious authorities discussed with subtlety and erudition the juristic precepts of the Pentateuch and developed exegetical rules and methods by which a scriptural basis could be given to many new doctrines and practices.[3] The result was that it became possible for Judaism to define a *halachah,* not expressly mentioned in the scriptural text, on the authority of the religious teachers, whom we call scribes or lawyers, and who interpreted the laws of the Pentateuch according to their own reason and conscience.[4] *Halachah,* so defined, was vouched for by oral tradition, was assumed to have come from Moses, and was accepted on the authority of the teachers who declared it.[5] The new method of defining a *halachah,* without necessarily connecting it with the biblical text, gave to the religious authorities of Judaism a liberty of interpretation which they never before had. Thus a way was opened for an advance from the literal meaning of the text toward a non-literal method of interpreting scripture. Judaism was no longer bound to take the Bible literally. The *halachah* and the *haggadah,* which were defined in terms of the oral law, represented a free interpretation of the scriptural texts in the light of practical experience and speculative meditation. H.A. Wolfson, writing about this method of exegesis, observes:

> What is known in Judaism as the Oral Law meant freedom of interpretation of the scriptural text, whether dealing with some legal precept or some historical event or some theological doctrine. Every verse in Scripture, whether narrative or law, was subject to such free interpretation.[6]

Something of the freedom which this concept allowed can be seen in such interpretations as those developed at Qumran and in the thought of Philo. Before turning to the very important work of Philo, we ought to consider briefly the method of exegesis employed by the sect of Qumran, precisely because in many respects it typifies the temper of the Old Testament apocalyptists. In the so-called biblical commentaries *(pešarim)* of Qumran are found expositions of biblical passages, for the most part from the prophets, which show marked differences from the traditional exegesis of rabbinical Judaism.[7] The sect of Qumran lived in an eschatological enthusiasm awaiting the dawn of a new age to be ushered in by Yahweh's mighty deeds. This eschatological expectation of an apocalyptic kingdom, which was molded by a common and continuous tradition of speculative interests in this cultic community, led the sectarian commentators to expound the prophecies of the Old Testament in accordance with the basic tenets peculiar to the religious sect. Their interpretation has an eschatological perspective, and strongly tends to see the oracles of the prophets fulfilled in the history of their own times or in the inner life of their cultic community. Such eschatological interpretation is an attempt to find in scriptural texts non-literal meanings referring to events which are to take place in the end of the days, such as the coming of the messianic age, and the world that is to come. This idea is clearly expressed in the *Habakkuk Commentary* 2:2:

> God told Habakkuk to write the things that were to come upon the last generation, but the consummation of the period he did not make known to him. And as for what it says, 'that he may run who reads it,' this means the teacher of righteousness, to whom God made known all the mysteries of the words of his servants the prophets.[8]

In the desert community of Qumran, it was held that little happened without an eschatological purpose. Convinced that all prophecy was being fulfilled in their generation, the sectarians searched the scriptures and commented upon prophetic texts in attempts to show that this was so. Their interpretation is neither rabbinical nor allegorical, but eschatological.[9] It is interesting to note that a very similar sort of interpretation was employed by the New Testament writers in presenting Christ as the fulfillment of Old Testament prophecy—that is, the Old Testament, apocalyptically interpreted, was the Bible of the early church.

Judaism in Alexandria, on the other hand, developed another method of scriptural exegesis under the influence of Greek philosophy. Philo is our best representative of this new method. The rules of interpretation observed by Philo combine two elements, namely, *midrashic* non-literal interpretations as used by the Palestinian rabbis, and allegoric principles characteristic of the Stoics.[10] These rules fall into two main classes: first, those according to which the literal sense is excluded, and the allegorical seems to be the only possible alternative; and, second, those according to which the allegoric sense is discovered as standing beside and above the literal sense.

Philo was the proponent of a complicated scheme of interpretation. His first exegetical principle held that, since scripture is inspired by God, it can never mean anything that would be unworthy of God or useless to man.[11] Consequently, whenever there is anything impossible, absurd or immoral in scripture, an effort must be made to find a meaning other than the literal one. Under the influence of the Greek philosophic interpretation of Homer and Hesiod, and because he himself was a trained philosopher, Philo assumed in his interpretation of scripture that biblical texts have a twofold meaning—a literal or obvious meaning, and an underlying meaning. The underlying meaning of a text is described by him in a variety of terms, but the term which is most dear to him is "allegory."[12] The allegorical meaning of a text as well as the allegorical interpretation of it is said by Philo to be "obscure to the many,"[13] to be clear only to "those who can contemplate bodiless and naked facts,"[14] to appeal only to "the few who study soul characteristics rather than bodily forms,"[15] and to be dear to "men who are capable of seeing."[16] Allegory was also described by Philo as "the nature which loves to hide itself" and into which one has to be initiated.[17] Allegorical method, whereby the true knowledge of God is to be extracted from the letter of the Bible, was regarded by Philo as a mystery.[18] If the underlying meaning of a biblical text was not immediately evident, the fault lay with the exegete, who was not yet well initiated in the mysteries of the allegorical method. Only those who have been initiated into the mysteries of the Bible are capable of understanding the hidden meaning of the texts. All this meant for Philo that only men of good ability and qualified education who have succeeded in mastering their passions and in acquiring a true knowledge of the existence and nature of God can be instructed in the theory and method of the allegorical interpretation of the Bible.[19] According to Philo everything in the Bible, whether narrative or law, is subject to allegorical interpretation.

In contrast to the allegorical method, Philo spoke of a literal or obvious method of interpretation.[20] After comparing the literal meaning of the scriptural text to "body," and the hidden inner meaning, which is to be discovered by the allegorical interpretation, to "soul," he suggested that the former is to be used with certain reservations. The formula with which he concluded his thinking on this subject was that everything in scripture has a figurative meaning, but not all of it has a literal meaning. The allegorical interpretation must discard the literal meaning of a term of expression and strive to grasp its deeper purport.[21] One general rule laid down by Philo, with regard to the literal sense of the texts, is that no anthropomorphic expression about God is to be taken literally. As proof-text for this general rule Philo quoted the verse, "God is not a man" (Num 23:19), which was thought by him to contain the general principle that anthropomorphic expressions must be discarded.[22]

Philo had no real interest in the Old Testament as a record of Israel's history or its religious experience. His objective was to interpret the theology of the Old Testament in terms of Greek philosophy and thus to create a Jewish philosophical literature based on Old Testament exegesis. The Pentateuch was his favorite document for study, and the greater part of his voluminous writings are devoted to expounding it. With regard to the historical events of the Pentateuch he maintained that their literalness should be rejected whenever, by the acceptance of such literalness, the inspired words of God would compel one to admit anything base or unworthy of their dignity.[23] Philo's adoption of the allegorical method of the Stoics was not only facilitated by his philosophical eclecticism, but also by the fact that in his time Palestinian Judaism was not bound to read the scriptures literally.

The effects of Philo's allegorical methodology are discernible not in subsequent Jewish exegesis but in the writings of the church fathers. Philo's method was inherited by Christian teachers along with the Septuagint.[24] It was after the close of the New Testament period that the allegorical method of scriptural interpretation became an accepted system of biblical exegesis and criticism for Christian scholarship. Through the work of Clement of Alexandria (ca. 150–215) the Philonic non-literal expounding of the Bible was introduced into the theological school of Alexandria, and the allegorical method of exegesis became the characteristic trait of this religious institution in the succeeding stages of its history. The leading Christian exponent of the allegorical interpretation of the Old and New Testament was the polymathic Origen (ca. 185–254), who was Clement's pupil and successor in the deanship of the school of Alexandria. Origen represents an advance in allegorical interpretation over his predecessors.[25] Starting off from the position of his Hellenistic predecessor, Origen held that the Bible is inspired by God and contains nothing unworthy of God; through the Logos or the Holy Spirit, God is the author of every detail of the Bible. The prophets and evangelists were instruments of the Holy Spirit, which filled their souls.[26] Origen also maintained, like Philo, that the Holy Spirit had deliberately inserted into scripture a number of obvious inconsistencies which looked like "stumbling-blocks and obstacles," not fitting in with the ordinary narrative and context where they are found, to remind the intellectual reader that there is something diviner in the text.[27] The "stumbling-blocks," Origen asserted, had been dictated by the Holy Spirit for the benefit not of the simple believers, who would not comprehend anyway, but for the benefit of people with inquiring minds, to make them apply themselves more to the careful scrutiny of the text and so convince themselves that they must in these cases seek a deeper spiritual meaning not unworthy of God.[28] But if the simple believers do not at once see the supernatural meaning of the biblical text there is nothing surprising in that, because the Bible is a tremendous sacrament, a vast allegory in which every detail is figurative and symbolic. In the fourth homily on Leviticus Origen wrote:

> As I try to expound the scriptures, I realize that the mysteries are too vast for my capacities. But even if we cannot explain it all, we still know that it is full of mystery, all of it.[29]

In a notable passage in the *De Principiis,* Origen divides the interpretation of scripture into three meanings or senses, corresponding to the triple division of human nature; as man is divided into body, soul, and spirit, so the scriptures yield three meanings: (1) corporeal or literal; (2) physical or moral; (3) spiritual or perfect. The spiritual or perfect meaning of the Bible is reserved for the perfect Christians, who will inherit eternal life in the aeon that is to come:

> The words of scripture should be printed in the soul in one of three ways. The uneducated should be edified by the letter itself, by what we call the obvious meaning; while he who has ascended a certain way may be edified by the soul. The perfect should be edified by the spiritual law, which has a shadow of good things to come. For as man is composed of body, soul, and spirit, so in the same way in scripture, which has been planned by God for man's salvation.[30]

In order to support his view that scripture is to be interpreted in three ways, Origen quoted the Septuagint version of Proverbs 22:20; the first part of that verse ("Have I not written for you thirty sayings?" R.S.V.), the Septuagint wrongly renders, "Have I not written unto thee in a triple way?"[31] With his triple division of scriptural interpretation, Origen succeeded in transforming the Old Testament into a record of Christian rather than Jewish revelation, and then he proceeded to interpret it christologically. For him, everything in the law and the prophets points to Christ through parables, images, oracles and allegories. As with Origen's mystical and speculative theology, so his exegesis is fundamentally unhistorical and spiritual.[32]

Origen's elaborated exegetical system as well as his voluminous commentaries and homilies appealed to Christendom at large, and they exercised an immense influence in the patristic age and later. Even Jerome favored a threefold division of all the senses of scriptural interpretation, in support of which he quoted Origen's biblical proof-text, "Have I not written unto thee in a triple way?" (Prov 22:20, LXX).[33]

But the "biblical alchemy," as the allegorical method of the Alexandrians has rightly been called, was challenged. It was rejected by the exegetes of the school of Antioch, who advocated a critical viewpoint and a historico-grammatical method of interpretation in their biblical studies.

In opposition to such Alexandrians as Clement and Origen, who approached the Bible in the interest of a pre-conceived and pre-established theological system and cultivated the allegorical-mystical method of interpretation, the Antiochians developed a deeper insight into the true nature of biblical interpretation. The fancies of allegory compelled the religious teachers of Antioch to employ a rigidly careful exegesis in interpreting what the Bible says in the light of its own historical and conceptual environment. The school of Antioch has been credited with the honor of being the first to have formulated a system of biblical interpretation that approached more nearly than any other early Christian school many principles of criticism which are now accepted by those who acknowledge the validity of the categories of modern biblical criticism.[34] This system was brought about by certain factors in training and background, and it also involved a strong reaction against the non-literal method of the Alexandrians. The Antiochians developed a christology which was concerned with both the divinity and the humanity of Christ. Another conspicuous trait of the Antiochians is their closer relationship to Jewish exegesis, which preferred, with the exception of the midrashic interpretations, to explain the Old Testament literally.[35] And, finally, the Antiochian scholars of the church had a predilection for the Aristotelian logic and methodology rather than the Platonic and Philonic philosophy.[36] These different doctrinal and methodological presuppositions led to quite different principles of interpretation.

The school of Antioch developed interpretation along its own lines, and sometimes acted as though deliberately correcting the methods of the school of Alexandria. The Antiochians insisted on the historical reality of the biblical revelation and refused to lose sight of it in a world full of symbols and cryptograms. In their judgment scripture is not full of secrets and mysteries—nothing is hidden behind and beneath its literalness. While the Antiochians regarded the Bible as the word of God, they nevertheless had a strong feeling for the human element in the biblical writers and an obvious understanding of the historical significance of the scriptural truths. They expounded the Bible, not to detect mystical parables pointing to metaphysical or super-temporal meanings, but to discover and hear the word of God in its historical truth and perspective, because each book of the Bible was written at a certain time and has, so to speak, a "situation-conditioned" nature, a *Sitz im Leben*. The first concern of the Christian interpreter, according to the Antiochian fathers, must be to hear God's words in scripture, and this involves a conscious attempt to live within the historical atmosphere of the biblical world, including its human idiom. This means that the interpreter must understand the biblical language, vocabulary, and history in order to take his stand with the prophets in their struggle to hear God's message of judgment and mercy in the midst of a providential drama. The interpreter has no right to depreciate the literal and historical sense of the Bible. He cannot separate himself from the biblical source and history, else he will not understand the reality of the biblical revelation.[37] A careful interpreter is characterized by his attempt to control interpretation by looking for the original meaning of a passage when such a meaning can be discerned. To this end the Antiochians used all available aids derived from philology and history. The emphasis always fell upon the literal meaning of the text. They recognized that the language of the Bible is often metaphoric, but this recognition did not lead them to deny the literal meaning of the text; it was the business of the interpreter to explain the figures of speech according to their literal image.

Diodore of Tarsus (d. ca. 390), who must be regarded as the true founder and theoretician of the school of Antioch, described the guiding principle of Antiochene exegesis in the following formula:

> We do not forbid the higher interpretation and allegory, for the historical narrative does not exclude it, but is on the contrary the basis and substructure of loftier insights. . . . We must, however, be on our guard against letting the *theoria* do away with the historical basis, for the result would then be, not *theoria,* but allegory.[38]

One has only to compare this sober statement with the quotation from Origen cited above to distinguish very clearly the real

contrast between the methods followed by the two schools, nota-
bly the Alexandrian with its bias toward allegorism, and the
Antiochene with its dedication to historico-literalism. Diodore
composed a manual of hermeneutics called *What Is the Difference between Theory and Allegory?* which has been lost.[39] According to Diodore, the true key to the deeper meaning of a scriptural
event which was not fully explicit was what he called *theoria.*[40]
By this term Diodore probably meant a loftier insight into the
nature of an Old Testament event quoted in the New Testament,
and as such it required a higher interpretation which had to be
firmly based on the letter. Presumably *theoria* presupposed a
kind of exegesis which has in modern times been given the convenient name "typology." This kind of typology had been practiced already by Paul (Gal 4:24) but under the name of allegory.
The antithesis which Diodore made between allegory and *theoria*
comes out in a remark by his pupil, John Chrysostom:

> Paul, by a catachrestic use of the language, called the
> type allegory. What he means is this: the history itself
> not only has the apparent meaning but also proclaims
> other things; therefore it is called allegory. But what did
> it proclaim? Nothing else than everything that now is.[41]

Here Chrysostom certainly reflects Diodore's concept of
*theoria.* He maintains that Paul used the term allegory in a loose
and catachrestic sense, and did not set aside the historicity of the
story of Sarah and Hagar.[42] Theodore of Mopsuestia brings out
the same point when, in explaining Galatians 4:24, he criticizes
those who appealed to the use of allegory by the apostle Paul himself. There is a great difference, Theodore asserts, between what
the apostle means and what the allegorists mean. The apostle
does not destroy history but believes in the historical reality of
the events he describes, and employs them for examples. The
allegorists, on the other hand, denied the historical significance
of the narrative, and their interpretation often differed only
slightly if at all from the speculations concerning pagan myths in
which pagan philosophers indulged.[43] Then Theodore goes on
giving his own interpretation of Paul's language in Galatians
4:24, which runs as follows: "Paul called allegory the comparison

by way of juxtaposition, of former events with present ones."[44] This quotation has been preserved by a catenist. Theodore did not try to correct the language of the Apostle as Chrysostom had done by calling the term "allegory," a misapplicated and misused word; rather he tried to express his own understanding of the Pauline expression. The comparison is an external one based on the resemblance (*similitudo*) of the persons (Hagar and Sarah); yet in their original biblical context these two women have their own historical identity and mission. Paul, by using the term "allegory," did not obliterate either the historicity of the biblical antiquity or its truth. Theodore time and again emphasizes this particular aspect because upon this Pauline text the Alexandrean "mythologues" had built their hermeneutical aberrations. The Apostle Paul preserved history, and the comparison is worthless unless the two persons or events being compared really existed. Theodore obviously was not happy with the application of the word allegory by Saint Paul. This phrase of Paul is not even a typology. Theodore's objective was to defend the Old Testament against the allegorists who wanted to reconstrue it arbitrarily into a book of mystical symbols. The allegorists turned everything askew by making no distinction between what the Bible says and "dreams in the night."

In his extant commentaries Theodore levels direct attacks against the methods of the allegorists:[45] The Mopsuestian had composed a work entitled *On Allegory and History*, which has been lost; Facundus had preserved a very brief quotation.[46] However, we know a good deal about Theodore's objections to the use of allegory from a Nestorian author, Isho'dad of Merv, who, echoing as usual the voice of the *Mephasqana*, dedicated the twelfth chapter of his *Introduction to the Psalms* to a polemic against those who insisted on interpreting the Psalms allegorically. The relevant chapter of Isho'dad deals with a subject which was highly meaningful to Theodore; this is reflected in the fact that the Mopsuestian limited the messianic Psalms to four, namely, 2, 8, 45, and 110. The Syriac writer states:

> One may ask what the difference is between allegorical exegesis and historical exegesis. We answer that the difference is great and not small. While the first leads to

impiety, blasphemy, and untruth, the other is con-
formed to truth and faith. It was the impious Origen of
Alexandria who invented the art of allegory. Versed in
the works of poets and Platonists, he believed that holy
scripture should be explained in terms of their fables.

Just as poets and geometricians, when they want to
raise their students from material and visible things to
things hidden and invisible, erring in regard to the eternity of incorporeal matter and to indivisible atoms, say:
"These visible signs are not signs for reading, but their
hidden meanings, one must elevate himself by the
image of thought from created natures to their eternal
nature"; just so, the insane Origen taught that the souls
existed, before the creation of the bodies and the uni-
verse, from time incommensurable. . . . Origen, stress-
ing this strange theory to his students, tainted all the
books of the Bible by an enigmatic interpretation. The
psalms and the prophets, who speak of the captivity and
the return of the people of Israel, he explained as teaching the captivity of the soul, far from truth and its return
to faith. Similarly with regard to the historical narratives of scripture, he diverted and emptied them from
their natural meaning and he delivered them into the
fancy of the imagination, and this was done in such a
fashion that we thought there was no creature nor Cre-
ator. The allegorists do not interpret paradise as it is, or
Adam, or Eve, or any existing being. . . .

And in order not to stretch the discourse beyond its
limit I am going to advance an example which will suf-
fice to illustrate the nature of the others. When the apostle writes: "This rock was Christ" (I Cor 10:4), he clearly
shows, the allegorists say, that even while appearing to
be a rock, in reality however this rock was Christ,
secretly working for the salvation of those who are like
him. Likewise in regard to Melchizedek, they assert that
he was the Son of God; for according to them our Savior
did not appear one time in this world, but many times;
he has revealed himself to the various ages according to
their proper measure, and he has been with all of them.

He even had to come for the inanimate rocks, in order to deliver those who were retained there.

Those insane people have not perceived that the apostles in quoting the sayings of the Old Testament do not quote them in only one way; sometimes they quote them to show their fulfillment, at other times as an example for the exhortation and correction of their readers, or else to confirm the doctrine of the faith, although these sayings were uttered for other purposes according to the historical circumstances.

Now when our Lord applies Psalms 8 and 110 to himself, and when Peter in Acts and Paul in his epistles apply to our Lord the same psalms as well as Psalms 2 and 45, they take them in their true sense.

But when our Lord says on the cross: "My God, my God, why hast thou forsaken me?" and again: "Into thy hands I commend my spirit," which saying is found in Psalm 31:6, these words are said by a comparison according to the resemblance of the events, although in their original place their application is different. Now the difference which exists between these things is evidenced with clarity from the context to those who want to know the truth.[47]

The exceptional importance of this text from Isho'dad's *Introduction to the Psalms* justifies the lengthiness of the quotation. In point of fact we do not know of any other source which provides a better glimpse into the nature of Theodore's exegetical principles. Isho'dad was not an original thinker and his writings are replete with quotations from Theodore and many lesser known Syriac authors.[48] Theodore of Mopsuestia was for him the *Mephasqana par excellence.* Those who are familiar with Theodore's extant commentaries will recognize Isho'dad's great indebtedness to him. Isho'dad's exegetical outlook was dominated by Theodore's influence, especially along the following lines:

1. Both exegetes agreed that the task of an interpreter is to discern the meaning of a text in its historical context, without

recourse to allegory. The literal sense, rightly understood, provides the fullest meaning.

2. Both commentators drew attention to the fact that the Old Testament must be interpreted in the light of its own historical environment. This hermeneutical principle requires full respect for the historicity of the biblical events. An interpreter has not the right to read into the history of Israel more than is actually there.

3. Lastly, both the Syriac exegete and Theodore stated that typological interpretation is acceptable, but it must strictly be related to, and be founded upon, the historico-grammatical meaning of the text. A "type" is a comparison of events in the two Testaments and not an interpretation of texts.

These Theodorean views were not presented in a formal treatise; they were set down during the course of Theodore's interpretation of biblical texts. We may now turn to a survey of Theodore's extant commentaries which will give an idea of what his historico-grammatical method of exegesis was like. First, we shall try to describe somewhat broadly Theodore's basic exegetical method, then his interpretation of biblical history, and, finally, his Old Testament typology.

First, the critical principles underlying Theodore's exegetical method must be determined. The materials on which our appraisal rests are mainly supplied by his commentaries on the book of Psalms and the minor prophets. Following the tradition of the school of Antioch, Theodore based his commentaries on the text of the Septuagint. His reliance on the Septuagint, however, did not lead him to accept it as a miraculously inspired translation, having as much authority as the original Hebrew. This is shown especially in his commentary on the book of Psalms, where the following statement furnishes a characteristic illustration of the author's thinking in this respect:

And the Hebrew text, which is the most authoritative of all and upon which the interpretation must be based, happens to be against this sort of exegesis.[49]

Further on, he evidenced an awareness that he relied on a translation which was not free of obscurities and ambiguous expressions. A translation cannot reproduce the conciseness of the Hebrew idiom, Theodore asserted, without occasioning damage to the clarity of its meaning.[50] And yet his ignorance of Hebrew compelled the author to follow the practice of his age in accepting the Septuagint as the authorized version. Nonetheless, Theodore's extant writings indicate that he respected the authority of the original Hebrew, and that he did not follow the Septuagint with completely closed eyes. In explaining Psalm 9 (LXX numbering) he wrote:

> Yet since this ninth psalm is divided in two in the Hebrew and Syriac texts, I do not know why it is found in our version redacted into one.[51]

In commenting upon Psalm 16:3, Theodore claimed:

> If, therefore, the text which reads "to the saints that are in the earth, and to the excellent, in whom is all my delight" be understood according to the Syriac text as meaning that the divine judgment has been visited upon the strong nations, and if this meaning which arises from the Syriac and Hebrew texts be held, then everything that follows is most fittingly joined with what was quoted above.[52]

The interesting point about all this is not the interpretation of the psalm which Theodore offered, but rather the fact that while he interpreted the Septuagint he seemed to prefer the Hebrew and Syriac variant which he invoked in order to link better the meaning of the second verse of the psalm with that of the third, and thus justify his interpretation.

In the commentary on the minor prophets Theodore showed little interest in textual criticism, and most of the time he chose his variant readings on the basis of arbitrary principles or subjective conjectures. It was on such grounds that in Amos 5:26 he explained the reading "and the star of your god Rephan" (LXX reading) by asserting that in the Hebrew language Rephan means morning star.[53] In Habakkuk 2:11 Theodore found another opportunity for exercising his arbitrary method in resolving a problem of variant readings:

> Some people say that the Syriac version reads "peg," but it would be nonsense to disregard the Hebrew language in which the prophets spoke and whose message was translated into Greek by the Septuagint, and pay more attention to the Syrian translator who translated the Hebrew scriptures into Syriac.[54]

The variant reading attributed by Theodore to the Syriac is actually an accurate translation of the original Hebrew, but he preferred the curious Septuagint rendering "beetle," contending that the translation of the "Seventy" is more faithful to the Hebrew.

It is in his commentary on the book of Psalms that Theodore's excellence as a textual critic is made very apparent. He frequently introduced variant readings borrowed from Symmachus, Aquila, and Theodotion. Theodore, as usual, followed the text of the Septuagint which stands as the basis of his study of the psalter, and apart from a certain number of instances in which he accorded equal probability to the readings of the other Greek versions of the Old Testament, the Mopsuestian did not seem to depart from the Alexandrian version.[55] Theodore's view of the Septuagint is, in a sense, summarized in his comparison of it with the other Greek version:

> Some exegetes, who do not care for the accuracy of the text, judging from the offhand clarity of Symmachus' version deemed it to be superior. But if one paid attention to the context as well as the mind of the scriptural text, he would never prefer another version other than that of the Seventy; not because they translated everything accurately—there are passages which they rendered very poorly, at times they failed, while the other translators carried it out with more clarity and consis-

tency—but because by a general comparison the Seventy are found to be surpassing the other versions even though they rendered much of the text in an unusual way.[56]

Theodore relies on the Septuagint, not because it is thought to be an inspired translation, but because generally he assumed it was reliably close to the Hebrew text. And the Hebrew text is the authoritative text. The comparison of the text of the Septuagint with those of Symmachus and Theodotion is made for the sake of clarity, and that comparison constituted the very first step toward an exact interpretation of the psalter. The variant readings quoted by Theodore, though not very important from the point of view of modern textual criticism, afford evidence of his steadfast intention to explain the literal meaning of the psalms as faithfully as possible. Theodore in his commentaries was concerned primarily with determining the text and then setting forth its literal exposition. Yet, even when all this has been said, Theodore's textual criticism was often weak.[57] The Mopsuestian was not an eminent textual critic. In this only two fathers have distinguished themselves.

After the emendation of the sacred text, the next preliminary step that Theodore felt he should undertake for a better determination of the literal meaning of the biblical text was to familiarize himself with the idiomatic expressions of the Greek Old Testament. He often drew attention to the difficulties of meaning arising from the unsatisfactory condition of the text which he was following. The peculiarities or the striking incongruities of the Septuagint were, he claimed, a reflection of the style and diction of the biblical authors.[58] A translation cannot reproduce the original accurately; and the Septuagint translators, in their attempt to render the "emphasis" of the original Hebrew, translated much of the text into idiomatic expressions.[59] In his constant care to expound the scriptures in terms of scripture rather than in terms of a pre-conceived theological system, he concentrated his attention on linguistic details which he commonly classified under the formula "Hebraic idiom."[60] He is reported to have written a book *On the Obscure Style and Diction of the Bible.*[61] And in the commentary on the book of Psalms he referred his readers to the "Hebraic peculiarities," which he had catalogued and explained in the Introduction with which he prefaced this writing.[62]

Generally speaking, the "Hebrew idioms" are some peculiar expressions which are found in the LXX text; they recur so frequently that acquaintance with them was imperative. In most instances the obscurity of these expressions was due to the idiomatic phraseology of the original text of which the LXX translators produced a rude and unpolished version. Theodore tried to make the meaning of the Greek text clearer by supplying comments intended to awaken the reader's interest in the wealth of detail contained in the text and by suggesting appropriate grammatical explanations. Lacking a knowledge of the Hebrew language, he nonetheless paid close attention to the mood of tenses and terminology of the LXX text. In doing so he believed that he could recapture the accurate meaning of the original. A few examples will illustrate his method.

In his opinion Hebrew verbs are rich in conjugational forms but poor in tenses.[63] Commenting upon Psalm 39:1 (H 40), Theodore made the following remark:

> This is also an idiomatic expression of sacred scripture when it wants to express the intensity of an action; just as it says: "The Lord chastening he chastened me" (Ps 117:18), instead of saying the Lord has truly chastened me exceedingly; just so it says "waiting I waited" instead of saying I waited continually.[64]

In two similar cases Theodore stated:

> The repetition of the same verb expresses intensity of action;[65] this peculiar grammatical usage derives from a certain idiom of the Hebrew language.[66]

Another grammatical usage peculiar to the Septuagint which Theodore singled out for special mention was its indiscriminate use of moods and tenses.[67] He frequently called attention to the fact that the translators of the Septuagint on several instances

failed to render the moods and tenses of the Hebrew verbs accurately. He was led to this conclusion by the sudden passing in a
text from one tense to another. He referred to this grammatical
usage as "interchange of tenses," and considered it to be harmful
to the sequence of thought and to exegesis.[68] Theodore, in han-
dling this grammatical problem, demonstrated a real exegetical
ability which was remarkable for his day. Instead of glossing his
text in order to simplify it, he maintained that in such cases the
interpretation should be based on the sequence of thought. In
commenting upon Psalm 36:13 (H 37:13) he said:

> Symmachus too interpreted the verbs according to the
> same sequence of thought, for it is evident that the
> change of tenses must be based on the interpretation;
> the Seventy translators instead of using the present tense
> used the future tense.[69]

The interesting point about all this is not how Theodore
resolved the indiscriminate use of tenses in the Septuagint (he did
not always hit upon the correct aspect of the matter),[70] but rather
the fact that he laid much emphasis on tracing the sequence of
thought, a procedure which is also emphasized in modern hermeneutical principles. Theodore examined the sequence of
thought carefully because he admitted that the language and
thought of the biblical writers is full of difficulties and ambigui-
ties, and an intimate knowledge of the Greek versions of the Old
Testament was not in his judgment adequate for working out the
arguments and intentions of its inspired authors.[71] He endeavored, therefore, to study the individual writers of the Bible, and
to understand their language and intentions. He made it a part of
his work as an expounder to point out what he considered to be
the characteristics of the "scriptural idiom."[72] Of Theodore's
careful attention to the language of the biblical writers there is
abundant evidence. He repeatedly stops to explain the force of
conjunctions and prepositions;[73] he takes notice of the punctua-
tion, sometimes proposing a new arrangement which has the
effect of modifying the construction of the sense;[74] he points out
an occasional use of a figure of speech.[75] He is indefatigable in his

efforts to comprehend the precise meaning of words and phrases. Thus we find him supplying pertinent and often striking definitions of biblical terminology. A few examples will illustrate his treatment of the terminology peculiar to the Old Testament.

In commenting on Psalm 73:11 (H 74:11) Theodore held that the Bible not infrequently styles God's protective energy and power as his "hand";[76] this anthropomorphic expression is used by the biblical authors as a metaphor signifying the various activities of God on behalf of or against his people.[77] On the other hand the expression "thy right hand" is used emphatically to denote the benevolent aid of God.[78] Words such as "way," "ways," and "paths" denote conduct or God's saving acts.[79] The terms "flesh," "soul," and "heart" signify the human personality.[80] At times scripture uses the term "flesh" in order to designate that part of the human personality which is temporary and perishable.[81]

According to Theodore the biblical writers considered the "kidneys" to be the seat of man's power and emotions.[82] The word "bone" or "bones" means either physical force or weakness.[83] The term *krima* (judgment), which is always used by the Septuagint translators in order to render the Hebrew word *mišpāt,* means justice, and connotes the idea of an effort toward attaining religious and ethical perfection.[84]

It was, however, in his exegetical rather than in his grammatical and rhetorical treatment of the Bible that Theodore's power chiefly showed itself. As Swete rightly says: "Theodore's interest in the language is professedly subordinate to his interest in the thought which it enshrines."[85] Theodore's exegesis itself is more suggestive and profound than the literary considerations and the critical assumptions which lie behind it. The Mopsuestian approached the sacred text of the Bible as an interpretor who was seeking to unlock the treasures of its teachings. This is evident in the *Commentary on the Book of the Twelve* in which Theodore was content with expounding the text verse by verse.

The first task that the author set himself when interpreting a book of the Bible was to determine its subject matter. A carefully constructed introduction is prefixed to each volume of the minor prophets; not one of the psalms interpreted in his *Commentary on the Psalter* is without such an introduction in which the subject of the poem is set forth. These introductions deal with such questions as date, authorship, historical occasion, and the purpose of the biblical writing, and include a summary of the plan and perspective of the book.

Conciseness is a second objective at which Theodore's interpretation aimed. Thus, in interpreting Psalm 1 he remarked:

> So we ought with the Lord's help to give attention throughout the writing to preserving the meaning. And if it be necessary in the consideration of matters which arise to explain anything at greater length, still we must not forget the brevity we have promised in the Introduction.[86]

The search for the true meaning of the Old Testament through its grammatical and historical context must be the source and condition of all truly Christian interpretation and exegesis. What is nowadays styled the grammatico-historical interpretation of the Bible, namely its grammatical, logical, and historical meaning, Theodore designated by expressions such as: "the literal exegesis,"[87] "the truth of the saying according to its literal meaning,"[88] "the literal notion of the word,"[89] "the context indicates,"[90] "the context of the language,"[91] "the historical interpretation of the psalms,"[92] "according to the historical testimony,"[93] "the historical circumstances."[94]

The foregoing expressions illustrate the esteem in which Theodore held the grammatico-historical interpretation of the Bible. In point of fact, in the field of patristic exegesis, no exegete, to our knowledge, stressed the principles of a rational exegesis with greater emphasis and universality than the bishop of Mopsuestia. He based his interpretation of the Bible on sound common-sense principles, being opposed on the one hand to the allegorical method of which the Alexandrians were the great exemplars, and on the other to crude literalism. He studied and interpreted the Old Testament in the light of its literal, conceptual, and historical environment. The Bible must be interpreted by the Bible. The business of the interpreter is to discover and define what the hagiographer intends to express.[95] To this end the interpreter should be guided by means which biblical literature and biblical history put in his hand. The emphasis must always fall upon the internal evidence of the biblical text, and not upon the external evidence which was formulated by the ecclesiastical tradition, to which the patristic commentators had attached so much importance.[96] No expounder of the Bible has the right to read into it his personal ideas, nor should he be allowed to violate the meaning of the texts by introducing arbitrary comments in the interest of a pre-conceived or pre-established theological system.[97] The expounder who dares to distort the significance of a biblical text by giving it an arbitrary explanation exposes himself to the greatest danger in regard to the religious or saving value of the Bible.[98] Theodore castigated the fathers for their obscuring of the literal or historical meaning of the sacred text.[99] Even Chrysostom was blamed;[100] while of Origen and his followers, Theodore said that they distorted, by their dreams, the meaning of the biblical history and scripture together.[101]

Indeed, Theodore's fundamental conceptions of biblical interpretation differed so sharply from those of the fathers who preceded him that we maintain he either had been influenced by currents of exegesis unknown to us or he evolved the exegetical tendencies of the Antiochian school to a marvelously full and free development. Of the members of the school of Antioch, Theodore, to our knowledge, is the only one who explicitly included all sorts of senses, whether metaphorical or symbolical, in the grammatico-historical interpretation.[102] Anthropomorphisms were not regarded by him as enigmas; figurative speech or *tropologia* was also associated by him with the literal interpretation.[103]

As noted above, Theodore's views on these matters are not set forth in a formal hermeneutical essay; they are included in the course of his explanations of specific biblical texts. Throughout his commentaries he reminds us that the primary task of an interpreter is to discover the literal meaning of the Bible. The literal sense, objectively understood, provides the highest and fullest meaning. An interpreter must avoid the extremes of crude literalism and fanciful allegorism.[104] In order to achieve this the interpreter must be controlled by what is actually there. This involves a comprehension of the biblical text and its context. In point of fact, Theodore pointed to the understanding of the context of a passage *(akolouthia tou logou)* as the most important single hermeneutical principle for the preservation and exposition of the biblical teaching. Consequently, the interpreter who attempts to speak about the biblical message must base his interpretation on the linguistic, philological, conceptual, and historical study of the context. The understanding of the passage in the light of its total context and background out of which it emerged, according to Theodore, provides the key principle to a valid exegesis.

As we have already noted, intrinsically connected with Theodore's regard for the literal and conceptual meaning of the scriptures is his effort to deal with the historical occasion and background which the texts suggest. This historical interest is prominent throughout; it is even to be found in his commentaries on the New Testament.[105] He considered the Bible the only true source of history for which the world offers no real parallel because it emphasizes the historical continuity and developmental growth of God's saving acts in Israel and in Jesus Christ. The special revelation which the Old and the New Testament claim to declare was mediated through the long series of events of Hebrew history which culminated in Christ.[106] According to Theodore, scripture is firmly grounded in history, and biblical revelation is based on events which have actually happened at a particular time and place in history, events of which the Bible is the record. Such a view of the biblical revelation impelled Theodore to interpret each book and passage in the Bible in the light of its historical background and its place in this continuity.

Theodore's reconstruction of the various historical contexts was based solely on biblical sources. His acquaintance with Jewish extra-biblical sources, however, seems to be pretty thorough; his use of Josephus and of the apocryphal 1 and 2 Maccabees resulted from his desire to describe Jewish religious and political life in Palestine under the Persians, Ptolemies, Seleucids, and Maccabeans.[107]

Theodore's sense of biblical history as well as his interest in the historical context is attested in the following three methods:

1. To each of his commentaries Theodore prefixed a general introduction in which he discussed each book of the Bible as a

whole. The authorship, date, and content were carefully studied.[108] The actual motives and insights of the writers were investigated, and great care was displayed in placing the books in correct historical settings.[109]

2. In his commentary on the minor prophets Theodore prefaced each book of the prophets with a prologue in which he carefully argued that the biblical God is revealed in the vicissitudes of Israel's history.[110] In the great crises of Israel's history, Theodore asserted, there arose a succession of prophets who proclaimed to those who would listen what God was doing in the upheavals of their national life.[111] Under Theodore's system of exegesis the prophetic literature is closely related to Hebrew history, and the Old Testament prophets are set within the historical framework provided by their oracles.[112] Theodore concluded that each prophet was called at a particular time to become an authentic herald of the divine revelation. The various stages of the revelation which were proclaimed by David through prediction are now cast by the prophets into the sequence of events contemporaneous with themselves.[113] Prophecy is firmly grounded in history; and prophetic insight arises from the illumination of the human mind by the spirit of God as that mind wrestles with the problem of interpreting God's will in the midst of the concrete historical situation:

> The blessed prophets Hosea, Joel, Amos, and Micah addressed their sayings to the entire nation of Israel, both to the ten tribes whose reigning city was Samaria, and likewise to the tribe of Judah and the inhabitants of Jerusalem. They denounced the people for their religious sins and for the moral transgressions which they were committing in many ways. And they also added to these sayings the list of impending evils which would come if the people continued to be unrepentant over their sins; I mean the disaster of the ten tribes which was caused by the Assyrians, and the events which happened to the tribe of Judah at the hands of the Babylonians later.[114]

The prophet Obadiah spoke about the punishments

to be inflicted upon the Idumaeans after the return from the exile. Jonah, the prophet, threatened Nineveh with destruction if its citizens did not refrain from their wickedness. The blessed Nahum heralded Nineveh's immediate fall and the destruction of the entire Assyrian kingdom by the Babylonians.

Habakkuk and Zephaniah, the blessed prophets, were contemporaries, and they preached after the ten tribes were taken by the Assyrians into exile, while Judah was left alone. They both denounced Judah and Jerusalem for their religious sins and transgressions and at the same time proclaimed that the punishment of the people by God through the Babylonians was imminent.[115]

Zechariah was a contemporary of Haggai; he began prophesying, according to the testimony of the sacred book, in the second year of Darius; he started his prophetic ministry after the return of the Israelites from Babylon to Judah. When Cyrus, who was the first Persian ruler to reign over Persia and Media simultaneously, allowed the Israelites to return to their homeland, a sizeable number of them returned to Jerusalem and Judah, and they laid the cornerstone of the temple and they erected an altar in it. Since the completion of the construction was interrupted partly on account of the wickedness of their enemies and partly on account of their own sluggishness, Haggai, the blessed prophet, induced the people to begin rebuilding the temple.[116]

Malachi is a post-exilic prophet who preached after Haggai and Zechariah. The prophet Malachi denounces both the priests and the people; the priests are criticized for offering defective sacrifices and the laymen are denounced for their many transgressions.[117]

Theodore, by setting each prophet upon the successive stages of Israel's national life, demonstrated that Israel's prophetic literature developed in closest relation to Israel's eventful history. He held to the belief that Old Testament prophecy becomes fully intelligible only when one sees the prophets as the interpreters of God's will in the midst of the concrete historical circumstances of their own day. The prophets expounded the problems of their day not *sub specie aeternitatis,* but under the guidance of the biblical God who illuminated their minds and shaped their messages in order that they might explain Israel's destiny to their countrymen.

3. As his commentaries developed, Theodore was careful never to break the thread of historical continuity. His determination to give a precise rendering of the grammatico-historical sense frequently led him to undertake an excursus into biblical history,[118] or to recall the historical situation underlying particular texts.[119] No historical or geographical data could go unnoticed; great stress was laid upon historical facts and events suggested by the texts. This historical interest often led Theodore to reconstruct the specific historical context in light of the total witness of biblical history. Here are some examples which illustrate Theodore's resolve to explain the historical sense of the Bible as faithfully as possible:

a. With regard to Psalm 76:67–68, Theodore taught that "the tent of Joseph" and the "tribe of Ephraim" mean the same thing because Ephraim was Joseph's son. The tribe of Ephraim rebelled against the tribe of Judah several times; even during the time of David the revolt was led by a certain Sheba (2 Sam 20:1ff), but the revolt ended through the efforts of a wise woman. Following the division of the united monarchy Ephraim was the leading power of the northern kingdom because it was the largest and strongest among the ten tribes. Its permanent capital city was Samaria.[120]

b. According to Theodore, "Tarshish" is used several times in the Old Testament in association with ships, trade, and ports. There were apparently several Tarshish cities built on the seashore, and so the ships of Solomon sailed to Tarshish for trading. Theodore concluded his comments on Tarshish by saying that some exegetes have identified it with Tarsus just because both sound alike, and others with Rhodes; he held that to argue over unknown cities is a superfluous minuteness.[121]

c. Theodore observed that Obadiah's oracles were addressed

to Edom, that Esau was the great ancestor of the Edomites, and that their attitude toward the Judeans was unfriendly from the days of Jacob. He noted that in the Old Testament the Edomites also are called "sons of Edom" or "Idumaeans."[122]

d. According to Theodore, the oracle in Amos 4:1–3 recalls the moral and social conditions of Samaria in the days of Ahab. The frivolous and corrupted life of the ladies of Samaria in the days of Amos was similar to that of Jezebel, who lived in the same city a century earlier. They took advantage of their husbands to oppress the poor and the needy; they acted like kine of Bashan. The region of Bashan is famous for its fertile land and its wild and untamed kine.[123]

e. Cyrus was the founder of the Persian empire who defeated Media and reigned over Persia and Media. After the conquest of Babylon he allowed the Israelites to return to their homeland Judah and Jerusalem. The Israelites suffered little if at all under the Persian rule. Cyrus is called messiah not because he was really anointed but because he was an instrument in the hand of God, carrying out his judgment in human affairs. Darius I was the fourth king who ascended upon Cyrus' throne.[124]

f. Theodore regarded Joel 1:4 as a prediction uttered in a highly figurative expression. The oracle does not deal with four different and actual locust plagues, devouring all the produce of the Judean fields, but with four dreadful national crises which were to be caused by four foreign rulers. He identified the four invasions of the insects with the campaigns of Tiglath-pileser, Shalmaneser, Sennacherib, and Nebuchadnezzar.[125] Most modern exegetes prefer the literal interpretation of the text, and they consider the devastations wrought by the plagues of locusts as historical incidents.[126] Patristic commentators, however, favored the symbolical interpretation. Jerome, for example, identified the four invasions of the insects with the expeditions of Shalmaneser, Nebuchadnezzar, Antiochus Epiphanes, and the Romans.[127] In this respect Theodore's interpretation is more sober and certainly more faithful to the history of the Old Testament because he insisted on casting the prophetic message into the sequence of events against which the prophets prophesied.

g. In his commentary on the minor prophets Theodore frequently mentioned the attack of Gog's hordes against restored Israel. The invasion of Palestine by Gog and all his hosts, according to Theodore, took place in the post-exilic period; the defeat of this foe was achieved either by the God of Israel without the collaboration of a Davidic prince or by Judah under the leadership of Zerubbabel.[128] It is in relationship to those prophetic oracles (Jl 2; Zech 9–14), which modern critics regard as late apocalyptic interpolations, that Theodore advanced his reflections on the mysterious personage of Gog. Although Theodore never quoted Ezekiel, nevertheless his theories on Gog seem to be influenced by Ezekiel 38–39, and particularly by Ezekiel's dictum in 38:17 which emphasizes the fact that the coming of Gog was repeatedly foretold by God through his servants, the prophets. Finally, Theodore associated Gog with the Scythians, in collaboration with whom he invaded Judea. Gog was not, of course, the sole chieftain of the Scythians but only the leading force within their tribal alliance.

Still further examples could be quoted to illustrate Theodore's sense of biblical history. These illustrations bear witness to his high regard for biblical history and give us data for evaluating his treatment of the historical material. Generally speaking, Theodore possessed a good background in biblical history and attempted to interpret the events of Israel's history in the light of his understanding of God's purpose in history. The Christian interpretation of revelation, in Theodore's view, derives from the Bible, which is essentially a book of history dealing with the acts of a covenanted God.

An examination of Theodore's exegetical method would be incomplete without a brief consideration of his teaching on Old Testament typology.[129] To begin with, typological interpretation of the Bible was approved by Theodore, but he was hesitant in applying the method.[130] In contradistinction to the Alexandrians,[131] the Mopsuestian regarded very few of the events of the Old Testament as types of the historical realities contained in the New Testament. In his commentary on the book of Jonah, Theodore found an occasion to evolve his theory on Old Testament typology. In point of fact the prologue he prefixed to this commentary is an essay on typology.[132] His teaching can be summarized as follows: typology is not an interpretation of biblical texts but an historical comparison of events. It is the external correspondence of the events themselves in the two Testaments that has to be compared and brought forward. Not every event of the Old Testament has its correspondence or imitation in the New Testament. Yet there are only certain events in the Old Testament which can be looked upon as the types of certain New Testament events. Theodore seems to have been opposed to those exegetes who stressed the esoteric and mystical correspondence between the type and the event rather than their external parallels and similarities. In Theodore's view no New Testament event is prefigured in the Old Testament in all its fullness, not even Christ himself. "For it is evident," Theodore asserted, "that every single type has some sort of imitation toward that which is said to be its type."[133] Typological interpretation must be related strictly to, and founded upon, the external similarities of the biblical events themselves. Besides, the authority of the typological interpretation must be supported by a New Testament proof-text. The result of this rigorous method for Theodore was a drastic limitation of the "types" in both Testaments. Contrary to the practices of many of his contemporaries who were prone to be extravagant in typology, Theodore refused to recognize more than three "types" which satisfied the strict criteria stipulated by him:

a. The sprinkling of the doorpost with blood by the Israelites on the eve of the exodus and the liberation from the Egyptian bondage typified our redemption from death and sin by Christ's blood. As proof-texts Theodore cited 1 Corinthians 10:11 and Hebrews 9:13.[134]

b. The brazen serpent in the wilderness was a "type" of our Lord's conquest of death and the benefits derived from it. The legitimacy of this typology was based upon John 3:14.[135]

c. Jonah's incarceration in the great fish and his mission is a type which illustrated Christ's entombment and resurrection and his summons of mankind to salvation. The miracles recorded in Jonah had been cited by Jesus in the New Testament (Mt 12:40–41).[136]

Throughout his discussion of typology Theodore returned tediously to the idea that, in spite of the resemblances existing between the types and the antetypes, the types of the New Testament are infinitely superior to the antetypes of the Old Testament.


## NOTES

1. George Foot Moore, *Judaism* (Cambridge, Mass.: Harvard University Press, 1948), I, 239.

2. Sir 51:23. In the literature of Palestinian Jews before the Christian era no reference is made to synagogues; sources of the first century A.D., both Jewish and Christian, imply that the synagogue was already an ancient institution.

3. Harry Austin Wolfson, *Philo: Foundations of Religious Philosophy in Judaism, Christianity, and Islam* (2nd ed. rev.; Cambridge, Mass.: Harvard University Press, 1948), I. 134–135.

4. G.F. Moore, *op. cit.,* I, 57.

5. *Pirque Aboth,* 1:1. It is not to be assumed, however, that there was no problem of interpretation for Judaism. The New Testament and Josephus testify that Palestinian Judaism at the beginning of the Christian era was by no means a united entity. There were, for example, differences in interpretation between the Pharisees and the Sadducees. The fundamental issue was the validity of the oral law (cf. Mt 15:1ff; Mk 7:1ff; *Jewish Antiq.,* xviii.1, 2–6; *Jewish War,* ii.8, 2–14).

6. *Philo,* I, 133. This conception of biblical interpretation, which was developed by the scribes during the last pre-Christian centuries, was carried on by the Pharisees and rabbis (Tannaitic and Amoraic) and found its fruition in the Mishnah. The codification of the Mishnah by Rabbi Judah ha-Nasi dates from about A.D. 200. Subsequent scholarly discussions of the Bible by rabbis in many Jewish academies produced the two great compilations known as the Jerusalem and Babylonian Talmuds, which were edited about A.D. 500. In form, each Talmud consists of the Mishnah together with *Gemara,* which is both a commentary on and a supplement to the Mishnah. The *Midrashim* are running commentaries on individual books of the Bible, and the best known collection of *Midrashim* is the *Midrash Rabbah* on the Pentateuch and the five *Megilloth* which were edited at a later

date (tenth century). But the term *midrash* originally had been used by the rabbis in their effort to discover a new meaning, in addition to the literal one, in the Bible. There have been two basic rabbinical methods of Bible interpretation: first, according to the plain literal meaning of the text; and second, the non-literal or the homilistic exposition of underlying meaning. The non-literal or homiletic method is described as *midrash,* a word derived from a root *(derash)* meaning "to seek out," in contrast to the literal method, which is described by the rabbis as *pashut,* from the root *(push),* meaning "to spread out." This method of exegesis resulted in *halachah* and *haggadah.* A *halachah* is essentially a legal decision, and the Mishnah is made up largely of *halachoth.* On the contrary, there are many facets to haggadah in both content and form; it includes principles of faith, moral instructions, parables, allegories, legends, messianic teachings, and astrology. *Haggadic* teachings are scattered throughout the *Gemara.* The non-literal midrashic method as it was employed in the Talmuds could lead to wild speculations which had little to do with the text of the Bible. It was held that anything which seemed to be lacking in the Bible was actually hidden in its literalness, and it was through the midrashic interpretation that the student had to discover it.

7. Frank Moore Cross, Jr., *The Ancient Library of Qumran and Modern Biblical Studies* (Garden City, N.Y.: Doubleday and Co., 1958), 163–164; Kurt Schubert, *The Dead Sea Community,* trans. John W. Doberstein (London: Adam & Charles Black, 1959), 88ff.

8. Millar Burrows, *The Dead Sea Scrolls* (New York: The Viking Press, 1957), 367–368.

9. F.M. Cross, Jr., *op. cit.,* 163.

10. A. Harnack, *History of Dogman,* I, 114.

11. H.A. Wolfson, *Philo,* I, 115.

12. The term *allegory* was not coined by Philo himself; it already was used in Greek rhetoric in the sense of metaphor. Cleanthes, the Stoic philosopher, was the first to use the term exegetically; cf. H.J. Rose, *A Handbook of Greek Literature* (London: Methuen & Co., 1934), 392.

13. *De Abrah.,* 36.200.

14. *Ibid.*, 41.136.

15. *Ibid.*, 29.147.

16. *Plant.*, 9.36.

17. *De fuga et inventione*, 32.197.

18. For this use of the term *mystery* Philo had ample justification, since by this time that term had come to be applied to all matters of science which required instruction; see G. Liddell and R. Scott, *A Greek-English Lexicon* (6th ed. rev.; Oxford: At the Clarendon Press, 1871), 1032.

19. H.A. Wolfson, *Philo,* I, 116.

20. *De Abrah.*, 36.200; 41.236; *De poster. Caini,* 2.7; *De migrat. Abrah.*, 16.93.

21. *Legum allegoria,* 1.13, 39.

22. *Quod Deus sit immutabilis,* 13.62.

23. H.A. Wolfson, *Philo,* I, 123.

24. The New Testament is uninfluenced by the allegorical method of exegesis, although in one book, the epistle to the Hebrews, there are marked tendencies toward it; see Heb 7:1–10; 8:2–5; 9:15–24; 10:1. Paul gives us several examples of the Palestinian variety of allegorizing, but these are practical rather than philosophical in their object; see 1 Cor 9:9f; 10:4; 2 Cor 3:13–15; Gal 4:21–23.

25. Jean Daniélou, *Origen,* trans. Walter Mitchell (London and New York: Sheed and Ward, 1955), 178.

26. Robert M. Grant, *The Letter and the Spirit* (London: S.P.C.K., 1957), 97.

27. Origen, *De principiis,* 4.2, 9, Migne, PG (11), 364 A.

28. Origen, *In Genesim. Hom.,* 10.1, Migne, PG (12), 215 D.

29. In *Leviticum,* 4.8, Migne, PG (12), 443 C.

30. *De principiis,* 4.2., Migne, PG (11), 364 B–366 A.

31. *Ibid.,* 364B.

32. J. Daniélou, *op. cit.,* 144ff.

33. *Comment. in Ezech.,* 5.16, Migne, PL (25), 153 D; *Comment. in Amos.,* 2.4, Migne, PL (25), 1027 D–1028 A.

In discussing the rules of biblical exegesis Jerome said: "We must interpret the sacred Scriptures, first, according to the letter, by doing all that is prescribed in the way of moral conduct; second, according to allegory, that is the spiritual sense; third, according to the bliss of things to come." For the text, see Harry Austin Wolfson, *The Philosophy of the Church Fathers* (Cambridge, Mass.: Harvard University Press, 1956), I, 66.

34. Frederic W. Farrar, *History of Interpretation* (New York: E.P. Dutton & Co., 1886), 210; Robert A. Aytoun, *City Centres of Early Christianity* (London: Hodder & Stoughton, 1915), 95.

35. R.M. Grant, *The Letter and the Spirit* (London: S.P.C.K., 1957), 105.

36. *Ibid.,* 105; G.F. Moore, "The Theological School at Nisibis," *Studies in the History of Religions,* 257. But for an opposite viewpoint see H.S. Nash, "The Exegesis of the School of Antioch," *The Journal of Biblical Literature,* XI, Part I (1892), 22–37.

37. G.F. Moore, "The Theological School at Nisibis," in *Studies in the History of Religion,* 261.

38. J.N.D. Kelly, *Early Christian Doctrines* (New York: Harper & Brothers, 1958), 76–77.

39. Diodore was a prolific writer and composed numerous treatises and commentaries which have disappeared with the exception of some fragments preserved in the *catenae.* For a listing of titles of Diodore's lost writings, see J. Quasten, *Patrology,* III, 398–401.

40. The Alexandrians used the term *theoria* as equivalent to allegory. Theodore of Mopsuestia employs the term in its plain etymological sense meaning vision. This suggests that patristic terminology at this stage of development was fluid.

41. *In epist. ad Galat.,* Migne, PG (61), 6 2 B.

42. While Chrysostom ordinarily restricted himself to typology, he did not reject the use of the term allegory altogether and continued to use that term but only *in* the Pauline catachrestic sense (cf. *In Math. Hom.* 52, 1, Migne PG [57], 579; *In Joan. Hom.* 85, 1, Migne, PG [59], 461).

43. H.B. Swete, *Theodori episcopi Mopsuesteni in epistolas Pauli commentarii,* I, 73–79.

44. *Ibid.,* 79.

45. *Commentarious in duodecim prophetas,* Migne, PG (66), 377 C, 417 D–420 A, 513 D–516 A, 517 D.

46. *Pro defensione trium capitulorum,* 3.6, Migne, PL (67), 602 BC.

47. J.M. Vosté, "L'oeuvre exégétique de Théodore de Mopsueste," *Revue Biblique,* XXIX, No. 4 (Octobre 1929), 544–546.

48. F.L. Cross (ed.), *The Oxford Dictionary of the Christian Church* (London: Oxford University Press, 1957), 705.

49. *Le commentaire sur les Psaumes,* 195, 11.23–25.

50. *Ibid.,* 512, 11.20–23.

51. *Ibid.,* 49, 11.32–33.

52. *Ibid.,* 93, 11.16–21; see also pp. 127, 11.9–10; 133, 1.30; 249, 1.23.

53. *Comment. in Amosi,* Migne, PG (66), 280 B.

54. *Comment. in Habac.,* Migne, PG (66), 437 C; see also pp. 452 C–454 B; 465 D–468 A.

55. Variant readings from other Greek versions of the Old Testament quoted by Theodore are numerous; see the appended index to *Le commentaire sur les Psaumes* under the headings Aquila, Symmachus, and Theodotion, pp. 564, 569–571.

56. *Le commentaire sur les Psaumes,* 365, 11.5–12.

57. H.B. Swete (ed.), *Theodori episcopi Mopsuestini in epistolas Pauli commentarii,* I, p. lxx.

58. *Le commentaire sur les Psaumes,* 512.

59. *Ibid.,* 394, 137.

60. *Ibid.,* 137, 244, 394, 512.

61. Assemani, *Bibliotheca Orientalis,* III, 30–35.

62. "Genuine difficulties would arise such as an ambiguity in understanding the interpretation, for truly many things would appear with the Hebrews, which from the fact itself is natural to ascertain the sense, and that is what we have established in the summary of idioms in the introduction," *Le commentaire sur les Psaumes,* 94. Unfortunately this introduction has not survived. In the same commentary he is reported to have said, "We, nevertheless, shall accomplish very little in a difficult place of major Hebraic peculiarities, which is very difficult to explain through the Greek translation," p. 108.

63. *In Malachi* 1:2, Migne, PG (66), 600; See also *Essai sur Théodore,* 59.

64. *Le commentaire sur les Psaumes,* 244, 11.21–24.

65. *Ibid.*, 500, 11.6–7.

66. *Ibid.*, 394, 11.10–11.

67. *Ibid.*, 211, 11.11–17; *In Zachariae* 9:9, Migne, PG (66), 560 A.

68. *Le commentaire sur les Psaumes*, 179, 11.8–9; 211, 11.15–17; 250, 11.9–10; 267, 11.17–19; 378, 11.9–10; 530, 11.11–13; Migne, PG (66), 197 A; 412 D–413 A; 569 D; 577 D.

69. *Le commentaire sur les Psaumes*, 211, 11.11–17.

70. In commenting upon Zechariah 11:4 Theodore erroneously claimed: "Sometimes the Bible is in the habit of disclosing the future by the imperative mood, just as when it says 'Rejoice greatly, O daughter of Zion'; at joyous events we have to rejoice, without pleasure joy is an impossibility. Scripture starts with an imperative because it declares Israel's future joy in Zerubbabel's government" (Migne, PG [66], 569 D).

71. *Le commentaire sur les Psaumes*, 94, 11.1–3; *In Amosi*, 6:9–10 Migne, PG (66), 284 A.

72. Cf. *Le commentaire sur les Psaumes*, 149, 11.15–17; 267, 11.8–9; 335, 1.24; 325, 11.4–5; 363, 11.19–25; *In Oseae*, 6:5 Migne, PG (66), 161 C; *In Zachariae*, 11:6, Migne, PG (66), 572 D; K. Staab, *Pauluskommentare aus der griechischen Kirche*, 147, 11.7–10.

73. *Le commentaire sur les Psaumes*, 66, 11.17–19; 131, 11.1–2; 149, 11.15–17; 239, 11.10–14; 240, 11.11–13; 322, 11.7–9; 337, 11.27–28; 384, 11.11–12; 411, 1.7; 436, 1.23; 468, 11.12–15.

74. *Ibid.*, 380, 1.19–381, 1.4; 386, 11.14–16; 401, 1.18; 487, 11.1–9; see also Migne, PG (66), 348 B, 444 B; K. Staab, *Pauluskommentare*, 154, 1.18–155, 1.9; 184, 1.17; 196, 11.17–20.

75. *In Joelis*, 2:9–11, Migne, PG (66), 221 D–224 A; 229 D–232 A; *In Zachariae*, 14:4, Migne, PG (66), 589 B.

76. *Le commentaire sur les Psaumes*, 491, 11.13–15. Hereafter this commentary is referred to as *Psaumes*.

77. *Ibid.*, 494, 11.16–17; 555, 11.1–3.

78. *Ibid.*, 97, 11.27–31; 408, 11.22–24; 513, 11.14–15.

79. Migne, PG (66), 160 D; 572 D; *Psaumes*, 318, 11.4–5; 364, 7–10; 478, 23–24.

80. *Psaumes*, 98, 11.15–18; 153, 11.1–12; 158, 1.19.

81. K. Staab, *Pauluskommentare,* 199, 11.11–15.

82. *Psaumes,* 97, 11.13–15; 128, 11.18–10; 225 11.2–17, 485, 11.18–20.

83. *Ibid.,* 179, 11.27–30, 223, 11.28–30.

84. Migne, PG (66), 196 C.

85. *Theodori episcopi Mopsuestini in epistolas beati Pauli commentarii,* I, lxvii.

86. *Psaumes,* 3, 11.15–19.

87. *Psaumes,* 334, 1.30.

88. *In Zachariae,* 9:10, Migne, PG (66), 557 A.

89. *In Joelis,* 2:32, Migne, PG (66), 232 A.

90. *Psaumes,* 491, 1.15; 281, 11.9–12; 365, 1.5; 467, 11.13–17; 501, 1.8.

91. *Ibid.,* 281, 1.3; *In Michaae,* 5:1–2, Migne, PG (66), 372 C; K. Staab, *Pauluskommentare,* 196, 1.16.

92. *Psaumes,* 194, 1.14.

93. *Ibid.,* 2, 11.4–5; 3, 11.25–27; Swete, *Theodori episcopi Mopsuestini in epistolas Pauli commentarii,* II, 234, 11.00–12.

94. *In Zachariae,* 9:8–10, Migne, PG (66), 556 D–557 D.

95. *Psaumes,* 249, 11.19–25.

96. Theodore, if we may judge from his extant biblical commentaries, never appeals to the authority of the earlier church fathers, but frequently attacks other commentators with derision. In his theological writings, however, Theodore seems to have attached much importance to the christological teaching of the fathers. In commenting upon the Nicene Creed Theodore said: "Our blessed fathers also followed the books and warned us against the unholy opinion and the ineptitude of the heretics, in saying: 'true God of true God.' The books had already stated that he was 'God,' and our fathers added prudently the word 'true.' . . . To this our blessed fathers added that the Son was 'consubstantial' with his Father, a word that confirms the faith of the children of faith and rebukes the unbelievers. Although this is not explicitly written in Holy Writ yet its meaning is found therein" (*Commentary on the Nicene Creed,* 47).

97. *In Oseae* (prologue), Migne, PG (66), 124 A.

98. H. Kihn, *Theodor von Mopsuestia,* 120.

99. Cf. Migne, PG (66), 377 C; 417 D–420 A; 513 D–516 A;

517 D; Swete, *Theodori episcopi Mopsuestini in epistolas Pauli commentarii,* II, 218, 228–229.

100. *In Amosi* (prologue), Migne, PG (66), 245 B; John Chrysostom, *In Isaiam,* cap. VI, Migne, PG (56), 67f.

101. Swete, *Theodori episcopi Mopsuestini,* I, 73–75; 82, 1.15; 83, 11.2–3; 86, 1.5ff.

102. Migne, PG (66), 232 BC; 233 A; *Psaumes,* 41, 11.18–20; 62, 1.20; 96, 1.16; 138, 1.10. *Fragmentum in Exodum,* 26:35, Migne, PG (66), 648 AB.

103. *Psaumes,* 302, 1.8; 430, 1.6; 473, 1.15; Migne, PG (66), 148 B; 213 B; 452 A; Staab, *Pauluskommentare,* 140, 1.1.

104. *Psaumes,* 470, 11.6–7.

105. Cf. *Les fragments Grecs du commentaire sur le quatrieme evangile* in R. Devreesse, *Essai sur Théodore de Mopsueste,* 305–306; see also H.B. Swete, *In epistolas Pauli commentarii,* I, 112; 116; 205; 310.

106. These views are developed by Theodore in the prologues he prefixed to his commentaries on the books of Amos and Jonah (cf. Migne, PG [66], 241 AB; 317 C).

107. Cf. *Psaumes,* 184, 11.10–11; 422 11.1–11; Swete, *In epistolas Pauli commentarii,* II, 227; *Psaumes,* 268–69; 306–07; 351–53; 360–61; 381; 391; 542.

108. Unfortunately Theodore's general introductions to his commentaries on the book of Psalms and on the minor prophets have been lost (cf. *Psaumes,* 94, 11.2–4; 334, 11.29–30).

109. J.M. Vosté, "L'oeuvre exégétique de Théodore de Mopsueste au II° Concile de Constantinople," *Revue Biblique,* XXXVIII, No. 3 (Juillet 1929), 391–395; R. Devreesse, *Essai sur Théodore,* 305–06.

110. *In Osese* (prologue), Migne, PG (66), 124 B–125 A; *In Amosi* (prologue), Migne, PG (66), 241 C–244 A.

111. *In Abdiam* (prologue), Migne, PG (66), 308 A; *In Nahum* (prologue), 400 D.

112. *In Joelis* (prologue), Migne, PG (66), 212 AB.

113. *In Jonah* (prologue), Migne, PG (66), 320 B.

114. Theodore claimed that both Amos and Hosea addressed their oracles to both the northern and southern kingdoms; the fathers gave full credence to the historical introductions con-

tained in the prophetic books as well as the references in the books of Amos and Hosea to the kingdom of Judah, which actually are interpolations by Judean editors who adapted the books for southern readers.

115. *In Aggaeum* (prologue), Migne, PG (66), 473 D–476 B.

116. *In Zachariam* (prologue), Migne, PG (66), 493 D–496 A.

117. *In Malachiam* (prologue), Migne, PG (66), 597 AB.

118. *Psaumes,* 74–76; 193–194; 300–301; *In Amosi* (prologue), Migne, PG (66), 245 BC; *In Abdiam,* 305 AC.

119. *Psaumes,* 218–221; 333–334; 517; *In Nahum* (prologue), Migne, PG (66), 397 A; *In Aggaei* 1:1–2, Migne (66), 477 AD; *In Zachariae,* 1:7–10, Migne, (66), 501 B.

120. *Psaumes,* 300; 539, 11.8–25. One might say that Theodore ignored the fact that Sheba was a Benjaminite and not an Ephraimite; but in the LXX Sheba's tribal relationship is not mentioned.

121. *Ibid.,* 312, 11.8–13; *In Jonam,* 1:3, 320 CD.

122. *In Abdiam* (prologue), 304–305 C.

123. *In Amosi,* 4:1–3, Migne, PG (66), 265 B.

124. *In Zachariae* (prologue) Migne, PG (66), 496 A–497 A; *In Amosi,* 4:13, Migne, PG (66), 272 A.

125. *In Joelis,* 1:4, Migne, PG (66), 213 B. Theodore and most early Christian commentators considered Shalmaneser the conqueror of Samaria because Sargon is not mentioned by name in 2 Kings 17:6–7; we know from extra-biblical sources that it was Sargon II who razed Samaria to the ground. In point of fact Sargon's name is mentioned only once in the Old Testament (Is 20:1), and the LXX rendered it Arna.

126. R. Pfeiffer, *Introduction to the Old Testament,* 574–575.

127. Migne, PL (25), 951 D. A curious aspect of Jerome's exegesis is his strong tendency to discover references to the Roman empire in the prophetic texts (cf. Migne, PL [24], 151 D; [25], 1349 D; 1452 CD; 1522 D).

128. *In Joelis* (prologue), Migne, PG (66), 212 C; *In Michaeam,* 4:11–13, Migne, PG (66), 369 C; *In Zachariae,* 9:10, Migne, PG (66), 561 B; 568 B.

129. It should be noted that the concept of typological interpretation of the Bible was no invention of the patristic writers; in

the Old Testament it was used by Deutero-Isaiah (51:1ff), and in the New Testament by Paul (1 Cor 10:1–11; Gal 4:24).

130.  Jean Daniélou, *The Bible and the Liturgy,* ed. and trans. Michael A. Mathis (Notre Dame, Indiana: University of Notre Dame Press, 1956), 13–14.

131.  The Alexandrians claimed that the Old Testament is a single outline of the New Testament because God selected countless items of the Old Testament as types, enigmas, and shadows of the Christian mysteries (cf. Origen, Hom. 10.1 *In Levitic.,* Migne, PG [12], 525 A; Cyril of Alexandria, *Glaphyr. in Genesim,* Migne, PG [69], 225 C).

132.  Migne, PG (66), 317 C–320 B.

133.  *In Michaeam,* 4:1–3, Migne, PG (66), 364 D. In refusing to go along with those exegetes who expounded Micah 4:1–3 as a messianic typology, Theodore said: "I do not know what made them think so; for this sort of interpretation is against what Christ is reported to have said to the Samaritan woman, 'Believe me, the hour comes when neither in this mountain, nor in Jerusalem, shall you worship the Father.'"

134.  *In Jonam* (prologue), Migne, PG (66), 320 C–321 A.

135.  *Ibid.,* 321 B.

136.  *Ibid.,* 321 D.

# Chapter Six

# OLD TESTAMENT
# MESSIANIC EXPECTATIONS
# AS INTERPRETED BY
# THEODORE OF MOPSUESTIA

As far back in the Church's kerygma as we can penetrate on the basis of the New Testament documents, it becomes evident that the early Christian evangelists and teachers did not hesitate to interpret the Old Testament as being prophetic of Christ. The primitive apostolic kerygma, much of which can be found in the various parts of the New Testament, is punctuated by citations from the Old Testament which are introduced by early Christian biblical scholars with the formulae "according to the scriptures," "this is that which was spoken by the prophet," and "thus it is written." These formulae draw attention to the fact that the early church was convinced that all the events of Christ's public ministry were predicted in the Old Testament, and that the proclamation of the gospel is "according to the scriptures." In the various parts of the New Testament we have a theological system based upon this tenet.

The question as to whether New Testament writers drew their Old Testament citations from a recognized anthology of isolated and disconnected proof-texts or from larger sections of the Old Testament scriptures lies beyond the scope of the present study.[1]

In adopting this use of the Old Testament, Christian evangelists were merely following the example of the primitive church in the years immediately before the New Testament was committed to writing. The early church was committed, by the very nature of its kerygma, to thorough and extensive biblical research for the purpose of justifying its own faith in Jesus the messiah, and also for the purpose of converting the Jews to this faith. The concept of "fulfillment" appears to dominate the early Christian interpretation of the gospel events in relation to their antecedents in the history of Israel. In adopting this conception the Christian thinkers of the pre-literary period appealed not only to select portions of the Old Testament prophecy but also to the "psalms of David." Such a way of interpreting the Old Testament, out of which the ground-plan of New Testament theology was developed, unquestionably antedated Paul's conversion (cf. 1 Cor 15:3) and may possibly be traced back to the Lord himself.[2] In the New Testament the risen Christ is reported to have considered the psalms as prophetic oracles having a far deeper meaning than Jewish readers had suspected (Lk 24:24–45), and he also is reported to have interpreted Psalm 110 as applying to an unnamed messiah.[3] In harmony with this kind of interpretation of the psalter the task of the primitive church was the search of the Old Testament for testimonies about incidents in Jesus' earthly life and career.[4] The authors of the New Testament filled their writings with Old Testament messianic quotations, drawn particularly from Isaiah and the psalter. In doing so, New Testament writers believed they could discern, by consulting the record of God's dealings with his people in scripture, "the determinate counsel and foreknowledge of God" which was fulfilled in the gospel facts.[5] One of the Old Testament books most often quoted by the New Testament authors was the book of Psalms. Several psalms were employed by the early church in a messianic sense. A similar usage of the psalms was common among the church fathers.

The church fathers, basing their arguments on the authority of the manifold testimonies of the New Testament documents, ascribed the authorship of the entire psalter or the greater part of it to David, and they interpreted the cult-lyrics of the public worship of ancient Israel as prophetic and messianic oracles through which David the king-prophet foretold the coming of the messiah, his kingdom, his priesthood, his suffering, and his glorification.[6] The veneration in which early church fathers held David, the psalmist, reappears in the writings of the Christian commentators of the fourth and fifth centuries. Whether we read the Latin or the Greek commentaries of the fathers on the book of Psalms, we are struck at once by how much Christianity they could find in the psalter. By using an arbitrary christological typology or allegory in interpreting each psalm the fathers could claim that in the psalter David revealed all the events recorded in the New Testament.[7] Augustine's explanation of Psalm 59:

> It is difficult for one to find in the psalms any utterance
> except those of Christ and the church, or of Christ only,
> or of the church only, inasmuch as we belong to both.[8]

The christological interpretation of the psalter was thus securely established in the patristic literature; nevertheless a vigorous reaction against this sort of exegesis made itself manifest in Theodore of Mopsuestia's commentary on the book of Psalms. In it the *Mephasqana* followed an interpretive approach which differed sharply from that of his predecessors and contemporaries.[9] This marked difference is seen clearly in Theodore's tendency to eliminate the messianic element in the psalms by repudiating the conventional views concerning the psalter as a repository of christological information for the exegetes and theologians.

In dealing with the psalmic *testimonia* or proof-texts which had been applied to Jesus the Messiah by the New Testament writers, Theodore demonstrated a marked originality that was strikingly novel for his day and at the same time in agreement with several tenets of modern biblical scholarship. His teaching on this very subject may be indicated by a consideration of the points stated in his commentary.

In the opinion of Theodore, David, the author of the psalter, anticipated the future vicissitudes of his people in history through an extraordinary illumination of his mind by God's Spirit.[10] It was only, however, in the prophetic psalms that God revealed to David the fullness of Israel's destiny in history.[11] In David's prophetic contemplation of time and history there is no

messianic element involved. The range of David's telescopic
view of Israel's consummation in history covered only the main
events from the era of Solomon to the Maccabean insurrections.[12]
David's "prophetic psalms" in their scope and perspective are
thoroughly theocentric and Israelitic, and not messianic. The
psalmic passages used by the New Testament writers which have
a messianic connotation lent themselves to this use, not because
they were messianic, but because their phraseology and the rich
meaning and symbolism contained in them supported analogous
spiritual conditions in Christian revelation. This point is elo-
quently affirmed in Theodore's commentary on the psalter. In
commenting upon Psalm 68:22 (H 69:22) he made the following
point (much of which could be endorsed by many modern Old
Testament students):

> The evangelist made use of this text as referring to the
> Lord (Mk 15:35; Jn 19:29), and the Lord himself applied
> the utterance "the zeal for thy house shall eat me up" to
> himself;[13] the blessed Paul, on the other hand, talking
> about the Jews, quoted from the same psalm the text,
> "Let their table be made a snare, and a trap, and a stum-
> bling block, etc.";[14] and finally the blessed Peter, speak-
> ing about Judah, quoted the utterance, "Let his habita-
> tion be made desolable";[15] although the circumstances
> for each case have been entirely different. Shall we say
> that this psalm must be understood to speak at one
> moment of those people, at another of him, and at
> another moment of somebody else? No, the psalmic
> utterances in question are referring to the apostatized
> Jews and reproach their ingratitude. But the use of
> the testimonies has been applied to analogous cir-
> cumstances.[16]

Openly reacting against those who claimed that the recitation of a psalmic text by Jesus Christ himself was sufficient evidence of its messianic character, Theodore maintained that the
practice of Jesus means nothing else but a free and at the same
time perfectly coherent accommodation of the original psalmic

text for the purpose of expressing a similar predicament which the psalmist confronted long before Christ. The surprising thing about all this is that Theodore advanced this interpretation when he was dealing with Psalm 21 (H 22), which is regarded even by the gospel writers as a clear foretelling of the crucified messiah:

> Those commentators who claim that this psalm is related to the person of Christ ought to know that they can be accused of recklessness because the second half of the opening saying of the psalm does not allow such an interpretation. How could Christ ever speak of his sins?
>
> There is no doubt that the Lord pronounced the opening words of the psalm when he was hanging on the cross in order to express his passion as well as his submission to his Father's will; but this does not mean necessarily that the psalm is related to him. Actually he does not use the words as if they had been accomplished by him; but only in the sense that during the turmoil of his pathos he found the occasion to use them in a right way, because they fit suitably to all pious men whenever they find themselves in the agony of suffering.[17]

A similar statement came from Theodore's pen when commenting on Psalm 30:6 (H 31:5), which text, according to Luke's narrative (23:46), Jesus adopted and applied to himself at the moment of his death. In the author's opinion the central idea in the entire psalm is God's judgment upon the hostile powers which precipitated the Babylonian captivity; and, therefore, the utterance "into thy hand I commit my spirit," quoted by the Lord as his final words spoken from the cross, could not be a messianic oracle, as several commentators have claimed, but rather a simple and meaningful expression which Jesus applied to himself. In quoting this psalmic utterance all that Jesus meant was that he was committing his soul to his Father before the resurrection of his body.[18]

More striking still is the approach that Theodore took with regard to those psalmic texts which are cited in the Pauline writings and the epistle to the Hebrews. Theodore, being aware of the fact that the work and mission of Christ are interpreted in the Pauline writings by categories derived from the pages of the Hebrew scriptures, advanced the theory that the isolated texts quoted by Paul should not be regarded as prophetic oracles accomplished in the experiences of the early church, but rather as proof-texts for the advancement of his own theology.[19] Paul was not searching in the psalter, Theodore asserted, for christological prophecies but for arguments and testimonies that would support on the one hand his polemic against the Jews, and, on the other, the scheme of his doctrinal system by basing it upon unimpeachable scriptural evidence.[20] The psalmic texts quoted by Paul are excellent adaptations, convenient illustrations, and suitable transpositions to conform his own theological purpose. In brief, it is by a simple accommodation of the original at the cost of a slight twist that Paul has applied these texts to new circumstances which, however, were not without resemblance to those envisaged by the psalmist.[21] Paul's example was also practiced by the Christian lecturers and preachers. From the very beginning of the church preachers quoted the Bible in their sermons, and the theologians cited biblical texts in supporting their doctrinal viewpoints.[22] The example set by the New Testament writers and the earlier fathers still goes on; our writings and sermons presuppose and often quote from the books of the Bible. Scriptural references are often used to suit the cast of our theological thought:

> Paul did not make use of this biblical quotation as if it had been uttered prophetically, but because the sayings of David concerning those who had fallen morally fitted comprehensively into this subject. Similarly, we Christian writers, even today, are still practicing the same procedure; we quote in our writings biblical passages which are coherently adapted in order to suit the cast of our theological thought. So did Paul. However, that psalm had not been communicated to David as a prophecy concerning all humanity; this becomes evident when he says, "Have all the workers of iniquity no knowledge, who eat up my people as they eat bread?"[23]

With regard to Psalm 15:10 (H 16:10), which is quoted by Peter (Acts 2:31) as a messianic text, Theodore made a statement which throws further light on how he dealt with the psalmic proof-texts:

> It must be noted here that the blessed apostle Peter is reported in the book of Acts to have used the sayings of this psalm as if they had been spoken about Christ. However, it must be made known that even in Acts this psalmic utterance is understood by Peter as it was understood by the psalmist. In Acts, of course, the psalmic text is quoted with a more stimulating force and in accordance with its true signification. What I mean is that this psalmic utterance as far as its verbal literalism is concerned has received its issuance in the Lord Christ. The apostle applied this biblical testimony to the Lord Christ because the issuance of the new circumstances had pronounced it more fittingly suited to him.[24]

The argument of the two foregoing quotations represents a view of interpretation which merits consideration in its own right. It suggests that the New Testament writers in quoting certain texts from the Hebrew psalter manifest a considerable freedom of selection. The selection of the proof-texts is not based on a mechanical or artificial process of bringing together detached and isolated citations having accidental or verbal resemblances with certain gospel facts; rather it is based upon a carefully calculated method of accommodation and transposition. The method of accommodation as applied in the New Testament, while recognizing the original meaning of the psalmic texts, nevertheless transposed them into a new and fresh situation of Christian revelation and doctrine. Thus, it provided for the New Testament writers a scriptural sub-stratum upon which they both built and tested the authority and the validity of their theological constructions. Such accommodation into a new setting involves a certain shift from the original meaning of the passage, and at the same time implies a kind of expansion of the historical context of the ancient Hebrew poem; yet, the accommodation of the psalmic texts is applied in such a manner as to fit suitably into the cast of thought of the New Testament writers. In the application of scriptural texts to their doctrinal system most of the Christian theologians followed practically the same method. They interpreted and applied the scriptural texts upon the basis of a certain theological understanding, which is substantially that of the theologians themselves.

Finally, the psalmic proof-texts or *testimonia* should not be considered as a kind of pious messianic foreknowledge which found its exact accomplishment in the life and destiny of Jesus, but as meaningful scriptural utterances which in their literalness fitted suitably with the events of his earthly life. There is here a principle of interpretation which expounds the texts not in accordance with the whole context of the original, but in accordance with the meaning of the gospel facts.

Such a line of reasoning, which was otherwise absent from the writings of ancient Christian commentators, was not bound, however, to be pressed by Theodore to its logical outcome. The objective and unorthodox treatment of the psalmic testimonies about Jesus advocated by Theodore should logically have led him to the rejection of the so-called messianic psalms. But Theodore never took this step. In his endeavor to investigate the Bible through a critical approach, Theodore's mind was limited by his own age in many respects. While he betrayed an anxiety to eliminate the messianic references in the psalter, that did not prevent him from committing himself to the belief that the Hebrew psalter includes "some special psalms" which he understood to be direct prophecies of the incarnation and the church.[25] He limited these "special psalms" to Psalms 2, 8, 45, and 110.

How did Theodore come to justify the presence of some christological psalms in the psalter? The answer is not found in his commentary. Presumably, he had discussed the case in the introduction to his commentary on the book of Psalms, which unfortunately has been lost. It is probably the New Testament usage that best explains Theodore's view regarding the deeper meaning and interpretation of Psalms 2 and 110.[26] Both are often quoted in the New Testament where they are given a prophetic and messianic interpretation.[27] As for the interpretation of Psalm 8 in the New Testament there is an established tradition which applied this psalm, at least by implication, to the Son of man,

Jesus Christ.[28] Hence we must conclude that it was the New Testament usage of this psalm, as well as its highly imaginative phraseology and thought, that led Theodore to interpret it as a prophetic oracle perceiving the deep mystery of the incarnation and the *homo assumptus.*[29] However, Theodore's interpretation as applied in his commentary is strange to the original meaning of this Hebrew hymn because the most distinctive elements in it are the majesty and glory of God as revealed in the calm of an oriental night, and the place of man in the scheme of creation.

Theodore's exposition of Psalm 45 makes it clear that the secular language of this ancient royal wedding song presented to him serious interpretive difficulties and many related and subordinate problems. He devoted much thought and concern to the matter. Theodore's argument for a christological exposition may be briefly summarized: contrary to the current Jewish interpretation which read Psalm 45 as a nuptial song written by David to be sung at Solomon's wedding, we, the Christian commentators, must maintain that the imagery is altogether too exalted, and the thought too peculiar to suit a royal epithalamium song. David, who was one of the greatest personalities of the Old Testament, could not have written such a secular song celebrating the marriage of an earthly king. A literal interpretation of this psalm will make it look like a joke or mockery. The only way out of this predicament is to "spiritualize" the whole content of the psalm, and then interpret it as a prophetic metaphor. The psalm is more than a love canticle celebrating the sumptuous nuptials of an ancient Israelitic king; it is written in the prophetic style and spirit. According to Theodore, it is a prophecy of Christ and his church. Consequently, we need not bewilder ourselves with fruitless attempts to identify the "king" with an earthly monarch (Solomon or Hezekiah), and the "queen" with a mortal princess, but we may at once see our Savior wedded to his bride, the church, in these adoring words of the psalm. Prophecy is here clothed with "spiritual metaphor."[30]

Theodore's interpretation of Psalm 45 was inconsistent and irreconcilable with the main lines of his exegetical method and analysis. He had insisted that Old Testament literature be interpreted and investigated in the light of its own literal, conceptual, and historical context, without recourse to allegory. However, in the case of Psalm 45 he tried to prove its christological nature from the allegory itself, but only under the excuse of "spiritual metaphor." The Mopsuestian is neither the first nor the last biblical scholar who has been forced to compromise his guiding methodology and basic presuppositions. The esteem in which he held David would not allow him to accept his hallowed hero as a rhapsodist and entertainer composing wedding songs. With his emphasis on grammar and literalism, the secularism of the psalm forced Theodore to sacrifice irrationally his method of interpretation on the altar of allegory. After all Psalm 45 was interpreted messianically in the Targum,[31] the epistle to the Hebrews (1:8–9), and the Peshitta.[32]

## MESSIANIC PROPHECIES

Another way to study Theodore's interpretation of the Old Testament may be found in his treatment of Hebrew prophetic literature. In the traditional scheme of Christian apologetics the "argument from prophecy" has played a significant part from the apostolic age to the present. The argument from prophecy in its traditional form laid stress upon the literal fulfillment of messianic prediction, and as such it goes back to the New Testament itself. In Old Testament prophecy, it was commonly thought, the Christian could prove that the advent of Jesus the messiah had been predicted, that in many incidents of Jesus' birth and public ministry, and in the subsequent outpouring of the Spirit, the ancient prophetic oracles had been fulfilled. In the words of A. Harnack:

> A glance at the early Christian writers, and especially at the apologists, reveals the prominent and indeed the commanding role played by the argument from prophecy, and this argument could only be led by means of the Old Testament.[33]

From the first century onward the demonstration of the witness of Old Testament prophecy to the truth of Christ by means of prediction and fulfillment became commonplace among Christian theologians and teachers.

There is no section of the Old Testament literature which has been so much abused at the hands of patristic writers as the so-called "messianic passages." The fathers in reading the prophetic writings were seeking above all things an Old Testament christology. The orthodox assumption underlying this argument from prophecy in terms of prediction and fulfillment was grounded in the belief that both Testaments form one single saving Testament, given by one God by means of one Lord;[34] and that the prophets in their oracles contemplated the mysteries of Christ before their accomplishment.[35] But since in the prophetic literature the passages which are clearly and unequivocally messianic comprise but a small part of the whole, the fathers were tempted to read in the remainder of the literature a christology which the oracles themselves do not imply, and of which the authors were completely unaware. To attain this end, the fathers relied on a method of exegesis which has in modern times been given the convenient name "christological allegory" or "christological typology." By the application of this exegetical principle the actual history of Israel's prophetic movement loses its validity as an eventful history in Israel's life drama, and we are expected to see as the true meaning of these facts nothing but Christ, his new covenant, his cross, his resurrection, and the founding of his church. The way was thus early paved for the classic doctrine which Augustine was to formulate in the following epigrammatic statement:

> Prophecy without any understanding of Christ was only water.... Read all the prophetical books omitting Christ, what will you find so insipid and meaningless? Understand Christ there and not only is your reading full of savor but also inebriating, diverting the mind from the body so that forgetting the past you strain forward to the future.[36]

Christian traditionalism in regard to this argument from prophecy was not accepted without opposition in the history of patristic literature. It was seriously challenged and modified by Theodore of Mopsuestia. The bishop of Mopsuestia, again, has some suggestive and original views on the subject; and among early Christian commentators he gives a different approach to the issue, an approach clear and intelligible and one which at several points anticipates the views of modern critical biblical scholarship.

In the first place, while Theodore's conception of prophecy seems to be one of foretelling the future, he nevertheless showed little if any interest in understanding and interpreting the phenomenon of prophecy as a religious institution whose primary mission was to predict, in a series of particular oracles or verses, the mysteries of the messianic times and their fulfillment in the events of the New Testament. As a matter of fact, he demonstrated, as his extant writings indicate, a remarkable ability to free himself from the conventional preconceptions of Christian traditionalism and return to an historical view of the prophet and his teaching. Theodore argued that every prophecy has a "situation-conditioned" nature because each was given in a particular circumstance of Israelitic history. The primary meaning and application of such prophecies has to do with the prophet's time and the immediate future.[37] Theodore insisted that there was no necessary or obvious double reference in Hebrew prophecy and that each oracle had but one sense and meaning. In point of fact, he was astonished at those theologians and exegetes who diverted their attention from the plain meaning of the text and searched for strange notions; such an interpretation, he exclaimed, is the utmost folly, since it drags the texts in different directions and makes prophecy look like strange uncouth utterances.[38]

Secondly, he firmly refused to allow that the Son-Logos and the Holy Ghost were revealed as separate persons and *hypostases* to the prophets; and in addition, he maintained that no prophet spoke concerning Christ in a direct predictive oracle.[39] The following passage clarifies Theodore's view:

> We learned from the holy books of the prophets to shake off from us all the aberrations of pagans, whose gods are different and numerous, and to believe that Divine

nature which ought to be called God and Lord is one,
because He alone is from eternity and is the cause of
everything. . . . This is the reason why we say that there
is only one God as the blessed prophets taught us. . . .
Beyond this they did not teach us anything clearly. The
doctrine concerning the Father and the Son was kept (to
be promulgated) by Christ our Lord, who taught His disciples that which was unknown before and was not
revealed to men, and ordered them to teach it to others
also in saying to them plainly: 'Go ye and teach all
nations, baptizing them in the name of the Father, and
of the Son, and of the Holy Ghost'. As the blessed Moses
said when he promulgated his doctrine: 'The Lord, thy
God is one Lord'—a doctrine that was taught and
handed down by all the prophets—so Christ our Lord
gave his teaching in the name of the Father, of the Son,
and of the Holy Ghost, but did not say what we had to
learn and to teach others concerning the Lord and God,
as this had been clearly done by the prophets. He
ordered his disciples to teach all the nations that which
was lacking to make the teaching of the prophets
perfect.[40]

According to Theodore, then, the Old Testament prophets
were teachers of monotheism, preachers of a true religious knowledge, interpreters of the purpose of God in history,[41] and revealers of the nature and character of God:

In this way the teaching of the Old Testament is in harmony with the teaching of the New Testament, and the
words which the prophets uttered concerning God are
not foreign nor contradictory to those which Christ our
Lord delivered to the Gentiles through the apostles, as
his words are in full harmony with the true knowledge
of religion according to the teaching of the prophets.
Through the prophets we only understood God and the
being to whom an uncreated nature belongs, but the

teaching of our Lord Jesus Christ gave us also with certainty the persons in whom is divine nature.[42]

In Theodore's view Old Testament prophecy, taken as a whole and on its own merits and terms, does not present Christ to us; it rather prepares the way for, and leads the way to, Christ. Actually, not only prophecy but the entire movement of the Spirit of God within Israel, as it is represented in the old covenant, served as a shadow, sign, and symbol in the preparation of the new covenant:

> He who rules over the Old and the New Testaments is one and the same God, the Lord and Maker of all creation; looking toward a single providential purpose he accordingly dispensed both in the former and in the latter.[43]

In another passage Theodore clarifies his position on this relationship:

> The words of the New Testament concerning Christ were found in the prophets of the Old Testament; they were indeed found in the prophets as a symbol and a sign whereby the Jews expected Christ to appear to them as a man, but none of them was aware of the divinity of the Only Begotten Son—the Word-God.[44]

These quotations show that for Theodore, Christ is not the Lord of both Testaments, but God himself; and the old and the new dispensations are not identical forming together a single saving Testament given by one God by means of the Lord Christ, but two distinct phases of revelation initiated by God himself for the purpose of furthering his saving acts in Israel and in Jesus Christ. So, while the significant words of the prophets are in no sense a direct prophecy of Christ, and not even an explicit promise of God's ultimate purpose for all humanity, yet in the larger light of revelation they can be seen as an implicit sign and symbol of God's saving deeds in Christ, his Son. The Old Testament did not predict so much as foreshadow Christ by symbols and signs. Theodore by signs and symbols probably meant types.[45]

When Theodore's commentary on the minor prophets is examined, it can be seen that in his treatment of those texts traditionally accepted as messianic,[46] he manifested a definite break with the current notion as far as the fulfillment of prophecy is concerned. He followed a bold and independent line of interpretation and not the old static rules of the Alexandrian tradition. Theodore was not interested in messianic eschatology and made no effort to discover Christian history in Hebrew prophecy because he knew, and so stated emphatically, that prophecies dealt primarily with the prophet's time and the immediate future. In many prophetic oracles or particular prophetic verses which both the New Testament authors and the fathers took as plain predictions of the Messiah, Theodore could find neither a direct messianic element nor a typological prediction of Christ, but referred them exclusively to persons and events in Israel's national history. In doing so, he based his rigidly careful interpretation on the literal, historical, and conceptual context of the texts. The immediate result of such an interpretation was the elimination of all purely messianic exegesis from texts in which many exegetes found direct or indirect predictions of things Christian.

Yet Theodore readily conceded that in these very same prophetic texts, which the authors of the New Testament quoted and applied in matters of Christian revelation, the prophets spoke in "exaggerated terms."[47] The phrasing of these oracles, Theodore argued, is saturated with a "hyperbolical element," and their expression is animated by a highly "imaginative mood," envisaging for Israel a glorious and blessed future which never materialized as such in Old Testament times.[48] In their hyperbolically stated literalness, Theodore claimed, these prophecies did not come into permanent historical reality in the years that followed their delivery. And yet the prophets delivered them with reference to the future of Israel. There certainly came a prince from David's line, but he failed to restore his ancestor's throne to eternal pre-eminence; God bestowed upon Israel many blessings, but no outpouring of God's spirit upon all his people ever took place; the return from the exile materialized, but there followed no flocking of nations to acknowledge God's mighty deeds and submit to his rule. The blessings and promises anticipated by the prophecies remained the unfinished business of Hebrew prophecy. The exaggerated promises of the prophets continued to exist in expectant waiting and without conclusion. It was, Theodore concluded, only from the point of the incomplete outlook of prophecy that the hyperbolically stated oracles of the minor prophets found their true and durable issue in the person and work of the Lord Christ. These prophecies were not fulfilled by Christ in the sense that they were direct messianic references to the Lord Christ but only that they found their issue, their true end and perfection, in the person and work of Christ. As we have already seen Theodore was not interested in the argument from prophecy in terms of prediction and fulfillment. In point of fact, the verb "to fulfill" and its derivative "fulfillment," as well as the formulae "thus it is written," "according to the scriptures," "this which was spoken by the prophets," are not even used by Theodore.[49] On the contrary, the bishop of Mopsuestia, in phrasing his interpretation of the traditionally accepted messianic prophecies, tried hard and conscientiously to create a new terminology which would not suggest the idea of fulfillment as it was understood by the Christian apologists, even by implication.

Before we proceed it would be appropriate to make a comment on the data just reviewed. The relevant prophetic passages which were termed by Theodore "hyperbolically stated prophetic utterances" are the very same ones which many modern liberal scholars have claimed to be late post-exilic interpolations or detached apocalyptic visions inserted in the original writings of the twelve by some anonymous annotators or authors in order to depict, in a series of pious and obscure eschatological visions, the bliss and glory of the messianic age. No doubt Theodore fell short of understanding the messianic prophecies inserted in the Twelve in any nineteenth or twentieth century mode of thought. Nevertheless, we venture to say that Theodore's suggestive language adumbrated in a primitive way the current teaching of critical scholars.

Possibly enough has been said to show that Theodore followed an independent and progressive line in the interpretation of the messianic prophecies. He exercised a great freedom in that, in all cases, he rejected the validity of the argument from prophecy in terms of prediction and fulfillment. In other cases he reinterpreted the messianic proof-texts of the New Testament, particularly in the sense of penetrating to the deeper spirit which underlies the application of Hebrew prophecy to the gospel events. Theodore's treatment of the prophetic *testimonia* can be seen clearly in his commentaries, selections from which follow in translation.

Hosea 11:1, which is quoted in Matthew 2:15 as a prophecy of Christ, and introduced with the formula "that it might fulfill that which was spoken by the Lord through the prophet," did not appear to Theodore to indicate a wonderful foreknowledge on the part of Hosea of the circumstances of the Savior's birth (though it seemed so to the author of the gospel). Insofar as the reference of the passage to Christ is concerned, Theodore made no comment at all; evidently the citation did not appear to him to have much relation to the immediate context and it was based on an arbitrary interpretation. But let us read his comments on this verse:

> God called Israel a child in reference to her sojourn in Egypt, which marked both the beginning of Israel's formative period and the providential acts that God bestowed upon her. The bestowal of these providential privileges was confirmed by the deliverance of the Israelites from Egypt. But the Israelites, in defiance of God's love and blessings, showed their wickedness by becoming apostates, and even worse than that, they switched their allegiance, which should belong to God, to idols. This is what God said through the prophet.[50]

Theodore approached the prophecy of Joel from the point of view of its historical context rather than of its fulfillment. He claimed that its primary meaning could be determined by examining the religious disposition of the prophet Joel and the circumstances under which he prophesied. According to the historical, literal, and conceptual contexts, Theodore argued, the oracle is a forecast of the future bliss and glory which would prevail in Israel following the return from the Babylonian exile. However, the entire oracle, Theodore conceded, is stated in hyperbolical terms and its phrasing is animated by a highly imaginative spirit. Contrary to Joel's forecasting of the glorious future of Israel, history moved on in its usual course and the anticipated blessings and promises failed to come to fruition in Israel's religion and history. But let us read the rest of Theodore's argument:

> It is an oracle which deals with the blessings which would prevail in Israel following the return from the Babylonian exile. This is what the expression 'I will pour out my spirit' means, because the Holy Ghost was never seen as a person and *hypostasis,* as true God of true God in Old Testament times. The expression 'holy spirit' is always used in the Bible to signify God's grace, solicitude, and will. This is the meaning of this prophecy according to its literal and conceptual contexts.
>
> But the blessed Peter made use of this prophecy (Acts 2:17–21) while he was addressing the Jews on the day of Pentecost. It was quite fair for him to do so. The religion of the law foreshadowed future events; and the people of Israel became worthy of God's solicitude for what was going to be manifested in the future at the advent of the Lord Christ.
>
> But the prophetic words are rather stated in a hyperbolical manner and they do not directly correspond to the realities of history. And so the truth of what has been said by the prophet Joel seemed to the apostle Peter to be receiving its issue in the Lord Christ. In like manner the blessed David said: 'For thou will not leave my soul to Sheol; neither will thou suffer thine Holy one to see corruption' (Ps 16:10).[51] It is an expression which it is not possible to understand literally, because David spoke metaphorically, in other words in hyperbolical terms. But the truth of the matter can be

demonstrated by the Lord Christ whose soul was not abandoned in Sheol, neither did his body suffer corruption. While David's saying seems like an enigma, Christ's case is a true one. For the same reason the blessed Peter made use of Joel's utterance which was somehow stated then in imaginative language, but now it has received its true issue in the realities of the New Testament history.

There are several such passages in the Old Testament; manifestly the present one is of the same nature. In accordance with the tradition of the Old Testament, God spoke through the prophet Joel to the Israelites, heralding the abundant blessings that he was going to bestow upon them in the years following the return from exile; but all these blessings have been issued with a truer sense in the Lord Christ. At the manifestation of our Lord Christ's salvation many wonders took place in the heavens as well as on earth; the sun's light darkened, and there appeared tongues as of fire the day that the Spirit heralded the salvation, just as that which was long ago stated metaphorically or hyperbolically by the prophet; but the display of the events took place after a serious depreciation in value of the original pronouncements. The reason that the blessed apostles apprehended either Joel's utterance or other prophetic utterances which were spoken by the prophets in regard to the old dispensation, in the economy of Christ, should be assumed to be a just one; for on the one hand the history of the former events would not seem to be fictitious, and on the other hand, the greatness of the latter affairs could be tested by a contrast with the former. There always is a fitting suitability between the former and the latter.

But since the prophet Joel heralded, by his early oracles, the hope of the return from the Babylonian exile, he also ventured to describe within the same context the blessings which were going to be bestowed upon the people at the time.[52]

In the prologue to his commentary on the book of Amos Theodore claimed that the oracles of the prophet from Tekoa deal primarily with the fate of Samaria and its subjects. Amos, Theodore maintained, exercised his prophetic ministry not in Jerusalem but in the court of the sanctuary in Bethel.[53] It was from Bethel that he addressed certain short oracles to Jerusalem concerning its impending end.

In Theodore's opinion the national calamities involving both kingdoms were brought about by the Assyrians and the Babylonians respectively. Though the invasions alluded to were separate in time, there was only one captivity, and it was initiated by the Assyrians and consummated by the Babylonians; the former attacked the ten northern tribes, the latter the two southern ones.[54]

The evils that eventually overtook both kingdoms, Theodore argued, were not inflicted by God out of cruelty, but rather out of care for his chosen people, with a view to chastising them thoroughly and to inducing them to do better. The last part of the book of Amos, Theodore concluded, ends with a solemn divine assurance that God's grace at the proper time will shine forth and magnify Israel by re-establishing the united kingdom of Israel under the legitimate Davidic dynasty, as it had been in David's time. In his commentary on Amos 9:11, Theodore stated:

> What is said here refers only to the return from the Babylonian exile and the certainty that, after the return, the entire nation was to have in Zerubbabel a king from David's line. As it is stated in the Acts of the Apostles (15:14–17) the blessed apostle James seems to have interpreted this very same oracle as referring to Christ the Lord; as though this oracle by Amos had received its true issue at the time of Jesus when David's kingdom was truly fallen and was raised up again and reached perfection after throwing off all its corruption.
>
> The utterance was spoken by Amos in heralding what was to happen in Israel following the return from the captivity; and, on the other hand, that which was said by the prophet Amos, according to the blessed

> James' interpretation, was proved and confirmed with
> truth and certainty by Christ the Lord. Therefore the
> prophetic utterance has been rightly quoted by the
> apostle.[55]

The passage that we have quoted indicates that the Antiochian exegete approached Amos 9:11 from the point of view of its historical context rather than of its messianic fulfillment. The oracle, according to Theodore, is a prediction of the restoration of the Jewish kingdom under a Davidic prince. The return from Babylon became a fact in Israel's history, but the Israelites under Zerubbabel's leadership failed to restore David's house. And thus the prophecy of Amos remained incomplete. It is only because of this inconclusiveness that the apostle James interpreted the oracle as finding its true issue in the person and work of the Lord Christ. Although the oracle of Amos, literally and historically understood, promises a national restoration to Israel, yet the tenor of the interpretation of James is wholly different and does not conform to the original meaning of the prophet's words. James considers the accomplishment of this oracle not in a national sense but in a truer and more certain interpretation: "the raising up of David's fallen hut" commenced with the coming of Christ and the founding of the Christian church by his apostles.

In advancing his arguments for a correct interpretation of Amos 9:11 Theodore could not sense that the phrase "I will raise up the tabernacle of David that is fallen" presupposes both the actual downfall of the kingdom of Judah and the Babylonian exile.

Basing his information on the opening verse of the book of Micah, Theodore claimed that Micah's call to the prophetic ministry occurred after that of Hosea and Amos. The oracles contained in the book that bears the name of the prophet from Moresheth were delivered in the days of Jotham, Ahaz, and Hezekiah, kings of Judah. Micah's visions and oracles concerned events that would happen to both Samaria and Jerusalem.[56] However, the historical perspective of the oracle 5:1–4, Theodore argued, refers to the national calamities of Jerusalem which were inflicted by the Babylonians, and at the same time it envisages

Israel's future restoration and glory under a united monarchy.[57] The oracle predicts that during the captivity there will be no king reigning in Jerusalem, but following the return from Babylon, he who will restore the fortunes of Israel will be a Davidic prince coming from Bethlehem. In this prophecy there is no direct messianic element; the predicted restorer from Bethlehem was Zerubbabel. This can be detected from the literal and conceptual contexts of the prophecy itself. Besides, God had promised on several occasions in the past that he would eternally reserve the throne of Jerusalem to David's house and descendants. As a matter of history it was Zerubbabel, a descendant of David, who led the Israelites after the return from captivity, but he failed to restore David's throne to eternal pre-eminence. Theodore continued:

> From the context of the prophetic text it becomes evident that the oracle was spoken by the prophet in reference to Zerubbabel who was a true descendant of David; but even so the perfection of what had been said in Micah's utterance had found its true issue in the person of the Lord Christ.[58]

After this general statement Theodore made no further comment in regard to Bethlehem as the birthplace of Jesus the messiah; nor did he take pains to remind his readers that Micah's oracle is quoted in Matthew 2:4–6 as a direct messianic testimony.

In his prologue to the commentary on Zechariah, Theodore affirmed his belief in the unity of the authorship of the book, as well as his belief that the whole prophecy is an authentic and genuine work of the prophet Zechariah, the son of Iddo, who lived and preached in Jerusalem during the reign of Darius I.[59] However, as this opinion is no longer accepted by modern liberal scholarship, and the composite character of the book of Zechariah has generally been recognized since J.G. Eichhorn, in the fourth edition of his introduction to the Old Testament (3 vols., Leipzig, 1924), attributed Zechariah 9–14 to a post-Zecharian date,[60] it will be interesting to give some attention to certain sug-

gestive remarks made by Theodore in regard to the historical perspective of Zechariah's prophecy in chapters 9–14.

Zechariah, according to Theodore, was like Haggai in rous-
ing the courage of the people to the task of reconstructing the
temple, but whereas the oracles of Haggai envisage this work
alone, the visions of Zechariah embrace a much wider horizon.
Zechariah guarantees that Jerusalem will regain her former splen-
dor; her divinely-appointed king will rule there in glory and dignity; the priesthood, too, will regain its ancient excellence in the
person of the high priest Joshua. In an explicit reference to Zechariah 9–14 Theodore made the following statement:

> It seems that the prophet Zechariah experienced many
> other and different apocalypses and he tried to interpret
> the force of their meaning. He heralded the attack of the
> hosts of Gog against Israel and reported that their
> destruction would be complete. He mentioned also the
> sorrowful events that would take place in Israel follow-
> ing the destruction of Gog's forces, namely, the tribula-
> tions inflicted by the Macedonian *diadochi* during the
> Maccabean times.[61]

Zechariah 9:9 portrays the triumph of an eschatological king
of Israel riding into Jerusalem "upon an ass and upon the foal of
an ass" (Mt 21:5; Jn 12:15). Theodore's rather long comments on
this verse could be summarized as follows: the whole passage not
only implies that the exile is an historical fact but also presupposes that most of the exiles are back and the city of David is
without a king; since the oracle gives no hint of a king in Jerusalem, the prince of peace riding into Jerusalem upon a despic-
able animal should be identified with an historical personality
contemporary with the prophet Zechariah. This person is
Zerubbabel.[62]

The oracle as a whole, Theodore argued, cannot be taken as
messianic because it is not a prediction of Christ; nor can it be
taken to have a double sense. Those who claim that Zechariah
visualized at one moment Zerubbabel and at another time the
Lord Christ should know that their interpretation lacks logical

coherence and makes prophecy look like a strange and paradoxical phenomenon; in addition, such an attitude runs the risk of confusing the plane of human history with that sphere which belongs to God. The oracle has but one meaning and sense; it envisages Zerubbabel.[63] Yet the prophet spoke of Zerubbabel in language so hyperbolical that the passage is out of agreement with the realities of Israel's history. There are, however, several passages in the Old Testament characterized by hyperbolical and excessive spirit which found no fruition or issue in the actualities of the Old Testament times. The oracle of Zechariah (9:9) is of the same nature as the ones mentioned above; it was uttered by the prophet in direct reference to Zerubbabel.[64] It definitely contains an idea that is not specifically Christian. However, it acquires a Christian signification when seen against the background of the gospel facts. In the gospel narratives the prophecy of Zechariah is quoted as having found its true issue in the person of the Lord Christ. Such an interpretation is suitable and fitting, because Christ alone is the real possessor of all the attributes already imputed to Zerubbabel by the prophet. To claim that the prophet envisaged Zerubbabel and Christ at one and the same time is nothing else but an exaggeration showing complete ignorance of the Bible and making prophecy a paradoxical phenomenon.[65] Even those who claim that the saying "he was led as a sheep to the slaughter" is a clear reference to the Lord Christ should know that the literal context of the passage shows that it refers to an already accomplished fact, while the advent of the Lord Christ took place after many centuries.[66]

Malachi, according to Theodore, was the last in the line of the great Hebrew prophets and as such his ministry marked the end of a great and fruitful tradition in the history of Israelite religion.[67] Malachi's call to prophecy occurred long after that of Zechariah, though we do not know whether it took place before the time of Ezra and Nehemiah.[68] Malachi, Theodore argued, was chiefly concerned with the internal problems of the post-exilic community of Israel, and the issues the prophet discussed with his own generation were religious, moral, and social. He was the only prophet who did not pronounce a judgment against the Gentiles, and the first, moreover, to confess that the sacrifices offered by the Gentiles to their gods were actually offered to the Lord of all creation.[69] The only judgment predicted by Malachi in a rather vague and obscure way was one upon the unfaithful Israelites whose transgression and iniquity will be punished by the Macedonian rulers in the Maccabean times.[70]

As far as Theodore's interpretation of Malachi 3:1 is concerned, it can be explained as follows: the theme of this oracle is nothing else but a direct answer by the prophet Malachi to those who were protesting against God with the complaint that the evildoers were a pleasing object in the sight of God, or, as they put it, "Every one that does evil is good in the eyes of the Lord, and he takes pleasure in such; and where is the God of justice?"[71] The answer is: God shall send his angel to execute justice among the pious and the wicked; the commissioned angel in his ministry will be assisted by God himself who shall direct his angel from the temple of Jerusalem.[72] The ministry of every angel is an expression of the will of God. God will not come and appear in person. It is in the execution of the angel's ministry that God's presence will be manifested and experienced. In the earlier sources of Israel's religious history angels were more active, working on behalf of God and assisting him in the preparation of the various covenants that God concluded with the Israelites. Malachi's messenger should not be identified with the prophet himself or with any other known personality of the Old Testament, least of all with Elijah.[73] Elijah will reappear in person to convert the Jews to Christianity in the second advent of the Lord Christ. After these remarks Theodore concluded his commentary on Malachi 3:1 with the following statement:

> However the fact that this prophetic utterance has been applied to the advent of the blessed John the Baptist should not excite wonder; for this prophetic voice was proving itself to be true only by the course of events of the New Testament times. Simultaneously there appeared not only the blessed John the Baptist, the precursor and servant of the appointed things from above, but also he to whom John the Baptist was called to be a witness, that is, the Lord Christ who was destined to dispense the salvation of all mankind.[74]

Of still greater interest than the commentary itself is Theodore's complete silence over the fact that Malachi 3:1 in conjunction with the "Elijah" passage (4:5) is more or less explicitly cited by all three synoptic gospels in identifying the messenger referred to in Malachi with John the Baptist.[75]

It seems Theodore was quite aware that there were some serious differences of opinion in the early church over the messianic proof-texts from Malachi. The Johannine tradition rejects this identification, and according to that tradition John the Baptist denied that he was Elijah. For the author of the fourth gospel John the Baptist is the "voice of one crying in the wilderness, 'Make straight the path of our God.'"[76] In Theodore's opinion the whole prophecy of Malachi was alien to New Testament times and it deals with the internal problems of the late postexilic congregation of Israel. And that is why Theodore warned his readers not to get wondrously excited by the application of this utterance (not the oracle) of Malachi to John the Baptist. Theodore viewed this application as a perfectly coherent accommodation and transposition of the original oracle into a new and fresh situation in Christian revelation which, however, was not without some resemblance to that envisaged by the prophet.

The preceding analysis of Theodore's interpretation of the psalmic and prophetic texts traditionally accepted as "messianic proof-texts" provides quite specific data about Theodore as a biblical exegete. The Antiochian exegete in his treatment of the messianic *testimonia* showed little interest in the messianic type of exegesis. This may be seen in the fact that he repudiated the old traditional view which regarded the recitation of a psalmic or prophetic text by a New Testament author as sufficent evidence of its messianic character. On the contrary he boldly maintained that the New Testament writers interpreted the person and work of Jesus by categories derived from the pages of the Hebrew scriptures, and consequently the Old Testament testimonies they quoted should not be accepted as direct or indirect messianic predictions finding their exact fulfillment in the person of Jesus and his church; rather they should be admitted as perfect and coherent illustrations and adaptations fitting to the theological objectives of the New Testament writers. The Hebrew psalter is not a repository of messianic information, because its scope and perspective is thoroughly Israelitic. Theodore considered only four psalms (2, 8, 45, 110) to be direct or metaphorical predictions of the incarnation and the church.

In Theodore's opinion Hebrew prophecy in its essence is predictive. It is predictive in the sense that it not only points to the outcome of events contemporaneous with the prophet's present or immediate future, but it also predicts forthcoming episodes in the national life of Israel. These distant predictions by the prophets almost always refer to the captivity, exile, return, restoration, and the Maccabean period. The predictive range of prophecy did not foresee Israel's future beyond these points. Needless to say, Theodore, in claiming that the prophets of Israel had predicted distant events, was misled by the eschatological and apocalyptic interpolations which were added to the genuine oracles of the prophets by some post-exilic anonymous annotators in order to counteract the depressing effect of the denunciations and doom contained in the prophetic oracles. After all, it would be unfair to expect from Theodore the critical accuracy of a twentieth-century critic.

## NOTES

1. For a full discussion of the problem, see C.H. Dodd, *According to the Scriptures* (London: Nisbet & Co., 1952), 126–138.

2. Cf. R.H. Pfeiffer, *Introduction to the Old Testament,* p. 5.

3. Mt 22:41–46; Mk 12:35–37; Lk 20:41–44. This psalm is often quoted, and the New Testament references leave no doubt as to its messianic character (Acts 2:34–35; 1 Cor 15:25; Eph 1:20; Col 3:1; Heb 1:13; 5:6; 6:20; 7:11, 17, 21; 10:12–13). This psalm, of course, has been subjected to many interpretations by modern critics; but most probably it was addressed to a king at his enthronement.

4. R.H. Pfeiffer, *Introduction,* 5–6.

5. Acts 2:22–36.

6. Tertullian, *Against Praxeas,* 11, Migne, PL (2), 167; Eusebius of Caesarea, *Demonstratio Evangelica,* I.4, Migne, PG (22), 41 AB; Athanasius, *Epist. ad Marcellinum,* Migne, PG (27), 37

C; Cyril of Jerusalem, *Catachesis Mystagogica,* IV, Migne, PG (33), 1101 B–1104 B. For a discussion of Jerome's stand on the subject, see J. Guillet, "Les Exegeses d'Alexandrie et d'Antioch. Conflit ou malentendue?" *Recherches de Science Religieuse,* XXXIV (1947), 281–283.

7. Alexander Kerrigan, *St. Cyril of Alexandria: Interpreter of the Old Testament* (Roma: Pontificio Instituto Biblico, 1952), 229–231.

8. *In Psalm.* 59 Migne, PL (36), 713.

9. Theodore's views on the authorship, purpose, and teaching of the book of Psalms have been discussed previously in this study.

10. *Psaumes,* 43: "The revealed grace of the Spirit led David to the contemplation of the future events, which was supplied with enormous amazement, and in the midst of this psalm he sent out the initial voice of admiration"; see also pp. 74, 194, 260, 282.

11. In his commentary Theodore recognized that the psalter comprised psalms of different types, and he even tried to classify them according to their subject matter along broad lines. The principal types which he detected in the psalter are: doctrinal psalms, hymns of praise, penitential psalms, exhortatory psalms, and prophetic psalms (*Psaumes,* 205–206).

12. R. Devreesse, *Essai sur Théodore,* 73.

13. Jn 2:17; it refers to Ps 69:10.

14. Rom 11:9; it refers to Ps 69:23.

15. Acts 1:20; it refers to Ps 69:26.

16. *Psaumes,* 454–455.

17. *Psaumes,* 121. In the narratives of the crucifixion, as they are preserved in the gospels, the inner correspondence between the sufferings of Jesus and those of the psalmist is noted in detail (cf. Mt 27:35; 27:43; Mk 15:29; Lk 23:34; Jn 19:23–24). Theodore, despite the gospel references to the psalm, claimed that the psalm is not a divine oracle addressed to the messiah but an historical psalm in which David means to describe his personal experience during Absalom's rebellion. Since we do not have Theodore's comments on the entire psalm, we do not know how he explained these verses which are quoted by the gospel writers.

18. *Psaumes,* 137–138: "Since the Lord has used this saying

while he was fixed on the cross, we note that the prophecy did not predict that, just as some had imagined so, but on the contrary toward the peril of suffering, he adapted these words through custom."

19. *Ibid.,* 248–249. Theodore advanced these thoughts in commenting upon Psalm 39:7–9 (H 40:7–9), which is quoted by the author of the epistle to the Hebrews (10:5–7). In Theodore's opinion this epistle is an authentic Pauline writing.

20. *Ibid.,* 85–86.

21. *Ibid.,* 85; 249; 276; 439.

22. *Ibid.,* 86.

23. K. Staab, *Pauluskommentare,* 117. The argument was advanced by Theodore in relation to Psalm 14:1–3, which is cited by Paul (Rom 3:10–12) in order to prove that "all have sinned, and fallen short of the glory of God."

24. *Psaumes,* 99–100; see also Migne, PG (66), 232 BC: 557 B.

25. *Psaumes,* 469–70.

26. We do not possess Theodore's commentary on Psalm 110, but there is evidence indicating that he understood it in a christological sense; on this subject see R. Devreesse, *Essai sur Théodore,* 77–78; E. Amann, "Un nouvel ouvrage de Théodore de Mopsueste," *Revue des Sciences Religieuses,* XX No. 3 (Septembre–Decembre 1940), 514.

27. Psalm 2 is interpreted messianically in Acts 4:25–26; 13:33; Heb 1:5; 5:5; Rev 2:27. It is notable, however, that apart from the cited New Testament quotations, the gospels do not refer to the psalm. Psalm 110 is quoted in Matthew 22:41–46; Mark 12:32–37; Luke 20:41–44; Acts 2:34–35; 5:31; 7:55; Hebrews 1:13; 7:11–21.

28. Mt 21:16; 1 Cor 15:25–28; Heb 2:6–8.

29. *Psaumes,* 44–46.

30. *Psaumes,* 277ff.

31. R. H. Pfeiffer, *Introduction,* 620.

32. In this Syriac version the superscription to Psalm 45 reads: "A writing for the sons of Korah contemporaries of Moses: an apparition of Christ and of the church, as well the glorious moral perfection of the Lord," *Revue des Sciences Religieuses,* XX (1940), 521 n.1.

33. *The Mission and Expansion of Christianity in the First Three Centuries,* trans. J. Moffatt (2nd ed. rev.; London: Williams and Norgate, 1908), I, 282.

34. Clement of Alexandria, *Strom.* 7:17 Migne, PG (9), 552 B; Cyril of Alexandria, *Commentarius in Isaiam,* Migne, PG (70), 656 A.

35. As an illustration of how impressive the argument from prophecy was we may cite a passage from the *Preaching of Peter* (a Christian writing of the early part of the second century), as quoted by Clement of Alexandria: "Having unrolled the books we possess, and in which the prophets named Christ Jesus partly through parables, partly through enigmas, partly authoritatively and literally, we found his advent as well as the death and the cross and all other punishments inflicted upon him by the Jews, and his resurrection and his ascension into heaven before the fall of Jerusalem. We found that what he was to suffer and what was to be after him was all written down. Learning all this, we believed in God by means of what had been written about him. For we have recognized that God has really ordained it, and we say nothing apart from scripture" (*Strom.,* 6:15, Migne, PG 9, 352 C–353 A).

36. *In Joan. Evang.,* 9:3.2, Migne, PL (35), 1459. Perhaps it should be stated here that Jerome too made several daring statements concerning the vision of the mysteries of Christ by the prophets of the Old Testament. For a detailed discussion, see J. Guillet, "Les exégéses d'Alexandrie et Antioche. Conflit ou malentendu?" *Recherches de Science Religieuse,* XXXIV, No. 3 (Juillet 1947), 281ff.

37. *In Oseam* (prologue), Migne, PG (66), 124 B; In *Amosi* (prologue), Migne, PG (66), 244 A.

38. *In Zachariae,* 9:9, Migne, PG (66), 556 D-557 D.

39. It would be interesting to repeat here that Theodore in his *Commentary on the Book of Psalms* had recognized direct predictions of Christ and had limited the number of psalms which he accepted to be directly predictions of the incarnation and the church to four (2; 8; 45; 110). Whether he changed his view on this subject we do not know, because in his extant writings the issue is not discussed.

40. A. Mingana (ed.), *Woodbrooke Studies,* Vol. V: *Commentary of Theodore of Mopsuestia on the Nicene Creed* (Cambridge: W. Heffer & Sons, Ltd., 1932), 27; see also *In Joelis,* 2:28, Migne, PG (66), 229 B; *In Zachariae,* 1:7–10, Migne, PG (66), 501 C-505 A.

41. *In Oseae,* 6:4–7, Migne, PG (66), 161 C.

42. *Commentary on the Nicene Creed,* 28.

43. *In Jonam* (prologue), Migne, PG (66), 317 C.

44. *Commentary on the Nicene Creed,* 25.

45. Theodore's theories and teaching in regard to Old Testament typology have already been considered.

46. The above statement refers to the following prophetic passages: Amos 1:11; Hosea 11:1; Micah 4:1–3; 5:1; Joel 2:28; Haggai 2:9; Zechariah 9:9; 11:12–14; 12:10; Malachi 1:11; 3:1; 4:5.

47. *In Joelis,* 2:28, Migne, PG (66), 229 B-233 B.

48. *In Zachariae,* 9:9, Migne, PG (66), 556 D-557 C.

49. The terms and expressions which Theodore used with greater frequency in setting forth his interpretation of the messianic proof-texts are the following: a. ecbasis which means "the issue of a matter" (its root idea [*ecbainein*] denotes "to go out," "to come to pass" or "the issue of an event"; cf. Liddell & Scott, *A Greek-English Lexicon*); b. *peras* which derives from the verb *perao* (to bring to an end, to finish), while the noun has the following meanings: the end, an object, the perfection of a thing. The following expression bears ample witness to the author's careful language which guided him while he interpreted the messianic text: "But the perfection of what has been stated in the utterance has received its true issue in Lord Christ" (Migne, PG [66], 372 C). Similar expressions and statements came from Theodore's pen while he was dealing with Amos 9:11; Joel 2:28; Zechariah 9:9; Malachi 3:1.

50. Migne, PG (66), 189 BC. Perhaps it is pertinent to state that in dealing with such traditionally accepted texts as Zechariah 11:12–14 and 12:10, Theodore not only refused their messianic nature but also he did not bother to mention that both passages are quoted respectively in Matthew 27:9–10 and John 19:37 as messianic testimonies realized in the life of Jesus (cf. Migne, PG

66, 576 C–577 B; 584 BC). Zechariah 11:12–14 is quoted in Matthew 27:9 as a prophecy by Jeremiah. According to Theodore both oracles describe the hardships and rivalries of the Maccabean leaders in their struggle against the Macedonian rulers and their Judaean sympathizers.

51. In the kerygmatic passages of the Acts of the Apostles, Psalm 16:10 is cited twice (2:25–28; 13:34–37) as a testimony of the Old Testament establishing the messiahship of the risen Christ.

52. Migne, PG (66), 232 A–233 B. J.N.D. Kelly offers a different explanation apropos of this passage from Theodore: "Yet Theodore was prepared to concede that some Psalms (e.g. 16:10) and prophecies (e.g. Joel 2:28), although not messianic if taken literally, could legitimately be interpreted as such in so far as they were types which reached their true fulfillment in the Christian revelation" (cf. *Early Christian Doctrines,* 77–78). Louis Pirot (*L'oeuvre exégétique,* 261–262) holds a similar opinion. We respond only by recalling that neither the word "type" nor the word "to fulfill" is used by Theodore in his comments on the oracle.

53. Migne, PG (66), 244 D.

54. *Ibid.,* 241 A–245 D.

55. Migne, PG (66), 301 D–304 A.

56. Migne, PG (66), 345 B.

57. *Ibid.,* 372 A–375 B. After stating that Micah's ministry took place in the days of Jotham, Ahaz and Hezekiah, Theodore's subsequent contention that Micah 5:1–4 refers to the return from the Babylonian captivity might seem absurd, but let us keep in mind that the patristic notion of prophecy seemed to be one of predicting the future. This conception of prophecy is shared by some conservative scholars. Numerous scholars are certain that Micah in 5:1–4 prophesied the coming of the messianic king; cf. E.J. Young, *An Introduction to the Old Testament* (Grand Rapids, Mich.: Wm. B. Eerdmans, 1958), 282–285.

58. Migne, PG (66), 372 C.

59. *Ibid.,* 493 D–497 A.

60. George A. Smith, *The Book of the Twelve Prophets* (4th ed.

rev.; New York: A. C. Armstrong & Son, 1900), II, 450–454; E.J. Young, *op. cit.,* 295.
61. Migne, PG (66), 496D.
62. Migne, PG (66), 556 BC.
63. *Ibid.,* 556 D.
64. Migne, PG (66), 557 BC.
65. *Ibid.,* 557 D.
66. *Ibid.,* 559 A. Johann P. Lange, a conservative scholar of the middle part of the last century, in his composite commentary on the book of Zechariah in giving the history of the interpretation of Zechariah 9:9 erroneously stated: "Among Christians the reference to Christ was uniform until the time of Hugo Grotius (1583–1645), who asserted that its first and literal application was to Zerubbabel, but that in a higher sense it referred to our Saviour. This view excited universal displeasure, and called forth a host of replies, the first of which was written by Bochart" (J.P. Lange, *A Commentary on the Holy Scriptures,* Vol. XIV: *Haggai, Zechariah, Malachi,* edit. by Philip Schaff [Grand Rapids, Mich.: Zondervan Publishing House, n.d.], 71).
67. Migne, PG (66), 629 D.
68. *Ibid.,* 597 AB.
69. *Ibid.,* 605 BC.
70. *Ibid.,* 620 D; 624 B.
71. Mal 2:17 (LXX reading); Migne, PG (66), 617 D–620 A.
72. *Ibid.,* 620 AB.
73. *Ibid.,* 632 BC. Jewish scribal speculation was much interested in trying to determine when the messianic era would come (Mt 17:10; Mk 9:11–13); and the words of Malachi (3:1; 4:5) and Ben Sira (Sir 48:10f) had given rise to the popular view that the messianic era was to be initiated by the precursor of the messiah who was Elijah, the angel of the covenant of Malachi. This common belief has been universally held by the Jews (cf. Justin, *Dialogus cum Tryphone,* Migne, PG [6], 581 B-584 C; Cecil Roth [ed.], *The Standard Jewish Encyclopedia,* 614–616). In this interpretation, the Jews have been countenanced by the majority of the patristic commentators, such as Origen, Tertullian, Chrysostom, Jerome, Augustine, and Theodoret; the fathers held that there are two Elijahs in prophecy, one, John the Baptist, and the

other, Elijah in person, who was to reappear to convert the Jews and prepare the way for the second advent of Jesus Christ. The fathers based their interpretations on Matthew 17:9–13, Mark 9:11–12, and Revelation 11:1ff.

74. Migne, PG (66), 620 C.

75. Mt 11:10, 17:10–13; Mk 1:2, 9:11–13; Lk 7:27.

76. Jn 1:23.

# Chapter Seven

# CONCLUSIONS

The primary purpose of this study has been to examine Theodore's critical methods in Old Testament study and evaluate them in the light of modern methods of scriptural study.

Theodore of Mopsuestia belongs at once to the history of Christian theology and to the history of biblical criticism. Our interest, however, is in the biblical rather than the theological field. Theodore spent his whole life in teaching and writing during one of the most intensely dramatic periods in the history of the church at Antioch. According to the testimony of the patristic sources, he wrote commentaries on nearly all the books of the Bible, and he was called by those who appreciated the outstanding quality of his exegesis the interpreter *par excellence.* Considering the large number of biblical commentaries Theodore wrote, surprisingly few have come down to us, mainly due to the fact that the bishop of Mopsuestia was associated posthumously with Nestorianism.

The *coup de grâce,* however, against the literary work of the Mopsuestian was dealt by the Fifth General Council (553) which consigned Theodore's person to perpetual anathema and condemned his writings in toto.

As we have noted earlier, in the New Testament field only Theodore's commentaries on the gospel of John and on the minor epistles of Paul survive, the former in a Syriac version and the latter in a Latin translation. Only two of his Old Testament commentaries have survived, those dealing with the minor prophets and the book of Psalms. However, our task has been facilitated by a large number of fragments of Theodore's commentaries which have been recovered in the last decades from manuscripts preserved in the libraries of western Europe. In addition to these new sources, the discovery by Alphonse Mingana in 1932 of Theodore's *Catechetical Homilies* in a Syriac version must be mentioned, as these homilies have contributed significantly to a better understanding of Theodore's teaching about the religion of the Hebrew prophets. Last of all, we mention our great indebtedness to the Nestorian commentator of the ninth century, Isho'dad of Merv. He was not an original thinker but his writings are packed with quotations from earlier exegetes, especially from the commentaries of the Mopsuestian. Theodore of Mopsuestia was for this Syriac author the *Mephasqana* (interpreter).

Owing to the fact that Theodore's commentaries on the major books of the Old Testament, which were written during the more mature stages of his scholarship, have been lost, it has been impossible to determine adequately the depth and dimensions of the biblical system of the Antiochian exegete. It has thus been impossible to restore a complete picture of Theodore's biblical scholarship. This fact is an important qualification of our study. And yet significant exegetical data suggest that Theodore was a precursor of biblical criticism. In some of his views, Theodore often sounds like a nineteenth or twentieth century critic. In some instances he anticipated in primitive and general ways the broad lines of contemporary critical biblical scholarship.

Like all patristic commentators Theodore was a man of his age. Like other fathers, he was not complete, consistent, or unified. In his biblical system there are views and elements which he inherited from the Christian theology of his time and which we today have largely abandoned. For example, unquestioning acceptance of miracles and a rigorous holding to the idea of biblical inerrancy played important roles in his interpretation of the Bible. He also subscribed, in his earlier works, to the traditional doctrine of plenary and verbal inspiration according to which revelation was dictated to the inspired author by the Spirit of God in mechanical and propositional form and sense.

But in spite of these views, Theodore's differences from his age stand out against his likenesses to it. Modifications and improvements were made by him with a view to satisfying his own critical leanings or the demands of his intellectual growth in the study of the Bible. The Mopsuestian started in his early commentaries with a strong notion of inspiration; indeed he sometimes stressed the divine and miraculous element to such an extent that he obliterated the human factor in revelation. However, in his later works Theodore showed more flexibility in his understanding of biblical inspiration. He gave such prominence to the human factor that inspiration later appeared to him to be a collaboration between the Spirit of God and man. Prophetic inspiration, Theodore asserted, is the result of a psychological state which the prophet experiences in a direct confrontation with the deity at a particular time and place in history. It was especially in his New Testament commentaries that Theodore attempted to break with the plenary view of verbal inspiration. In explaining how the gospel writers composed their accounts of Jesus' public ministry, Theodore explicitly stated that the evangelists drew on their own memories and each one assumed full responsibility for his gospel narrative. In Theodore's commentaries on Pauline letters the autonomy of Paul was so carefully safeguarded that there seems to have been only limited room for divine intervention.

In his interpretation of psalms, Theodore presents to the modern reader a real dichotomy between fidelity to his Christian tradition and his critical propensity. He contended, under the manifold influences of the New Testament, that the content of David's psalter was far deeper than Jewish biblical authorities had suspected. On the other hand, he recognized that the Hebrew psalter comprises psalms of various literary types, and he even attempted to classify them under certain categories, according to their diversified religious moods and content. Among the types of psalms he detected are hymns of praise, doctrinal psalms, prayers of penitence, congregational laments, songs of thanksgiving, exhortatory psalms, and prophetic psalms.

In view of the tremendous advances which have been made in the field of biblical literature and exegesis in modern times, it would admittedly be most unfair to pass a value judgment on Theodore's Old Testament work according to modern standards of biblical interpretation. This is a field in which research methods and tools have changed radically. In view of this fact, it would also be a mistake to review Theodore's writings on the Old Testament with any expectation that the outstanding representative of the Antiochian school of theology could offer to the modern student original suggestions contributing to the elucidation of Hebrew history and biblical exegesis. The overriding issue, however, is to determine Theodore's place in the history of the critical interpretation of the Old Testament by stating conclusions from this study which give us reason to accept the Mopsuestian, along with Origen (185–254), Jerome (342–420), Ibn Ezra (1088–1167), and Baruch Spinoza (1632–1677), as an antecedent of the modern era of criticism.

1. In Theodore's interpretation of the Bible there is remarkable freedom for research with strikingly few dogmatic preconceptions. Theodore's time was not conducive to a critical attitude toward the Bible. And yet, Theodore, following in the footsteps of his teacher Diodore, made a strong and fearless plea for independent and critical interpretation free from encumbering official tradition, Jewish or Christian. He maintained that such interpretation should be based largely on internal evidence from the text.

2. While Theodore praised the Nicean fathers for their creedal efforts concerning questions of faith, nevertheless he taught that the interpretation of the Bible should not be subordinated to the consensus of the fathers because the patristic authorities confronted the texts with preconceptions, arbitrariness, and subtleties. His criticism was particularly strong against allegorists and *official* biblical tradition, so far as it then existed. In thus doing, he cleared away the old structure of allegory and the tyranny of theological preconceptions, and proceeded to lay a new foundation, the so-called historical and literal interpretation of the Bible.

3. Theodore refused to accept the view uncritically that the two Testaments form but one single, saving covenant, given by one God by means of one Lord. He was courageous enough to teach that the Old Testament is not one single book but many, coming from different periods of history, and exhibiting diverse spirits and teachings. The teaching of Christ and the apostles, in

his opinion, is not identical with that of the Old Testament but essentially harmonious with it. This harmony, however, was confined to the teaching of the law, the psalms, and the prophets because these three groups of writings owed their origin to the initiative of God's Spirit.

4. Theodore's scientific method is best seen in his literary and historical criticism of the Hebrew canon. He was practically the only one among early Christian scholars, not excluding even Jerome, who restricted canonicity to the Palestinian Jewish Old Testament. His acquaintance with Maccabean history was quite thorough but he considered 1 and 2 Maccabees to be extra-biblical sources. He also treated problems of biblical introduction in his commentaries and elsewhere with considerable freedom. He rejected, for example, the superscriptions of the psalms, regarding them as no part of the original text and as having little significance for interpretation. He referred seventeen psalms to Maccabean times. Theodore's critical judgment placed the book of Job at the beginning of the post-exilic era; he held that it had been written by an anonymous Jewish poet, that Job was an Edomite, and that his undeserved sufferings had become a folktale among the people of the near east. He concluded, amazingly, that Job's story in its oral version was very ancient, and that the book as it stands is not history but fiction, the product of an imaginative writer who was well versed in poetry and religion. He regarded the wild behemoth of Job as a purely mythological animal. Theodore considered the Song of Songs to be an erotic epithalamium which was written on the occasion of Solomon's wedding to Pharaoh's daughter, and expressed astonishment that such a secular book, in which God's name is not mentioned, could be included in the Hebrew and Christian canons. Theodore referred Proverbs and Ecclesiastes to the Solomonic era and regarded both as being of purely human origin. There was in his judgment little if any divine inspiration involved in the writing of the Hebrew wisdom books.

5. Because of his ignorance of the Hebrew language, Theodore was forced to rely on the Septuagint, the official Old Testament of the Greek church. His information concerning the origin

of the Septuagint appears to rest on the pseudepigraphic letter of Aristeas, although Theodore never mentions it by name. However, the legends and miracle stories with which the history of the translation was embellished by Philo and some of the fathers were not accepted by Theodore. On the contrary, he emphatically stated that the translation was achieved by men of sound scholarship without the intervention of any divine agency. He appreciated the fact that this version for years declared the ideals of Hebrew monotheism to the Gentile world even though the Gentile world persisted in idolatry. He held that it was by the practice of the apostles that this version was introduced into the Apostolic church. Furthermore, he compared the Septuagint text with those of Aquila, Symmachus, and Theodotion, in order to obtain a better textual reading for his interpretation.

6. In his teaching about the phenomena involved in a prophetic call and prophetic inspiration Theodore expounded careful views. His interpretation is highly appreciative of the psychological aspects of the phenomenon of prophecy. In his opinion all the prophets of Israel were ecstatic personalities, and this state of mind resulted from their certainty that they clearly stood in a personal relationship with the living God. Prophecy was not open to any man of good will; it was not a vocation which could be mastered through the medium of a sacrament; it was not even a hereditary office.

Prophecy, in Theodore's judgment, was independent of any particular state of life because it originated from a positive action of God's Spirit without the influence of a religious institution. And he who has been the object of that divine action can only point to a call that emanated freely from the will of God. It was the irresistible command of the deity experienced by the prophet in the midst of a terrifying theophany that consecrated him to the prophetic ministry. From the moment of this charismatic experience these men were prophets, although they were not constantly under the influence of the prophetic inspiration. The prophets spoke whenever they felt the presence of God's Spirit. Typically oral preaching preceded the writing of the prophetic oracles. Prophetic inspiration is not a mechanical communication of truths dictated in Hebrew or Aramaic but an experience known during an ecstatic state in which the prophet witnessed in his inner soul unutterable and terrifying things. And when the terrifying experiences receded into the background the prophet spoke the words of God in his own human idiom.

7. In defining both the nature of prophecy and the legitimate spheres of prophetic activity, Theodore represented another remarkable point of contact with contemporary conceptions of prophecy. The Mopsuestian showed only a very nominal interest in theories about prophecy as long-range prediction. In most emphatic terms he taught that most of the prophets of Israel seemed to be proclaiming oracles the resolution of which appeared to be near at hand. Most oracles were given in partic- ular historical settings, and in primary meaning and reference had to do with events contemporaneous with the prophet or the immediate future.

Theodore held that the primary meaning of each prophetic oracle is to be found in determining the historico-grammatical sense of the revelation and must proceed from the whole context of both. To him each oracle has only one meaning and applica- tion, be this of the letter simple and plain, or of the letter which is intonated in hyperbolical terms. However, it must be conceded that Theodore as a man of his own age could not escape entirely from the traditional view which regarded prophecy as prediction. Prophecy is predictive in the sense that it not only points to the outcome of events contemporaneous with the prophet's present or immediate future, but it also predicts forthcoming episodes in the national life of Israel. These distant predictions by the proph- ets, according to Theodore, almost always refer to the captivity, exile, return, restoration, and the Maccabean period. The predic- tive range of prophecy did not foresee Israel's future beyond these points. In reality the oracles which Theodore accepted as predictions of the future, resulting from a certain historical con- text, are the very same oracles which modern critics have termed eschatological and apocalyptic interpolations which were added to the genuine oracles of the prophets by some post-exilic anon- ymous annotators in order to counteract the depressing effect of the denunciations and doom contained in the prophetic oracles.

8. The concept of "fulfillment" and the messianic interpretation of the prophets and psalms was securely established in the theological and exegetical system of the early Christian thinkers but a vigorous reaction against this sort of interpretation is evident in the writings of Theodore. Dealing with the so-called "messianic proof-texts" Theodore maintained that the isolated passages quoted from the Old Testament by the New Testament writers with a messianic connotation were not originally messianic predictions which found their exact fulfillment in the person and work of Jesus the messiah, but free and coherent accommodations of the original texts to analogous settings in the Christian revelation. The Old Testament texts, he held, lent themselves to this use because of their "hyperbolical" imagery and blessings, rich metaphorical meaning, and phraseological symbolism. The doctrinal viewpoints of the New Testament authors are interpreted by categories derived from the Hebrew Bible. He held that the Old Testament quotations in the New Testament serve the lines of thought of the apostles and evangelists. Strictly speaking, however, Old Testament prophecy in Theodore's judgment is not predictive of Christ and (although elsewhere he held that a few psalms do contain such predictions) contains no messianic element. Theodore did not press this conclusion very far. His denial of messianic elements in Old Testament prophecy did not prevent him from holding the belief that the psalter comprises "some special psalms" which he accepted to be predictive of the incarnation and the church; as we have noted these were Psalms 2, 8, 45, and 110. The grounds for this conclusion are not to be found. Evidently, he discussed the problem in his introduction to the commentary, and that introduction unfortunately has been lost. There is, however, evidence for assuming that the Mopsuestian corrected his view about these psalms because in one of his latest works Theodore is reported to have said: "The words of the New Testament concerning Christ are found in the prophets as a sign and symbol." Theodore's final verdict was that the Old Testament taken on its own terms does not present Christ to us; it rather prepares the way for Jesus the messiah.

9. Theodore was a declared trinitarian who fought against all unitarian movements. His belief in the lordship of Christ was

absolute. Yet he refused to confess Christ as Lord of both Testaments because this would substitute the ethical monotheism of the Old Testament for a new kind of monotheism based on an over-simplified Christomonism. The Mopsuestian was more than convinced that the Old Testament is the record which registers the initial dealings of God with his chosen people of Israel before he "spoke at the end of these days unto us in his Son."

10. In Theodore's theology of the Bible there is a real conception of progressive revelation. He stated explicitly that the Son-Logos and the Holy Ghost as independent persons and *hypostases* of the Trinity were never revealed in the Old Testament. The doctrine of the resurrection of the dead as such is rarely mentioned in the Old Testament where the notion of sheol prevails generally. He also held that the Hebrew prophets were teachers of monotheism, progressive revealers of God's true character, and preachers of increasingly perfected religious knowledge.

11. Theodore, as the chief theoretician of the Antiochian school of theology, must be credited with having been the first Christian commentator to have explicitly taken into consideration all figures of biblical speech—parabolical, metaphorical, figurative, numerical. He held that these figures in any text, taken together, should produce one clear, primary interpretation of meaning. Multiple meanings in one biblical text were, in Theodore's judgment, absurd. Allegorical interpretation he held to be mythological. No one has the right to risk reading into the faith of Israel more than is actually there. The task of interpreter is to discern the meaning of each text by proceeding from the historical, literal, and conceptual context. The historico-grammatical sense, rightly understood, he held, provides the fullest meaning of the text. Given this methodology, Theodore's greatest weakness as an expounder of the Old Testament was his inability to undertake serious textual criticism because of his ignorance of the Hebrew language.

12. In Theodore's exegetical system typological interpretation is almost completely absent. There is only one clear exception in his extant writings. When Theodore was writing his commentary on the book of Jonah he found an opportunity to set

forth his theory concerning Old Testament typology. In his view typology is not an interpretation of texts from the two Testaments having an inner and mystical correspondence with each other, but merely an external comparison of events in the two Testaments based on their outward resemblances and similarities. A typology, he concluded, must always be sustained by a New Testament proof-text.

13. Much of Theodore's critical method has been suppressed for centuries by a conservative spirit in orthodox Christianity. The critical spirit exemplified by Theodore has been revived and extended in the post-reformation era and in our times.

In these days when the ecumenical dialogue within the World Council of Churches is becoming a pan-Christian endeavor and experience, biblical differences which actually exist among the various churches, especially with regard to their respective approaches to the study of the Bible, are bound to be raised up for serious consideration. Biblical issues ought to be discussed in the light of all great Christian traditions and of schools of thought within Christendom which have made contributions through the centuries. As this happens the contribution of the Antiochian tradition to ecumenical biblical study, especially as seen in the work of Theodore, should prove constructive and reconciling.

# Appendix One

# ANCIENT ANTIOCH AS A POLITICAL AND CULTURAL CENTER

Theodore of Mopsuestia was born in A.D. 350 in Antioch on the Orontes and lived there until 392 when he became a bishop in Cilicia. Antioch was a center of Hellenism with no dominant semitic elements. Damascus, the ancient capital of Syria, was overshadowed by Antioch during the Seleucid, Roman and Byzantine ages. The founding of Antioch in 300 B.C. by Seleucus I Nicator was a typical project in the mass production of new cities which took place under Alexander and the Diadochi.[1]

Archaeological remains from the stone age have been found in the neighborhood. Recent excavations on the site of ancient Antioch have not brought to light any evidence of semitic or Persian settlements prior to the Macedonian founding of the city.[2] As in the case of other sites in the area, the cuneiform texts we possess furnish virtually no evidence of any Aramean settlement in the region of Antioch except for a reference to the Orontes which was called Arantu by the Assyrians.[3] Like Alexandria, Antioch was a new city and the permanent capital of the Seleucid kingdom. The Macedonian conquerors established it for monarchic considerations, as a fitting geographical position for a kingdom which ruled Asia Minor, the region of the Euphrates, Coele-Syria and the Eastern Mediterranean. It grew under successive Seleucid monarchs until it became the chief center of the east. As a center of culture, Antioch was surpassed only by Rome and Alexandria, and later by Constantinople. It was often referred to as Antioch the great.

When the Romans came to Syria in 64 B.C., Antioch became the central seat for their civil and military control of the Asiatic provinces. All Syria was incorporated under one title, *Provincia Syria,* with Antioch as the capital, and it was placed under the direct rule of a proconsul with power to levy troops and engage in war.[4] (Judea was left a subject state within the framework of the new province under the Roman legates of Syria.) Owing to its position as the administrative center of a frontier province bordering on Parthia, Rome's most dangerous foe, Antioch was naturally of particular interest to emperors, both as the strategic military and as the cultural focus of Syria. Here the emperors resided when they were campaigning in the east. Many of them carried out projects which further adorned the already famous city. Serious efforts were made by Pompey, Caesar, Anthony, Trajan and Hadrian to enlarge the city of Antioch and to restore it to the position of prestige that it had enjoyed under the Macedonians.[5] All the outstanding emperors of later times contributed to the bountification of Antioch as well as its famous suburb Daphne. The Christian emperors, too, were eager to beautify Antioch. As a consequence the city became the second imperial center of the Roman empire until the establishment of Constantinople as the eastern capital.

The original settlers of Antioch were brought from various locations in Greece. Among the original inhabitants were Macedonians, Argives, Cretans, Cypriots and Athenians. Theodore's teacher, Libanius, proudly informs us about the population of Antioch:

Let a man consider our nobility of birth, and remark that the best elements in any place have come together here as though to some land chosen by the gods to hold man worthy of admiration. We alone have origins which have brought together what is admired in each race—the antiquity of the Argives, the Cretan respect for law, a royal race from Cyprus, and the line of Heracles. As for those whom we receive from Athens and all the other Greek breeds with which we have been blended, the tale will be told when we come to those times.[6]

The nucleus of the population in the early Seleucid era consisted of colonists who had been established in the new city by royal decree. The colonists were primarily soldiers and mercenaries. To the colonial population were soon added throngs of civilians who were attracted by hopes of commercial advantage or driven from their old homes by political change and came seeking fortunes in the new capital of the Orient. The last Greek immigrants into Antioch, of whom we are informed, were those brought in by Antiochus the Great. According to Libanius, Antiochus, after his defeat at Magnesia at the hand of Lucius Scipio (190 B.C.), brought in Hellenic stock, Aetolians, Cretans and Euboeans.[7] Perhaps the growth of Roman power in Asia Minor had compelled a considerable number of Hellenes to leave their cities, now under Roman dominion, and to seek out a city still free from imperial power.

Thus, in its ethnic composition, Antioch, in the Seleucid era, was a typical Greek city built according to the policy instituted by Alexander.[8] The founders of the city populated the site with strategic care; they settled Macedonians and Greeks to insure the security of the new regime; and they provided a constitution which had as its basis not the tribal system, but the urban community, the typical practice in Greek city-states.

It is interesting to note that the population seems to have included a major Oriental element during all periods of the history of Antioch. The indigenous Syrians were not included in the city-state.[9] In time, however, native Syrians, who had accepted Hellenism as a way of life, were added to the colonial settlers, and this assimilation contributed to the ease with which the Greco-Syrian synthesis was accomplished.

In addition there were many Jews at Antioch though they cannot be compared with those of Mesopotamia or Egypt in antiquity, nor can the Jewish community of Antioch be compared with those of Alexandria and Rome in size.[10] Antiochian Jewry goes back to the days of Seleucus I Nikator. Some of the Jews, according to Josephus, participated in the military expeditions of the Seleucid kings.[11] We do not know what the size of the community was during this early period, but the references to Antioch in the Palestinian Talmud and Tosephta indicate that the Jewish community at Antioch increased in number almost continuously, and especially in the early years of the Roman period.[12] This is suggested by the phrase "as large as Antioch" which appears in a number of *baraithas*. At a later period, probably after the destruction of the second temple in A.D. 70, a synagogue, *Knesheth Hasmunith,* existed; it was named for the mother of the seven Maccabean martyrs who were executed, according to the apocryphal 2 Maccabees, by the order of Antiochus IV Epiphanes for refusal to abandon their religion.[13] In the early fourth century A.D., the Jewish community flourished and there were no fewer than three synagogues in or near Antioch, one in the city proper, one at Daphne, and one east of the city in the plain of Antioch.[14]

Though the Romans did not plant a colony in Antioch, the city did include a great number of Roman civil servants, officers, veterans, contractors and businessmen many of whom already knew Greek and could communicate with the natives and other ethnic groups through that tongue. The Caesars instituted a comprehensive building program at Antioch in attempts to enhance Roman prestige and to introduce the Roman way of living into the Hellenized Orient. But Hellenistic life with its characteristic traditions continued much as before. When the Empress Eudocia, the daughter of a pagan professor at Athens, visited the city in 438, she delivered an encomium of Antioch before the local senate, and in the closing paragraph of her address she complimented the Antiochenes by paraphrasing a line of Homer: "Of your lineage and race I declare myself to be."[15] Obviously she thus alluded to the fact that her own Athenian origin united her racially with the ancestors of the people of Antioch. The courtesy was warmly received and the senate of Antioch voted a bronze statue of the empress to be set up in the *bouleuterion* in which she had delivered her address, and another bronze statue of her outside the museum.[16]

The population of Antioch in the fourth century cannot be determined exactly for lack of evidence. In the time of Bishop

Ignatius, who was martyred in A.D. 115, there were, according to Chrysostom, twenty myriads of inhabitants.[17] Concerning his own time, Chrysostom spoke of 100,000 Orthodox Christians alone.[18] On the other hand, the Antiochian chronicler, John Malalas (d. ca. 577), reports that in the earthquake of the year 551 approximately 250,000 people perished in one day.[19] Malalas was never exact in giving numbers. If one takes as a basis Chrysostom's numerical estimate of Orthodox Christians and adds the Arians, semi-Arians, Apollinarists, and other Christian sects, then, including the Graeco-Syrian pagans and Jews, one might arrive at a total of fewer than half a million people, probably little more than 300,000.[20]

The general picture of Antioch in the fourth century must have been strikingly brilliant. Our sources for the cultural, social, economic, and political life of this time in the Syrian capital are abundant. They are largely the writings of native sons who rose to fame and distinction, men like Libanius, Ammianus Marcellinus, Diodore of Tarsus, John Chrysostom, and Theodore of Mopsuestia.

The fourth century was a period of prosperity and creativity, and Antioch, by virtue of its connections with most of the known world, was destined to become a focal point for the collection and diffusion of ideas. Both our earlier sources and the great discoveries made during the excavations between 1932 and 1939 show that Antioch, in the century with which we are concerned, was a leading academic center.[21] A number of factors contributed to the distinction of the city as a center of the ancient world: wide commercial activities especially after the overthrow of Palmyra (A.D. 273); large artistic and technical workshops;[22] intense intellectual and social life; several schools of Greek classicism with students coming from all places;[23] and finally the rapid development of Christianity and the controversies which ensued, both between antagonistic sects and between believers and pagan sophists.

The Syrian capital was also famous for its theatrical performances and Olympic games which drew visitors from all over the Roman world. On the paved and colonnaded streets of the city moved a multitude of gay and pleasure-loving people. Besides the Greeks and Syrians one could see there the togas of the Romans, the turbans of the proud Persians, the shrewd Armenian tradesmen, the militant Scythians, Hindus, Arabians and Jews.[24] This mingling of nationalities made Antioch a city of notable cosmopolitanism with an international character comparable to that of Alexandria. Libanius conveyed some sense of this quality when he asked: "In what land or sea has the fame of this city not entered?"[25] He continued his encomium with the remark, "Attractions of all kinds bring people from all sides, from Africa, Europe, Asia, from the Islands, from the mainland."[26]

Religious activities in such a great city were varied. At the time of Emperor Julian's visit the ancient Phoenician fertility rites to Adonis were celebrated.[27] The local temples, altars, shrines and festivals were mainly dedicated to Zeus, Tyche, Apollo, Demeter, Hermes and Muses. Greeks and Romans were hospitable to Oriental deities, and a few such foreign gods had gained admission into Greece and Rome.[28] During the Hellenistic age increased contacts between east and west tended to blend together the Greek and Oriental religions.[29] This fusion of religions, which is called by modern scholars "religious syncretism," identified Oriental deities with Greek gods. Presumably, this process of syncretism could best explain why Syrian deities, aside from those of the Tammuz-Adonis cult, do not figure prominently in the writings of the Antiochene authors.

The old Greek religion, with its cults and practices, persisted for a long time, and their most obstinate adherents and champions were chiefly the rhetoricians of Antioch. The rhetoricians clung with almost fanatical zeal to the gods and goddesses of their classical Pantheon. There were also many influential pagans, especially among the state and army officers. But as a whole the religion of the Olympian gods was declining after Constantine, and especially after the Edict of Milan (A.D. 313) which declared Christianity a legal religion. The last battle for survival of Olympian religion was launched by Julian the Apostate (361-363) at Antioch. After Julian's failure no one could any longer hope for the revival of Greek religion. It came to its end with the edicts of Theodosius I (379-395) which repressed paganism and closed its temples throughout the Roman empire. Nonetheless, the people of Antioch retained the same fondness for classical Greek studies, Greek theatrical performances, and Olympic games.[30]

Throughout these changes the Jewish community of Antioch flourished in the fourth century. The Jewish population was large and influential; several Jews practiced medicine, and others were engaged in merchandising and finance.[31] The relationship between Antiochian and Palestinian Jewry was very close. We have a record of attempts by rabbis to identify the city of Antioch with places mentioned in the Old Testament, such as Hamath and Riblah.[32] Jewish rites retained a curious attraction for some Christians, especially women, and they would visit synagogues on the sabbath of festival days.[33] The relics of the Maccabean martyrs, preserved in a synagogue in Antioch, were thought to have miraculous powers and attracted the attention of many Christians. The local church authorities in their mounting intolerance toward the Jewish influence on the Christians solved the problem by taking over the synagogue where the relics of the martyrs were preserved and turning it into a Christian church.[34] The effect of this Jewish cult on the Christians was so strong that eventually the Maccabean martyrs were accepted by the church of Antioch on a par with Christian saints and martyrs and later were placed in the records of Christian martyrological literature.[35]

In the time of Emperor Constantine, Antioch reached its zenith as an educational center; from this period came most of the records which suggest Antioch's contribution to the evolution of the post-classical Graeco-Roman culture. A distinguished group of pagan and Christian writers elevated the Syrian capital to a center of both classical and Christian *paideia*. Like Tarsus and Alexandria, the city of Antioch became a famous academic seat of sophists and rhetoricians. There were also grammarians and lawyers. Together these learned men constituted the University of Antioch.[36]

The head of this institution was Libanius, the successor of such famous teachers as the sophist Ulpian, a leading lawyer in Antioch; his pupil, Prohaeresius; and Zenobius who had been Libanius' teacher. Higher education was in the hands of rhetoricians, and Libanius, the leading rhetorician, was in charge of matters pertaining to teachers, curriculum and schools. Around this sophist of Antioch a regular university system was organized with classes and courses extending over the winter and spring months. The principal subject was the Greek classics. Rhetoric, logic and philosophy were emphasized, as were Latin and Roman law. We have no evidence that there was an established chair for Syriac, the popular language of the country, freely spoken not only in the hinterland but also in the streets of the city of Antioch.[37]

Intimate relationships existed during this period between Greek *paedeia* and Christian families. Not only did the sons of the pagan nobility study in the school of Libanius, but also many future theologians attended university classes in order to receive a classical education. The initial step in this process had been taken at Alexandria by Clement and Origen, and was then continued by the three Cappadocians, Basil of Caesarea, Gregory of Nazianzus, and Gregory of Nyssa.[38] In Antioch, too, several promising young men, who were born in Christian families and were destined to become the future leaders of the church, were studying classical culture in the pagan institution run by Libanius. Socrates, the ancient church historian, tells us that Theodore of Antioch, later to be called Theodore of Mopsuestia, and John, the future patriarch of Constantinople, had Libanius as their teacher in oratory.[39]

In addition to the school of sophistry, Antioch could boast of a Christian theological school. Among its famous biblical scholars and theologians were personalities who have exercised a lasting influence on the history and development of Christian doctrine. The Antiochene fathers, as the modern scholars prefer to call them, were doctors of the church who brought profound erudition to the new faith and its institutions.

## NOTES

1. Richard E. Wycherly, *How the Greeks Built Cities* (London: Macmillan, 1949), 35.

2. Glanville Downey, *A History of Antioch in Syria from Seleucus to the Arab Conquest* (Princeton: Princeton University Press, 1961), 46.

3. James B. Pritchard, *Ancient Near Eastern Texts Related to*

*the Old Testament* (Princeton, N.J.: Princeton University Press, 1955), 246, 276, 277, 279. The original names of the river, however, are given by various ancient historians as Typhon, Drakon or Orphites. The ancient historian of Antioch, Ioannes Malalas, in his *Chronographia* states that Tiberius changed the name of the river that flowed past Antioch from Drakon to Orontes which, according to Malalas, means "eastern" in Latin (cf. *Chronographia in Church Slavonic Version,* trans. M. Spinka [Chicago: University of Chicago Press, 1940], 45). In the light of the Assyrian documents, it would appear that all these early names, which were given to the river by the Greek authors, suggest aetiological legends which were devised for the purpose of casting glory on the origin of Antioch.

4. Joseph, *Antiq.* xiv, 4.4; Josephus reports that Vitellius, the proconsul of Syria, dismissed Pontius Pilate who was in reality procurator of Judea (A.D. 24–37) for his cruel treatment of the Samaritans (*Antiq.,* xvii, 4.1, 2).

5. Chrysostomus Baur, *John Chrysostom and His Time,* trans. M. Gonzaga (Westminster: The Newman Press, 1959) Vol. I, 34-35.

6. *Orat.* 11.57: this English translation from the Greek has been made by Glanville Downey in "Antiochikos," *Proceedings of the American Philosophical Society,* 103, (1959), 652-686.

7. Glanville Downey, *A History of Antioch in Syria,* 92.

8. Theodore Mommsen, *Provinces of the Roman Empire,* trans. W.P. Dickson (New York: Charles Scribner's Sons, 1887), 131.

9. Glanville Downey, *op. cit.,* 80.

10. Carl H. Kraeling, "The Jewish Community at Antioch," *The Journal of Bibilical Literature,* LI, Part II (June 1932), 130ff.

11. *Against Apion* ii. 39; *Antiq.* xii. 119; *War* vii. 43ff.

12. *Talmud, Erubin* 5.22; *Taanit* 3.66; *Tosephta, Erubin* 4.13.

13. 2 Mac 6–7. On the martyrdom of the seven Maccabean brothers and martyrs John Chrysostom has delivered three orations which have come down to us (*In Sanctos Maccabaeos,* Migne, PG [50], 617–628). *Knesheth Hasmunith* is mentioned in the Judeo-Arabic Martyrology of Nissim Ibn Shahin of Kairowan (J. Obermann, *The Arabic Original of Ibn Shahin's Book of Comfort* [New Haven: Yale Oriental Series 17, 1933], 25–28).

14. John Chrysostom, *Adversus Judaeos,* Migne, PG (48), 852.

15. Evagrius, *Hist. Eccles.* 1.20, Migne, PG (86), 2473–2476.

16. *Chronicon Paschale* 316, Migne, PG (92), 805.

17. *Hom. in Ignatium* 4, Migne, PG (50), 591.

18. *Hom. in Matth.* 36, Migne, PG (58), 762–763.

19. *Chronographia* 17, Migne, PG (97), 620.

20. Chrysostomus Baur, *John Chrysostom and His Time,* 36.

21. The exploration of ancient Antioch was not undertaken until, on the initiative of the late Prof. Charles Rufus Morey (1877–1955) of Princeton University, the Syrian government, in 1931, granted permission to Princeton University and the Musees Nationaux de France to excavate there over a period of six years. The committee for the excavation of Antioch and its vicinity was formed under the chairmanship of Morey and included several American institutions and individuals. Princeton University was made responsible for the direction of the exploration and for the publication of the results. So far four volumes have been published containing archaeological reports of the campaigns of 1932–1939 under the general title *Antioch-on-the-Orontes* and in the following order: G.W. Elderkin (ed.), Vol. I: *Antioch-on-the-Orontes, The Excavations of 1932* (Princeton: Princeton University Press, 1934); R. Stillwell (ed.), Vol. II: *The Excavations, 1933–1936* (Princeton: 1938); R. Stillwell (ed.), Vol. III: *The Excavations, 1937–1939* (Princeton: 1941); F.A. Waage (ed.), Vol. IV, Part I: *Ceramics and Islamic Coins* (Princeton: 1948); Dorothy B. Waage (ed.), Vol. IV, Part II: *Greek, Roman, Byzantine, and Crusader's Coins* (Princeton: 1952). In addition several shorter studies have been published. Two large volumes on the mosaics of Antioch have been published by Doro Levi under the title, *Antioch Mosaic Pavements* (Princeton: Princeton University Press, 1947).

22. Certain scholars support the view that the local art school was the fount of Byzantine art which constituted an essential element in the devotional and liturgical life of Greek Orthodoxy (C.R. Morey, *Early Christian Art* [Princeton: Princeton University Press, 1953], 55).

23. Libanius, *Orat.* 31.40.

24. John Chrysostom, *Ad. popul. Antiochiam,* Migne PG (49), 188; *De Mart.* Migne, PG (50), 648.

25. *Orat.* 1.1.

26. *Orat.* 11.264.

27. Glanville Downey, *A History of Antioch in Syria,* 383.

28. R.H. Pfeiffer, *History of New Testament Times,* 147.

29. *Ibid.,* 147-148; Franz Cumont, *The Oriental Religions in Roman Paganism,* trans. Grant Showeman (Chicago: The Open Court Publishing House, 1911), 10ff.

30. Chrysostom, *Contra ludos et theatra.* Migne, PG (56), 263-270; *In Julianum* 4. Migne, PG (50), 672-674.

31. S. Kraus, "Antioch," *Revue des Etudes Juives,* 45, (1902), 26-42.

32. *Ibid.,* 29.

33. Chrysostom, *Contra Jud.* 1, Migne, PG (48), 843: *Contra Jud.* 2, 860.

34. Jerome, *De situ et nomin. Hebraic.* Migne, PL (23), 958.

35. Gregory Nazianzus, *Orat. 15* Migne, PG (35), 912f; Chrysostom, *In sanctos Maccabaeos* 1-3, Migne, PG (50), 617-628.

36. J.W.H. Walden, *The Universities of Ancient Greece* (New York: Charles Scribner's Sons, 1912), 275.

37. Chrysostom, *Ad popul. Antioch.* Migne, PG (49), 188; *De sanct. martyribus.* Migne, (50), 646.

38. Werner Jaeger, *Early Christianity and Greek Paedeia* (Cambridge: Harvard University Press, 1961), 46, 51, 75.

39. *Historia Ecclesiastica* 6.3 Migne, PG (67), 665.

# Appendix Two

# THE CHRISTIAN CHURCH AT ANTIOCH IN THE FOURTH CENTURY

Christianity was brought to Antioch directly from Jerusalem and found in the city a highly receptive audience.[1] This region was a kind of crossroad for religions, many of which were already organized into syncretistic combinations under the powerful influence of the Olympian religion and the theories and dogmas, more or less popularized, of the Hellenistic philosophers.

Antioch formed the great intellectual center of Asia where ideas and beliefs met and merged. Besides the local cults, as we have seen, many other religious influences flowed in from the near east, including the Jewish faith which attracted a number of Gentiles.[2] The city of Antioch presented a challenging opportunity for the future of Christianity.

The religious syncretism of the Greco-Roman world created a situation in which a way was prepared for the coming of Christianity. It was in Antioch and similar centers that the first Gentile Christian communities were born and grew.[3] According to Acts 11:19-20 after the execution of Stephen, the Hellenistic followers of Jesus gave up the idea of making converts in Jerusalem and went to preach as far as Phoenicia, Cyprus, and Antioch. In Antioch, however, they spoke to the Greeks (i.e. Greek-speaking Gentiles, not necessarily Greeks by birth), and many of these Greeks became Christians. This projection of Christianity as a world system beyond Palestine was a decisive step in the evolution of the Christian *kerygma*. The church was not to confine itself to Judah, like the pietistic religious sects living at that time in Qumran; it overcame primitive isolation by declaring its universalism

197

through its mission to the world. It was upon the plain of Antioch that the church began to emerge as a world religion. And it was in Antioch that the infant Gentile congregation received the name "Christian," which, in all probability, was originally a nickname.[4]

The church of Antioch was of cardinal importance, for it served as the original home of Christian missions. From it Paul and other early propagators of the new faith went out on each of their three missionary journeys and they returned to Antioch to report. In addition to the activities of Paul in Antioch, Peter, too, had a small share in the development of the local community. However, judging from one New Testament reference he played no glorious role in the dispute between Jewish Christians and Gentile Christians over matters pertaining to the observance of the torah.[5] It was in Antioch that for the first time a Christian church, free of ties with rabbinical Judaism and no longer submitting to the constraint of the Pharisaic teaching, was formed. The idea that the church of Christ was totally independent from the synagogue was determined in the free atmosphere of Antioch which could later claim to be the mother of the churches of Asia Minor and Europe.

In those early days, the spiritual leaders of the church were prophets and teachers.[6] There is no mention of a council of elders as was the case in the community at Jerusalem which was governed by a board and a presiding officer.[7] Later, the church of Antioch began to follow the practice of other Christian communities and had a bishop as its head, as well as presbyters and deacons. Bishop Ignatius of Antioch, writing at the close of the apostolic age, was fully convinced that the threefold hierarchy constituted the only hope for unity in the maintenance of a healthy and vigorous fellowship in the shared experience of the faith and worship.[8] Ignatius, traveling from Antioch through Asia Minor on his way to martyrdom at Rome (ca. 107-117), wrote seven letters which give a vivid picture of the popular faith of the early church and of the religious life of the times.[9] The letters also show that by Ignatius' time there was, in Antioch at least, a settled hierarchal ministry, to whom the laity were urged to be obedient. Ignatius presents the local clergy as normally consisting of three orders, and asserts that apart from these three orders "there could be no church."[10]

Our knowledge of the period following Ignatius' death and of the church at Antioch after the apostolic fathers is scanty, and we have no sources dealing with the development of the Christian community. This obscurity for the first three quarters of the second century ends with the beginning of the episcopate of Theophilus. The teaching of Theophilus is important in the history of Christian thought because it represents an early attempt to formulate a learned system of theology based on the literal interpretation of scripture. His work in this respect marks him as a precursor of the methods that later characterized the biblical studies of the Antiochene fathers.[11]

Our knowledge of the church at Antioch after Theophilus is again obscure until the third quarter of the third century. Church history has preserved for us only shadowy personages.

Of all the great sees of Christian antiquity, Antioch was the first to fall into heresy. The elevation of Paul of Samosata on the Euphrates to the episcopal throne of the Antiochian church in A.D. 260 marks the beginning of an era which witnessed heresies, schisms, and divisions in many local congregations. The circumstances of Paul's election to the bishopric, at a time when Syria was within the Palmyrean sphere of influence, are not recorded, and it is not easy to describe his theology, because there is no evidence that he wrote anything. However, he is generally regarded as the celebrated heresiarch who paved the way for Arianism.[12] We possess few fragments with accounts of his teaching, and most of the records, in the opinion of Hans Lietzmann, appear suspiciously as if they presented his teaching unfairly.[13] Theodore of Mopsuestia, writing more than a century later, calls Paul of Samosata "an angel of Satan because he taught that Christ our Savior is a simple man and he did not recognize that hypostasis of the divinity of the one before the ages."[14]

The first church councils which were called at Antioch and of which we have record were held in connection with the Samosatene doctrine. Within a period of four years (264-268), two or three synods were convoked and each time a large number of bishops attended. This fact suggests that by the end of the third century the Syrian diocese had assumed a considerable ecclesiastical authority within the Oriental province of the Roman empire.[15]

Beginning with the fourth century the ecclesiastical head of a Christian province was usually also the bishop of the capital city. In each province the bishop of the capital city came to possess certain rights over his comprovincial bishops. The ecclesiastical superiors, exercising provincial and not merely diocesan powers, were called "metropolitans," and their jurisdiction was probably determined by local custom before the Council of Nicea. In the fourth canon of that council, the title "metropolitan" first appears and we have the beginning of the gradual process of defining that title in canon law.[16]

From the fourth century, there were also some church dignitaries who might be called chief metropolitans, whose hierarchical status within the church, the sixth canon of the Council of Nicea expressly says, was of long standing.[17] This canon included the bishops of Rome, Alexandria, and Antioch. Here we have the beginnings of the later patriarchal organization. The see of Antioch ranked, after Rome and Alexandria, as the third patriarchial *ecclesia* of Christendom, reaching its most extensive jurisdiction at the end of the fourth century. John Chrysostom termed the see of Antioch "head and mother of all the churches of the east."[18] However, it is not known exactly when this patriarchial cathedra originated.[19]

At the time of the Council of Nicea, the eloquent prelate Eustathius of Antioch was not only one of the presidents of the synod, if not the actual president of the hierarchy, but also the primate of Coele-Syria, Cilicia and all Mesopotamia.[20] No fewer than one hundred and fifty bishoprics in fifteen ecclesiastical provinces belonged to the patriarchate of Antioch, and in normal times the bishops of the provinces assembled with their patriarch for an annual conference in the first half of October.[21]

On the eve of the Arian controversy the church at Antioch was full of life and promise for the future. Prominent presbyters were industriously copying biblical manuscripts and studying the scriptures in order to come to a fuller understanding of the Bible and their faith. In doing this, they were perhaps unwittingly preparing the foundations of the theological school of Antioch. Henceforth Antioch was to take a more definite place in the evolution of Christian letters and dogmas. In this same period Antioch was the scene of the biblical studies of Dorotheus and Lucian. Dorotheus, according to Eusebius, was a highly learned presbyter, well versed in Hebrew and capable of reading the Old Testament in the original.[22] Eusebius' description of Dorotheus' understanding of the Hebrew language seems to imply that such knowledge was rare at the time. Lucian is considered by some historians to have been the founder or at least the first teacher of a sort of theological school in Antioch.[23] Unfortunately, historical information about the exact time of the establishment of this school is lacking.[24] Whether or not he was the actual founder of the school, Lucian's activity in textual criticism betokens the beginning of serious theological studies at Antioch, an academic tradition which was to influence the development of Christian thought in the fourth and fifth centuries.

Lucian was among the few biblical scholars of the patristic church who were occupied with the textual criticism of the Bible. Jerome, in referring to the diversity of the editions of the Greek Old Testament, observed that three were current within the Greek-speaking churches of the Roman empire and that one of them bore the name of Lucian.[25] There seems to be some ground for maintaining that Lucian's biblical work was a significant factor in the eventual establishment of the theological school of Antioch by Diodorus, Carterius, and Flavian.[26]

During the first quarter of the fourth century, the patriarchate of Antioch found itself in the very midst of the Arian controversy. Although Arianism became prominent in Alexandria, its roots were in the city of Antioch.[27] Arius himself made this claim in a letter to the foremost spokesman of Arianism, Eusebius of Nicomedia. In this letter, Arius hails Eusebius as a Collucianist and declares that Eusebius is merely following Lucian's views regarding christology.[28]

The condemnation of Arius by the Council of Nicea turned Antioch into a stronghold of Arianism, and the clergy and believers were divided into four parties: the Arians, the semi-Arians, the Old Nicene party, and the New Nicene party.[29] The patriarchate was practically paralyzed. At this time there were four independent bishops. The spiritual leaders of the New Nicene party were two young and well educated monks, Diodorus and Carterius, the heads of a religious school or monastery, and presbyter Flavian, who later became bishop of Antioch. With their followers they held divine service in the *martyria* outside the city near the Orontes, and sometimes they gathered in a cave on a neighboring mountain, spending the night singing psalms and hymns.[30] Such was the state of affairs in the orthodox congregation of Antioch when Theodore was born, a state of religious confusion and ecclesiastical anarchy.

## NOTES

1. Acts 11:19 f; 13:1f.
2. Josephus, *War* 7. 45.
3. The syncretistic combinations in the religious life of the Graeco-Roman world were extremely complex. From the Aegean Sea and Phrygia down to Egypt and in Rome, it is clear that at the beginning of the Christian era a number of divinities were worshiped, many so closely resembling each other that they were occasionally confused. Principal among these were Attis, Tammuz-Adonis, Cybele, Osiris, Isis, Serapis, and Dionysos. For the factors which prepared the way for the spread of Christianity see A.D. Nock, "Early Gentile Christianity and Its Hellenistic Background," in *Essays on the Trinity and the Incarnation,* edited by A.E. Rawlinson (London: Longmans, Green & Co., 1928), 51–156.
4. Acts 11:26. There are, however, other interpretations of the origin of the word; the text clearly suggests that the name was devised by outsiders, whether by the Roman authorities in the city as the official identification of the group, or by the people who wanted to ridicule the new faith and its followers is not clear. The text does not allow us to suppose that the name *Christianoi* was coined by the Christians themselves.
5. Gal 2:11ff.
6. Acts 13:1f.

7. Acts 15:13-34; 21:18f; Gal 1:18f.

8. Ignatius, *Epist. ad Trall.*, Migne, PG (5), 676.

9. The controversy over the genuineness of the seven letters of Ignatius has begun to die down after J.B. Lightfoot's learned defense of their authenticity in his monumental edition, *The Apostolic Fathers* (London, 1891); on the same subject see V. Corwin, *Ignatius and Christianity in Antioch,* p. 50; C.C. Richardson, "The Church in Ignatius of Antioch," *Journal of Religion,* XVII (1937), 428ff.

10. *Epist. ad Trall.,* Migne, PG (5), 677. The advent and triumph, however, of the monarchic episcopate is the central problem in the organization and development of the early church, and various theories of this organization have been advanced, each one winning varying degrees of acceptance.

11. G. Downey, *A History of Antioch in Syria,* 302. Apart from his *Apology to Autolycus* (Migne, PG [6], 1023-1168), Theophilus' treatises have been lost. He seems, however, to have employed in his writings a biblical interpretation which is more literal and historical than the one employed by his contemporaries (cf. R.M. Grant, *The Letter and the Spirit* [London: S.P.C.K., 1957], 78-81).

12. R.V. Sellers, *Two Ancient Christologies* (London S.P.C.K., 1954), 107-118; John Romanidis, "Highlights in the Debate over Theodore of Mopsuestia's Christology and Some Suggestions for a Fresh Approach," *The Greek Theological Review,* V, No. 2 (Winter 1959-1960), 163.

13. *A History of the Early Church,* trans. B.L. Woolf (London: Lutterworth Press, 1950), III, 101ff.

14. R. Tonneau (ed.), *Les homélies catéchétiques de Théodore de Mopsueste* (Città del Vaticano: Bibliotheca Apostolica Vaticana, 1949), 387.

15. Paul of Samosata, as a theologian, stressed the unity of God and presented Christ as mere man by nature. His Logos doctrine had a strong adoptionistic tendency safeguarding the monarchy of the Godhead. Logos, according to Paul, is not a self-subsistent being having an independent person, but rather a manifestation of God's operation. The Logos is *homoousios* with the Father because it emanates from his essence. The title "Son

of God" applies only to the historical Jesus, because, according to the gospel account (Lk 1:35), he was born of the Holy Spirit and the Virgin Mary. Previously, the Logos had dwelt in Moses, in the prophets, and in many personalities; in the fullness of time, Logos revealed himself in Jesus and their conjunction was such that separability became impossible. Logos was never an independent person or entity; Christ differed only in degree from the prophets (cf. H. Lietzmann, *A History of the Early Church,* III, 101ff).

16. J.D. Mansi, *Sacrorum conciliorum collectio* (Graz: Akademishe Druck-U. Verlagsantal, 1960), II, 893.

17. *Ibid.,* 895. This synodal pronouncement was altered with the rise of Constantinople by the Second Council in 381 which accorded the new Rome the first place of honor after that of Rome (cf. Mansi, III, 560).

18. *Hom. III In profect. episcopi Flaviani* Migne, PG (49), 47.

19. Robert Devreesse, *Le patriarchat d' Antioche* (Paris: Librarie Lecoffre, 1945), 120.

20. Mansi, *op. cit.,* II, 881.

21. Chrysostom, *Hom. II Contra Anom.* Migne, PG (48), 709.

22. *Historia Ecclesiastica* 7.32, 2–4.

23. Philip de Barjeau, *L'école exégétique d'Antioche* (Toulouse Impremerie A. Chauvin & Fils, 1898), 19ff.

24. Chrysostomus Baur, *John Chrysostom and His Time,* trans. from the German by M. Gonzaga (Westminster, Maryland: The Newman Press, 1959), I, 89–91.

25. "Alexandria et Aegyptus in LXX sius Hesychium laudat auctorem; Constantinopolis usque Antiochian Luciani martyris exemplaria probat; mediar inter has provinciae Palaestinos codices legunt, quos ab Origene alaboratos Eusebius et Pamphilus vulgaverunt" (cf. *Preface to Chronicles,* Migne, PL [28], 1392).

26. Glanville Downey, *A History of Antioch in Syria,* 338–340, 363.

27. Lucian has been held responsible for the Arian heresy (cf. Theodoret, *Hist. Eccles.,* 1.4, Migne, PG [82], 912). Modern scholars hold different views with regard to Lucian's theology. Adolf Harnack describes Lucian as "the Arius before Arius" (cf. *History of Dogma,* trans. from the 3rd German edition by N.

Buchanan [New York: Dover Publications, 1961], IV, 3); see also
J.F. Bethune-Baker, *An Introduction to the Early History of
Christian Doctrine* (7th ed.; London: Methuen & Co., 1958),
111ff. This view, however, is not accepted by H.M. Gwatkin who
claims: "There is really nothing against Lucian except the leaning
of his disciples to Arianism" (cf. *Studies of Arianism* [Cambridge:
At the University Press, 1900], 17).

28.  Theodoret, *Hist. Eccl.,* 1.4, Migne, PG (82), 912; see also
Philostorgius, *Hist. Eccl.,* 2.4, Migne, PG (65), 477.

29.  For a detailed study on the schism of Antioch see F. Cav-
allera, *Le schisme d'Antioche* (Paris: Impr. Picard, 1905), 31ff and
71ff.

30.  Theodoret, *Historia Religiosa* 2, Migne, PG (82), 1317.

# BIBLIOGRAPHY

Altaner, Berthold. *Patrology.* Translated from the fifth German edition of *Patrologie* by Hilda C. Graef. Edinburgh-London: Nelson, 1959.

Amann, É. "Chronique d'ancienne littérature chretienne. Un nouvel ouvrage de Théodore de Mopsueste," *Revue des Sciences Religieuses,* XX, No. 4 (Octobre 1940), 491–528.

————. "La doctrine christologique de Théodore de Mopsueste," *Revue des Sciences Religieuses,* XIV, No. 2 (Avril 1934), 160–190.

————. "Théodore de Mopsueste," *Dictionnaire de Theologie Catholique Supplement,* Tome XV, Part 1, pp. 235–279. Edited by A. Vacant, E. Mangenot, E. Amann. Paris: Librarie Latouzey et Ane, 1946.

Ammianus, Marcellinus. *Historia.* Edited with an English translation by John C. Rolfe. (The Loeb Classical Library) 3 vols. Cambridge, Mass.: Harvard University Press; London: William Heinemann, 1952.

Anastos, Milton. "The Immutability of Christ and Justinian's Condemnation of Theodore of Mopsuestia," *Dumbarton Oaks Papers,* No. Six, pp. 125–160. Cambridge, Mass.: Harvard University Press, 1951.

Aytoun, Robert Alexander. *City Centres of Early Christianity.* London: Hodder and Stoughton, 1915.

Bardy, Gustave. *Recherches sur Saint Lucien d'Antioch et son école.* Paris: Gabriel Beauchesne et ses Fils, 1936.

Barhadbeshabba, Arbaya. *Cause de la fondation des écoles.* Texte syriaque publié et traduit par Addai Scher dans *Patrologia Orientalis,* Tome IV, pp. 337–340. R. Griffin and F. Nau (eds.) Paris: Firmin & Didot, 1903.

Barjeau, J. Philip de. *L'école exégétique d'Antioche.* Toulouse: Imprimerie A. Chauvin Et Fils, 1898.

Baur, Chrysostomus. *John Chrysostom and His Time.* Vol. I: *Antioch.* Translated from the German by Sr. M. Gozanga. Westminster, Maryland: The Newman Press, 1959.

Beagle, Dewey. *The Inspiration of Scripture.* Philadelphia: The Westminster Press, 1963.

Belkin, Samuel. *Philo and the Oral Law.* (Harvard Semitic Series, No. 11) Cambridge, Mass.: Harvard University Press, 1946.

Bethune-Baker, J.F. *An Introduction to the Early History of Christian Doctrine.* 7th ed. revised. London: Methuen and Co., 1951.

Bouchier, E.S. *A Short History of Antioch.* Oxford: Basil Blackwell, 1921.

————. *Syria as a Roman Province.* Oxford: Basil Blackwell, 1916.

Burrows, Miller. *More Light on the Dead Sea Scrolls.* New York: The Viking Press, 1958.

————. *The Dead Sea Scrolls.* New York: The Viking Press, 1957.

Cavalera, F. *Le schisme d'Antioche.* Paris: Imprimerie Picard, 1905.

Chabot, Joseph B. *Synodicon Orientale ou recueil des synodes nestoriens.* Paris: C. Klincksieck, 1902.

Chrysostom, John. *Opera Omnia.* Edited by J.P. Migne, *Patrologiae Graecae,* Vols. XLVII–LXIV.

Corwin, Virginia. *St. Ignatius and Christianity in Antioch.* New Haven: Yale University Press, 1960.

Cross, F.L. (ed.) *The Oxford Dictionary of the Christian Church.* London: Oxford University Press, 1957.

Cross, Frank Moore, Jr. *The Ancient Library of Qumran and Modern Biblical Studies.* The Haskell Lectures 1956–1957. Garden City, New York: Doubleday & Company, 1958.

Cumont, Franz. *The Oriental Religions in the Roman Empire.* Translated by Grant Showerman. Chicago: The Open Court Publishing Co., 1911.

D'Ales, Adhémar. "La lettre d'Ibas a Marès le Persan," *Recherches de Science Religieuse,* XII, No. 1 (Fevrier 1932), 5–25.

Daniélou, Jean. *The Bible and the Liturgy.* (University of Notre

Dame Liturgical Studies, Vol. III) Edited by Michael A. Mathis. Notre Dame, Indiana: University of Notre Dame Press, 1956.

―――. *Origen.* Translated by Walter Mitchell. London and New York: Sheed and Ward, 1955.

Devreesse, Robert. *Essai sur Théodore de Mopsueste.* Studi e Testi, No. 141. Città del Vaticano: Bibliotheca Apostolica Vaticana, 1948.

―――. "La méthode exégétique de Théodore de Mopsueste," *Revue Biblique,* LIII, No. 2 (Avril 1946), 207–241.

―――. "Le commentaire de Théodore de Mopsueste sur les psaumes," *Revue Biblique,* XXXVII, No. 3 (Juillet 1928), 340–360; XXXVIII, No. 1 (Janvier 1929), 35–62.

―――. "Le florilège de Leonce de Byzance," *Revue des Sciences Religieuses,* X, No. 4 (Octobre 1930), 545–576.

―――. *Le patriarchat d'Antioche: depuis la paix de l'église jusqu'a la conquete Arabe.* Paris: Librarie Lecoffre, 1945.

―――. "Les instructions catéchétiques de Théodore de Mopsueste," *Revue des Sciences Religieuses,* XIII, No. 3 (Juillet 1933), 425–436.

―――. "Par quelles voies nous sont parvenus les commentaires de Théodore de Mopsueste," *Revue Biblique,* XXXIX, No. 3 (Juillet 1930), 362–377.

Dobschutz, E. von. "A Hitherto Unpublished Prologue to the Acts of the Apostles (Probably by Theodore of Mopsuestia)," *The American Journal of Theology,* II, No. 2 (April 1898), 353–387.

Dodd, C.H. *According to the Scriptures. The Sub-structure of New Testament Theology.* London: Nisbet and Co., Ltd, 1953.

Downey, Glanville. *A History of Antioch in Syria.* Princeton, New Jersey: Princeton University Press, 1961.

Duchesne, Louis. *Early History of the Christian Church.* Translated by Claude Jenkins. 3 vols. London: John Murray, 1938.

Ebedjesus. *Catalogus.* In Joseph S. Assemani, *Bibliotheca Orientalis,* Tom. III, caput xix, pp. 30–35. Romae: Typis Sacrae Congregationis de Propaganda Fide, 1726.

Elderkin, G.W., Stillwell, R., *et al.* (eds.) *Antioch-On-The-Orontes.* 4 vols. Princeton: Princeton University Press, 1932–1952.

Eusebius of Caesarea. *Historia Ecclesiastica.* Edited by J.P. Migne, *Patrologiae Graecae,* Tom. XIX–XX.

Facundus of Hermiane. *Pro defensione trium capitulorum.* Edited by J.P. Migne, *Patrologiae Latinae,* Tom. LXVII.

Farrar, F.W. *History of Interpretation.* New York: E.P. Dutton & Co., 1886.

Festugière, A.J. *Antioche païenne et chrétienne.* Éditions E. de Boccard, 1959.

Florovsky, Georges. "Revelation and Interpretation" in *Biblical Authority for Today.* A World Council of Churches Symposium on 'The Biblical Authority for the Churches' Social and Political Message for Today.' Edited by A. Richardson and W. Schweitzer. London: SCM Press Ltd., 1953.

Grant, Robert. *The Bible in the Church. A Short History of Interpretation.* New York: The Macmillan Co., 1948.

————. *The Letter and the Spirit.* London: S.P.C.K., 1957.

Greer, Rowan. *Theodore of Mopsuestia: Exegete and Theologian.* Westminister: The Faith Press, 1961.

Grosse-Brauckmann, Emil. "Der Psaltertext bei Theodoret," Mitteilungen des Sepuaginta-Unternehmens der königlichen gesellschaft de Wissenschaften zur Göttingen, Heft 3 (1911), 83–93.

Guillet, J. "Les exégèses de'Alexandrie et d'Antioche. Conflit ou malentendue?" *Recherches de Science Religieuse,* XXXIV, No. 2 (Avril 1947), 257–303.

Gwatkin, H.M. *Studies in Arianism.* 2nd ed. revised. Cambridge: At the University Press, 1900.

Haddad, George. *Aspects of Social Life in Antioch in the Hellenistic-Roman Period.* (Ph.D. Dissertation, The University of Chicago) New York: Hafner Publishing Co., 1949.

Hanson, R.C.P. *Allegory and Event.* Richmond, Virginia: John Knox Press, 1959.

Harnack, Adolf. "Antiochenische Schule" *Realencyklopädie für protestantische Theologie und Kirche,* Erster Band, 592–595.

————. *History of Dogma,* Vols. II and III. Translated from the third German edition by Neil Buchanan. London: Williams and Norgate, 1894–1896.

————. *The Mission and Expansion of Christianity in the First Three Centuries.* 2 vols. Translated and edited by James Moffatt. 2nd ed. revised. London: Williams and Norgate; New York: G.P. Putnam's Sons, 1908.

Hedley, P.L. "The Göttingen Investigation and Edition of the Septuagint," *The Harvard Theological Review,* XXVI, No. 1 (January 1933), 57–72.

Hitti, Philip K. *History of Syria.* London: The Macmillan Co., 1951.

Jaeger, Werner. *Early Christianity and Greek Paideia.* Cambridge, Mass.: Harvard University Press, 1961.

Josephus, Flavius. *Complete Works.* Edited by S. Naber. 6 vols. Leipzig: Teubner, 1888–1896.

Junilius, Africanus. *Instituta regularia divinae legis.* Edited by Heinrich Kihn as an Appendix in *Theodore von Mopsuestia und Junilius Africanus als Exegeten.* Freiburg im Breisgau: Herder'sche Verlagshanbung, 1880.

Justinian, Emperor. *Confessio rectae fidei adversus tria capitula.* Edited by J.P. Migne, *Patrologiae Graecae,* Tom. LXXXVI, 993–1036.

————. Epistola adversus Theodorum Mopsuesteno. Edited by J.P. Migne, *Patrologiae Graecae,* Tom. LXXXVI, 1040–1096.

Kelly, J.N.D. *Early Christian Doctrines.* New York: Harper and Brothers Publishers, 1958.

Kenyon, Frederic G. *Recent Developments in Textual Criticism of the Greek Bible.* London: Published for the British Academy by the Oxford University Press, 1933.

Kerrigan, Alexander. *St. Cyril of Alexandria Interpreter of the Old Testament.* Roman: Pontificio Instituto Biblico, 1952.

Kidd, B.J. *A History of the Church to A.D. 461.* 3 vols. Oxford: The Clarendon Press, 1922.

Kihn, Heinrich. *Theodor von Mopsuestia und Junilius Africanus als Exegeten.* Freiburg im Breisgau: Herder'sche Verlagshanbung, 1 1880.

Kraeling, Carl H. "The Jewish Community at Antioch," *Journal of Biblical Literature,* LI (1932), 130–160.

Kraus, S. "Antioche," *Revue des Etudes Juives,* XLV (1902), 26–42.

Laistner, M.L.W. "Antiochene Exegesis in Western Europe During the Middle Ages," *The Harvard Theological Review,* XL, No. 1 (January 1947), 19–32.

Landman, Isaac. (ed.) *The Universal Jewish Encyclopedia.* 12 vols. New York: Jewish Encyclopedia Co., Inc., 1948.

Leontius of Byzantium. *Contra Nestorianos et Eutychianos libri tres.* Edited by J.P. Migne, *Patrologiae Graecae,* Tom. LXXXVI, 1267–1398.

Levi, Doro. *Antioch Mosaic Pavement.* Princeton, New Jersey: Princeton University Press, 1947.

Libanius. *Complete Works.* 12 vols. Edited by Richard Foerster. Leipzig: Teubner, 1903–1912.

Lietzmann, Hans. *A History of the Early Church.* Vol. III: *From Constantine to Julian.* Translated by Bertram Lee Woolf. London: Lutterworth Press, 1950.

————. "Der Psalmenkommentar Theodors von Mopsuestia," *Sitzungberichte der koniglich preussischen Akademie der Wissenscharten zu Berlin,* April (1902), 333–346.

Loofs, Friedrich. "Theodor von Mopsuestia," *Realencykopädie für protestantische Theologie und Kirche,* Neunzehnter Band, pp. 598–605.

Malalas, Ioannes. *Chronicle.* Bks. VIII–XVIII. Translated from the Church Slavonic by Matthew Spinka in collaboration with Glanville Downey. Chicago: University of Chicago Press, 1940.

————. *Chronographia.* Edited by J.P. Migne, *Patrologiae Graecae,* Tom. XCVII, 9–700.

Mansi, J.D. *Sacrorum conciliorum collectio.* Vols. VII–IX. Graz: Akademische Druk- U. Verlagsanstalt, 1960.

McKenzie, John L. "A New Study of Theodore of Mopsuestia," *Theological Studies,* X, No. 3 (September 1949), 394–408.

————. "The Commentary of Theodore of Mopsuestia on John 1:46–51," *Theological Studies,* XIV, No. 1 (March 1953), 73–84.

McNamara, Kevin. "Theodore of Mopsuestia and the Nestorian Heresy," *The Irish Theological Quarterly,* XIX No. 3 (July 1953), 254–278; XX No. 2 (April 1953), 172–191.

Metzger, Bruce M. "Antioch-on-the-Orontes," *The Biblical Archaeologist,* XI, No. 4 (December 1948), 70–88.

————. "Lucian and the Lucianic Recension of the Greek Bible," *New Testament Studies,* VIII, No. 3 (April 1962), 189–203.

Mingana, Alphonse. (ed.) "Synopsis of Christian Doctrine in the Fourth Century According to Theodore of Mopsuestia," Bulletin of the *John Rylands Library,* V, Nos. 3 and 4 (April–November 1919), 301–316.

Mommsen, Theodor. *The Provinces of the Roman Empire.* 2 vols. Translated by William P. Dickson. New York: Charles Scribner's Sons, 1899.

Moore, George Foot. *Judaism: In the First Centuries of the Christian Era. The Age of the Tannaim.* 3 vols. Cambridge, Mass.: Harvard University Press, 1927.

————. "The Theological School at Nisibis," in *Studies in the History of Religions,* pp. 255–269. Edited and presented to C.H. Toy by David G. Lyon and G.F. Moore. New York: The Macmillan Co., 1912.

Morey, C.H. *Early Christian Art.* Princeton, New Jersey: Princeton University Press, 1953.

Nash, H.S. "The Exegesis of the School of Antioch. A Criticism of the Hypothesis that Aristotelianism was Main Cause of its Genesis," *Journal of Biblical Literature,* XI, (1892), 22–37.

Obermann, J. (ed.) *The Arabic Original of Ibn Shahin's Book of Comfort.* (Yale University Oriental Series, No. 17) New Haven: Yale University Press, 1933.

Opitz, H.G. "Theodoros Bischof von Mopsuestia," in *Pauly-Wissowa Real-encyklopadie der classischen altertumswissenschaft,* Funfter Band, 1881–1890.

Orlinsky, Harry. "The Columnar Order of the Hexapla," *The Jewish Quarterly Review,* XXVII, No. 2 (October 1936), 137–149.

Pack, Roger. *Studies in Libanius and Antiochene Society Under Theodosius.* (Published Ph.D. Dissertation, The University of Michigan) Menasha, Wisconsin: George Banta Publishing Co., 1935.

Patterson, Leonard. *Theodore of Mopsuestia and Modern Thought.* London: S.P.C.K., 1926.

Pfeiffer, Robert H. *History of New Testament Times.* New York: Harper and Brothers Publishers, 1949.

————. *Introduction to the Old Testament.* 2nd ed. revised. New York: Harper and Brothers Publishers, 1948.

Philo. *Opera Omnia.* With an English translation by F.H. Colson and G.H. Whitaker. (The Loeb Classical Library) 11 vols. Cambridge, Mass.: Harvard University Press; London: William Heinemann Ltd., 1949.

Philostorgius. *Historia Ecclesiastica.* Edited by J.P. Migne, *Patrologiae Graecae,* Tom. LXV, pp. 459–624.

Pirot, Louis. *L'oeuvre exégétique de Théodore de Mopsueste.* Romae: Sumptibus Pontificii Instituti Biblici, 1913.

Pritchard, James B. *Ancient Near Eastern Texts Related to the Old Testament.* Princeton, New Jersey: Princeton University Press, 1955.

Quasten, Johannes. *Patrology.* Vol. III: *The Golden Age of Greek Patristic Literature.* Utrecht/Antwerp: Spectrum Publishers; Westminster, Maryland: The Newman Press, 1960.

————. "Theodore of Mopsuestia on the Exorcism of the Cilicium," *The Harvard Theological Review,* XXX, No. 3 (July 1942), 209–219.

Raven, C.E. *Apollinarianism.* Cambridge: At the University Press, 1923.

Romanides, John S. "Highlights in the Debate over Theodore of Mopsuestia's Christology and Some Suggestions for a Fresh Approach," *The Greek Orthodox Theological Review,* V, No. 2 (Winter 1959–1960), 140–185.

Rose, H.J. *A Handbook of Greek Literature.* London: Methuen and Co., 1934.

Roth, Cecil. (ed.) *The Standard Jewish Encyclopedia.* London: W.H. Allen, 1959.

Sachau, Edward. *Theodori Mopsuestini fragmenta syriaca.* Leipzig: Sumptibus Guilelmi Engelman, 1869.

Socrates, Scholasticus. *Historia Ecclesiastica.* Edited by J.P. Migne, *Patrologiae Graecae,* Tom. LXVII, pp. 33–841.

Sozomen, Hermiae. *Historia Ecclesiastica.* Edited by J.P. Migne, *Patrologiae Graecae,* Tom. LXVII, pp. 844–1269.

Sperber, Alexander. "The Problems of the Septuagint Recensions," *Journal of Biblical Literature,* LIV, Part II (June 1935), 73–92.

Staab, Karl. *Pauluskommentare aus der griechischem Kirche.* Aus Katenenhandschriften gesamelt und herausgegeben. (Neutestamentliche Abhandlungen, Band XV) Munster: Verlag der Aschendorffschen Verlagsbuchhandlung, 1933, pp. 113–212.

Sullivan, Francis A. *The Christology of Theodore of Mopsuestia.* (Analecta Gregoriana, cura pontificiae Universitatis Gregorianae edita, LXXXII) Romae: Apud Aedes Universitatis Gregorianae, 1956.

Swete, H.B. "Theodorus of Mopsuestia," in *A Dictionary of Christian Biography.* Vol. IV, 934–948. Edited by W. Smith and H. Wace. London: John Murray, 1887.

Théodore de Mopsueste, *Fragments syriaques du commentaire de Psaumes* (Psaume 118 et Psaumes 138–148). Edites et traduits par Lucas van Rompay. Louvain: E Petters, 1982.

Theodori Mopsuestini, *Commentarius in duodecim prophetas,* with an introduction and editing by Hans Norbert Sprenger, Wiesbaden: Harrassowitz, 1977.

Theodori Mopsuestini, *Expositio in Psalmos.* Translated into Latin by Bishop Julian of Eclanum. Edited by Lucas de Coninck. Turnholti: Brepos, 1977.

Theodore of Mopsuestia. *Opera Omnia.* (quae exstant 1864). Edited by J.P. Migne, *Patrologiae Graecae,* Tom. LXVI, pp. 125–1020.

————. *Catechetical Commentary on the Lord's Prayer and on the Sacraments of Baptism and the Eucharist.* Edited and translated from the Syriac by Alphonse Mingana. (Woodbrooke Studies, Vol. VI) Cambridge: W. Heffer and Sons Ltd., 1933.

————. *Catechetical Commentary on the Nicene Creed.* Edited and translated from the Syriac by Alponse Mingana. (Woodbrooke Studies, Vol. V) Cambridge: W. Heffer and Sons Ltd., 1932.

————. *Commentaire sur les Psaumes I–LXXX.* Edited by

Robert Devreesse. (Studi e Testi, No. 93) Città del Vaticano: Bibliotheca Apostolica Vaticana, 1939.

————. *Commentarius in evangelium Iohannes apostoli.* Edited by J.M. Vosté in *Corpus Scriptorum Christianorum Orientalium.* (Scriptores Syri, series quarta, Tomus III) Louvain: E Typographeo Republicae, 1940.

————. *Controverse avec les Macedoniens.* Edited and translated from the Syriac by F. Nau in *Patrologia Orientalis,* Tom. IX, pp. 637–667. Paris: Firmin and Didot, 1913.

————. *In epistolas beati Pauli commentarii.* Vol. I: *Galatians-Colossians.* Vol. II: *Thessalonians-Philemon.* (The Latin Version with the Greek Fragments). Edited with an Introduction, Notes, and Indices by H.B. Swete. Cambridge: At the University Press, 1880–1882.

————. *Les fragments grecs du commentaire sur le quatrieme Evangile.* Edited by Robert Devreesse as an Appendix to *Essai sur Théodore de Mopsueste.* (Studi e Testi, No. 141) Città del Vaticano: Bibliotheca Apostolica Vaticana, 1948.

Theodoret of Cyrrhus. *Historia Ecclesiastica.* Edited by J.P. Migne, *Patrologiae Graecae,* Tom. LXXXVII, pp. 880–1280.

————. *Historia Religiosa.* Edited by J.P. Migne, *Patrologiae Graecae,* Tom. LXXXII, pp. 1283–1496.

Tonneau, Raymond. *Les homélies catéchétiques de Théodore de Mopsueste.* Reproduction phototypique du MS. Mingana (Syr. 565).Traduction, introduction, index par R. Tonneau en collaboration avec Robert Devreesse. Città del Vaticano: Bibliotheca Apostolica Vaticana, 1949.

Vööbus, Arthur. "Regarding the Theological Anthropology of Theodore of Mopsuestia," *Church History,* XXXIII, No. 2 (June 1964), 115–124.

Vosté, J.M. "La chronology de l'activité litteraire de Théodore de Mopsueste," *Revue Biblique,* XXXIV, No. 1 (Janvier 1925), 54–81.

————. "Le commentaire de Théodore de Mopsueste sur Saint Jean, d'après la version syriaque," *Revue Biblique,* XXXII, No. 4 (Octobre 1923), 522–551.

————. "Le Gannat Bussame," *Revue Biblique,* XXXVII, No. 2 (Avril 1928), 221–232.

————. "L'oeuvre exégétique de Théodore de Mopsueste au II<sup>e</sup> Concile de Constantinople," *Revue Biblique,* XXXVIII, No. 3 (Juillet 1929), 382–395; No. 4 (Octobre 1929), 542–554.

Walden, John W.H. *The Universities of Ancient Greece.* New York: Charles Scribner's Sons, 1912.

Westcott, B.F. *A General Survey of the History of the Canon of the New Testament.* London: The Macmillan Co., 1870.

Wickert, Urlich. *Studien zu den Pauluskommentaren Theodors von Mopsuestia. Als Beitrag zum Verstandnis der Antiochenischen Theologie.* Berlin: Verlag Alfred Topelmann, 1962.

Wolfson, Harry Austin. *Philo: Foundations of Religious Philosophy in Judaism, Christianity, and Islam.* 2 vols. 2nd ed. revised. Cambridge, Mass.: Harvard University Press, 1948.

————. *The Philosophy of the Church Fathers.* Cambridge, Mass.: Harvard University Press, 1956.

Wright, G. Ernest. "From the Bible to the Modern World," in *Biblical Authority for Today.* A World Council of Churches Symposium on 'The Biblical Authority for the Churches' Social and Political Message Today.' Edited by Allan Richardson and W. Schweitzer. London: S.C.M. Press LTD., 1953.

Wycherly, Richard E. *How the Greeks Built Cities.* London: The Macmillan Co., 1949.

# Subject and Name Index

# THEOLOGICAL INQUIRIES:

Serious studies on contemporary questions of Scripture, Systematics and Moral Theology. Also in the series: